To Bryan
Follow your
Heart brother, always!

Mit

Healing
through
Awakening

Books may be purchased by contacting the publisher and author at:
holistic.mica@gmail.com

Cover Design: Mica Akullian and Susan Tower
Interior Design: Creatspace.com
ISBN-13: 978-1515259466

ISBN-10: 1515259463

May all beings be filled with peace, love, and joy

Healing *through* Awakening

~*~

Mica Akullian M.S.

Contents

Part II
The Awakening

Part III
The Path of Self-Mastery

Part IV
The Holistic Healing Process

Preface

Imagine for a moment what it would be like to wake up tomorrow completely free from the voice of fear, negativity, anxiety, or doubt. And imagine, instead, that you awoke feeling deep love, joy, gratitude, and a profound sense of connection to all of life. How would you create your life from this place of freedom and happiness? How would you experience yourself and your reality from this feeling of unconditional love?

The keys to awakening this heavenly realm within are available to everyone, but require a journey inward to the most essential part of yourself; your heart and Soul. Though it requires effort to embark on this path of awakening, it is not the effort of doing more, or trying to become something greater than what you already are. Instead, it is the effort of letting go—letting go of fear, and letting go of the false self that has been constructed in the mind over the course of a lifetime, uncovering the perfection of that which you have always been. The path to spiritual liberation requires honest self reflection, inward investigation, and a desire to know the truth of who you are beyond the limitations of your mind and emotions.

Our primary purpose on the planet is to reawaken to the truth of who we are; that of unconditional love, peace, and joy. Love is the unifying energy of the Universe, being expressed in infinite ways throughout all of creation. The loving energy that we are is ever changing, evolving, and expanding, and is beyond the mind's ability to fully comprehend. Though I am using these words to point to the truth of our beingness, who we are in our essence is not a concept to be grasped in the mind, but rather, can only be felt through direct

1

experience. By learning to let go of the ego and fearful mind, we can begin reconnecting to the truth of who we are.

It is this profound covering over of our true essence that causes suffering on an individual level, as well as within our collective experience, and perpetuates much of the pain and destruction on the planet at this time. It's as if the infinite loving energy that we are has been stuffed into a box that we call the mind, emotions, and body, reducing our experience to what can only be perceived with our five senses and the thinking mind. Throughout our lives we learn to become so attached to, and identified with the box, that we have forgotten our true nature as infinite creative energy. As one learns to transcend the limitations of the mind, the box becomes dissolved, and a deep sense of connection and oneness with all of life emerges, profoundly changing the experience of life.

I discovered this greater connection after years of living in pain and suffering. It was a physical disease that brought me to the doorway of transformation. I was diagnosed with a chronic digestive disease called ulcerative colitis after returning home from a trip to South America in 2001. I was told that there was no known cause, nor any known cure for this disease, and the only relief came from daily doses of medication, coupled with an extremely restrictive diet.

For the eight years I was challenged with this disease the quality of my life deteriorated significantly, with depression, anxiety, and a relentless sense of despair becoming my everyday reality. I didn't know it at the time, but the suffering I experienced on account of this illness would serve as the vehicle for a spiritual awakening, profoundly transforming my life. From the brink of despair a new world would become known to me, one where the underlying current is that of love, joy, connection, and peace.

As I integrated this more expansive and deeply joyful reality into my life, I also underwent what might be termed a "miraculous healing." I awoke one day to find that my symptoms were gone and that my body was healed. Although looking back on it now, I see that healing is more or less a systematic process, and I believe that almost anyone can heal from almost any disease. What makes healing possible is the willingness to move beyond what feels familiar and safe, allowing belief systems to dissolve, repressed emotions to be released, and behaviors to change.

We now stand upon the precipice of a profound collective choice. Do we continue creating the reality that we have grown accustomed to; a reality built around fear, ego, and limitation, or do we step more fully into the light of who we are, envisioning for ourselves a world built from unconditional love? Do we continue viewing the purpose of our lives through the small lens of the personal self, motivated by selfish desires, or do we expand ourselves to see the shared unity of all life, and the part that each one of us plays in the greater whole?

If we are to deeply and profoundly change the world in which we are living, we must first change ourselves. Personal transformation holds the key to healing the planet, and awakening within each one us our shared connection to all of life around us. One person living in truth, speaking truth, and being truth, can truly change the world in a way that the mind could never fathom, nor fully understand.

This is my story of healing, of stepping out of the mind-made reality of the ego, and directly experiencing the energy of God, the Universe, and unconditional love. This is a story of the magic, grace, and love that has accompanied my awakening process, uncovering more of my essential nature. The first part of this book is my personal journey, while the following chapters serve as a guide for the awakening and healing journey for anyone who desires to live in greater truth, connection, and happiness.

Though the scope of this book may seem ambitious, covering such a wide array of topics relating to the mind, emotions, and body, I feel that this is the most balanced approach to spiritual awakening. The reason for this is that the journey of awakening and healing is truly a holistic process, where each part of our human experience profoundly affects and shapes all other parts of the self. By learning to integrate back into wholeness on every level, we grow and evolve in a balanced way. The holistic approach builds a solid foundation to begin creating a new reality for oneself, a reality filled with infinite potential for peace, happiness, and well-being. May these words inspire you, and awaken within you the memory of a greater reality, and of your true nature.

Part I
A Journey of Awakening
~*~

A Happy Childhood

I am blessed to have had a wonderful childhood, filled with joyful moments spent with friends and family. My parents met in California in the 1970s after each migrating to San Francisco in search of a more meaningful way of life. They eventually settled down in the suburbs of northern California, where my sister and I spent the majority of our childhood. My parents questioned many of the cultural standards that they had been raised with, and were constantly exploring new ways of thinking and living.

Part of this exploration was an interest in Sufism. Our family belonged to a local Sufi church, and every week we would celebrate with the community through chanting, singing, and dancing. The Sufi community was a wonderful group of people, where potlucks, parties, and group camping trips were a regular occurrence. This provided rich experiences of connection early in my life, and I am so thankful to have been raised in such an open and accepting communal environment.

My parent's relationship also stands out in my memory as being particularly healthy and vibrant. My mother and father were deeply in love, and I am grateful to have had this model for relationship at an early age. I have fond memories of them relating in a loving and playful way, which contributed to a very positive environment for my sister and me. My parents placed an emphasis on honest and authentic communication, expressing one's feelings, and honoring one's own needs. This relatively enlightened style of parenting was the result of much inner work and spiritual investigation they had undergone throughout their lives.

From my parent's deep commitment to living authentically, a strong foundation of trust was fostered within our family. We spent many hours laughing and playing as a family, strengthening the bond between us. There were, of course, challenges that arose from time to time, and our life was not perfect by any means. Despite these challenges, however, the underlying experience of my early years was one of joy and peace.

From a very early age I was quite aware of the energy that I felt from the people around me. I often found myself less interested in the activities of my peers, and instead, focused on the relationship dynamics between other children, or between the adults and children in the classroom. I was labeled a "late bloomer" because of my introverted tendencies. As I remember it, my withdrawn tendencies allowed me to develop my skills of observation, and allowed me to remain connected to my inner sense of freedom and knowing.

As a child I never quite felt at home in my body, as though I knew this flesh and blood was not really who I was, but rather a temporary costume. Meeting an African American woman for the first time, and feeling a strong energetic connection with her, sparked a memory within me that seemed to come from another lifetime, as though being a woman with dark skin felt just as much "me" as what I saw reflected back in the mirror.

I was also fascinated with the topic of death at an early age, and wondered why nobody ever talked about it. Death was looming over all of us, and yet seemed to be ignored by most people around me. Out of concern, my parents invited the spiritual teacher from our Sufi church to our house one night to answer questions I had on the topic. I remember being aware that the teacher of our Sufi church didn't seem to have the answers to my questions, despite her best efforts. This meeting did little to calm my mind, but rather, piqued my curiosity even more. As I neared the end of 6th grade, my excitement to begin middle school was overshadowed by an unexpected event that would significantly change the course of my life.

A Profound Loss

Tragedy struck in the summer following my graduation from elementary school, when my father was killed in a hit-and-run car accident while riding his bike to work. The driver ran a red light, and my father was killed on impact. Our family was in shock. I had little time to process this life-changing event, as I was scheduled to begin middle school in a matter of weeks.

The death of my father sent my family into a tailspin. My mother became emotionally absent, and after a period of grieving, developed a pattern of spending time away from the house with friends or her boyfriend. Later she would admit that being in the house she and my father had raised our family was too painful for her. My sister, now a sophomore in high school, had turned to alcohol to numb the pain that she was feeling.

I, too, was deeply affected by the loss of my father, and felt the sense of safety and well-being that I had once known as a child disappear from my life. The activities I used to enjoy with friends no longer brought me much pleasure, and I often felt alone, confused, scared, and vulnerable. By the time I entered high school I had become withdrawn, depressed, anxious, and frustrated with life. I began having intense stomachaches and panic attacks on a recurring basis.

The unprocessed trauma from my father's death stayed with me, and I began acting out. I started stealing, drinking and smoking, sneaking out at night with friends, and breaking into cars. I had little interest in school, and my grades reflected this. It seemed to me that we were being taught to follow rules and please our teachers, rather than learning to truly think for ourselves.

Amidst my disillusionment I began seeking out spiritual material, reading books by Ram Dass, Timothy Leary, and Aldus Huxley. The suffering I was experiencing also propelled me to begin practicing meditation. And then one Sunday morning I came across some dusty books in my garage (relics from my parents earlier days of spiritual investigation) which had a profound impact on me. The books were called "Emmanuel's Books," and were authored by a woman named Pat Rodegast. There were three books in the series, which were based on the teachings of Emmanuel, who was a light-being, or angel. Emmanuel had come to Pat early in her life, and eventually Pat realized her role as a channel for this important spiritual wisdom.

The teachings of Emmanuel are so beautiful, so simple, and yet incredibly profound. When I first read these texts I felt alive, and had the feeling of suddenly seeing a bigger picture to life. The books focus on how we are all an expression of unconditional love, and that all of life is an extension of one source of energy. Emmanuel reminds us that we are all beings of light wearing human costumes, and that the suffering we experience is related to over identifying with these temporary human bodies. By choosing to embody love again and again, we can learn to reconnect to our true nature, dissolving the illusion of that which causes suffering.

These teachings resonated deeply in my heart, and I began observing in myself patterns of fear that had developed in my life. I also became aware of role-playing within myself, as well as in those around me, noticing how most people were looking for love outside of themselves in some way. These teachings helped me to see the world in a less serious and negative way, and I found myself beginning to enjoy life again. I was opening up to a greater reality, and beginning to see that life was far more interesting than I had previously thought.

During these few years my grades improved in school, and I began participating in life again. Beneath the surface, however, I could feel that something was not quite right. The teachings of Emmanuel had provided me with relief from my dreary everyday existence in high school, and yet on some level I knew that I was trying to escape something. It was hard for me to feel connected to other people, let alone my connection to the universe, when under the surface I still felt angry, judgmental, and negative towards life. In moments spent alone, I could feel an unresolved pain lying dormant within me, and I knew that it was only a matter of time before I would have to face it. Despite my inner turmoil I managed to graduate high school with honors, and made plans for college the following year.

An Energetic Awakening

It was the summer after I graduated high school that I had my first energetic awakening. I was at my friend's house one afternoon, when my friend's older brother, David, invited us to accompany him to see a holy woman. David had been planning to drive the three hours to a rural town to receive blessings from the woman at her ashram, and wanted some company for the drive. Having a strong interest in spirituality, I was eager to go on the journey. My friend declined, and so Dave and I headed out. I had no idea what was in store for me that night, but had a feeling that something significant lie ahead of me.

When we arrived at the ashram I was in awe of the magic and mystery of the place. The ashram itself was so beautiful, and the property, covered with fruit trees and sprawling meadows, was also breathtaking. There were people lined up in front of the ashram to receive blessings from the holy woman, who was known as Amachi. She was well known at the time as the "hugging saint," and had gained notoriety for offering a hug and a blessing to anyone who came before her.

I was a little skeptical at first, however, because the first thing that was requested of us was a donation. The donation seemed to be mandatory, so I begrudgingly dropped some money into the envelope that was being passed around. I began to have second thoughts about coming. The combination of a gift shop, a televised video of Amachi hugging people, and a certain fervor among her devotees, all left me feeling a little unnerved. Despite my cynicism I dutifully waited in line, which had become so long that it extended outside the building and down the long gravel drive. We waited in line for many hours, and as the night wore on I decided to get a closer look at Amachi to see what all the fuss was about. I had David hold my place in line while I peeked inside.

The ashram was a beautiful building, and had a side entrance for folks who wanted to peruse the gift shop and watch from the sidelines as devotees received their hugs. As I walked through the door I smelled incense, and noticed the gentle glow of candles and soft lighting. There was a palpable sense of peace and positivity emanating from the room, and I immediately felt at ease.

I had only taken a few steps into the ashram when I received a very strong wave of energy through my body. It felt as though someone had pushed me backwards. I was stopped in my tracks, and paused to collect myself, when another wave of energy passed through me. This time the energy was stronger than the first, knocking me down to my knees. I was in shock and didn't understand what was happening.

Then a third wave of energy moved through me, and this time an intense grief seemed to come pouring out of my heart as I collapsed to the floor, sobbing. I lay crumpled up on the floor, crying, unable to collect myself or stand up. A few nearby people helped me up and brought me back outside to where my friend David was. I stayed sitting in line while tears poured out of me, feeling this intense sadness and grief. I cried for the next hour, unable to talk about what had just happened. I was exhausted and confused, and now felt a pretty hefty dose of anxiety about receiving my hug. If simply going into the building knocked me over with energy, what would a hug from a holy woman do to me? By the time I received my hug from Amachi it was 2am. But despite my concern, the hug was relatively uneventful. I felt a strange peace and stillness during the hug. She whispered a mantra in my ear for me to repeat, which I forgot immediately.

As we left the ashram I felt that something had shifted within me. On the drive home I felt different, lighter, and more aware of myself and my surroundings. Though the event seemed profound, I had little context for it in my life, and over the next month it slipped out of my awareness. I returned to my every day life, and as summer reached a close, I began preparing for the next chapter of my life.

My life really began to unravel once I went off to college. I was holding onto the belief that I could start a new life in a new town, and that I could somehow leave my former painful experiences behind. Instead, the pain and sadness grew more intense, interfering with my ability to focus on my studies. I spent more time alone, walking in the woods, or drinking with my friends, rather than focusing on school, which seemed to me to be so contrived and inauthentic. The information that we were learning, and the way it was being presented, somehow felt false to me, and I did not know how to reconcile these feelings within. By the end of my first semester I had dropped out of college. I was miserable, hopeless, and lost. I was searching for greater meaning in my life, and decided to spend time traveling outside the U.S to get a different perspective on life.

By this time I had also come across another powerfully transformative book called, "The Miracle of Love," a compilation of stories about the Indian sadhu, Neem Karoli Babba (the guru of the well-known American spiritual teacher, Ram Dass). The stories in this book filled my heart with hope, inspiration, and thoughts of India. Stories of Neem Karoli Babba performing miracles, healing people, and bringing so much love into people's lives that they underwent powerful life changing transformations, often brought me to tears. One story, in particular, tells of Ram Dass' first encounter with Neem Karoli Babba, which left a strong impression in my mind and heart.

The story is written by Ram Dass, and recalls his initial meeting with the holy man at his ashram in India. Upon meeting Neem Karoli Babba, Ram Dass had a strong negative reaction, thinking all kinds of judgmental thoughts about the sadhu, whom he initially believed to be an imposter and a fraud. He stayed stewing in this negative state until the old sadhu directly addressed him. When Neem Karoli Babba recounted an intimate story, retelling events that Ram Dass had personally experienced earlier in his life, but had never shared with anyone, Ram Dass experienced what might be described as an "awakening"—a sudden opening to a greater reality. His mind couldn't compute how this stranger could have known such personal details about his life, and the result was that something within him cracked open. He began crying, feeling an overwhelming love flowing through his body, and from that point on, became a life-long disciple of Neem Karoli Babba.

Stories such as this one reminded me of a larger reality, one that was much greater than what I was experiencing in my day to day life. Having this awareness propelled me to investigate why my reality felt so limiting. I began looking at my life for clues. The emptiness I felt in life seemed directly related to being in an environment that did not inspire me. I knew I had to leave school, and after some reflection, I decided to drop out of college and travel. South America seemed to be calling me, and I made arrangements to travel through Peru and Ecuador for a few months.

The trip was wonderful in many ways, allowing me to expand my horizons beyond what I was accustomed in the U.S. During my travels I spent much time reflecting on my life, and began unraveling the trauma that lay dormant within me. Without the tools to process the trauma, however, I would often sink into patterns of self-pity and negativity. I remember one night, in particular, unraveling in a small town in Ecuador. I had bought a 40-ounce bottle of beer and got drunk by myself on the rooftop of a neighborhood apartment, drowning myself in a pool of pity and sorrow. I felt angry, alone, and depressed. I knew that the root of this sorrow was buried deep within me, but I didn't yet have the tools to access it.

By the time I arrived home, I had mustered a certain amount of resolve to do something with my life, and so I re-enrolled in community college. I was planning on majoring in fine art, as painting had become an important form of self-expression in my life. I was also involved in a relationship with a woman whom I was deeply in love with, and we spent most of our free time together, often cooking, creating art, and being domestic. Life seemed to be on the upward swing, if only temporarily.

The Grace Of Illness

Five months after I returned home from traveling I developed symptoms of what I thought was food poisoning. I had constant diarrhea, abdominal cramping, and eventually blood in my stool. It had gotten so serious that within an hour of eating I would have to go to the bathroom, which was often just a stream of blood. I made an appointment to see the doctor, and after many tests I was given the diagnosis of ulcerative colitis (U.C). The symptoms of U.C. were intense physical pain that often left me bed ridden with constant abdominal pain and urgent bowel movements. Living with U.C. took a toll on my mental and emotional health, and was a constant source of stress, anxiety, and depression throughout the eight years that I was inflicted with the illness.

Interestingly enough, during the initial weeks of my diagnosis, I underwent a huge emotional release, where repressed feelings of sadness and pain from my father's death surfaced unexpectedly in my life. Not only was I dealing with the diagnosis of this new disease, but I was also navigating strong emotions that seemed to come out of nowhere. Looking back on it now, I see that the process of my body becoming ill and physically weakened, also weakened my psychological defense mechanisms, allowing for a release of what was being repressed in my mind and body.

The first many months following my diagnosis I spent countless hours researching and investigating possible causes and cures for U.C. I tried every supplement, herb, and natural remedy that I came across. And though I often found temporary relief from the symptoms, nothing ever completely healed the illness. By the end of the first year I was losing hope that I would ever find a cure, and I resigned myself to living with this condition for the rest of my life. I felt like I was living in a bad movie, and that life had turned into a day-to-day struggle. My relationship with my girlfriend of many years had become one of the few things in my life that brought me any joy, and I am very grateful for her support during those challenging times. I was working at a restaurant, going to school part time, and just trying to survive.

By 2005 I had graduated with a degree in art and decided to get a master's degree in counseling. I had already begun investigating my own mental and emotional patterns, and intuitively knew that helping others heal would give my life a greater sense of purpose. My girlfriend and I moved to San Francisco so that I could be closer to the university.

Though I had direction in my life, I was still struggling just to make it through the day. There was a near constant background anxiety and sense of dread in my life, in addition to the relentless physical pain, bloating, and diarrhea. Moving to the city felt like a good move, but also seemed to intensify the anxiety I was feeling. It was during this transition that I experienced one of the most profound events of my life, one that would transform me in a powerful way.

The White Light

The experience occurred one night when my girlfriend and I were at a social gathering in Palo Alto, Ca. We had gone to a friend's birthday party and were sitting around an outdoor fire, enjoying the warm summer evening. I didn't feel particularly comfortable at the gathering, and I began having strong judgments towards myself and others. As I sat by the fire I unexpectedly began to feel very uncomfortable in my body. A strong sense of anxiety and dread set in, and I felt an urgent need to leave the gathering. Pulling my girlfriend aside, I explained what I was going through, and she agreed that we should leave. As we walked to the car I increasingly became very cold and began shaking, despite the warm summer weather.

We got into her car and she turned the heat on, which had little effect on my body temperature. As I sat in the car I noticed that everything around me—the interior of the car, the trees outside, the houses that lined the street—all seemed so foreign, cold, and threatening. By the time that we arrived home my anxiety and feelings of fear had intensified. I was still feeling very cold, and so we wrapped ourselves in blankets and lay down on the bed, my girlfriend holding me from behind.

The panic and fear continued to grow, and even though we were in a fully lit room, the edges of my vision started to become dark. I had experienced panic attacks in the past, and while they were uncomfortable and often frightening, this experience was exponentially more intense. It felt as though my entire reality was crumbling on a core level, and everything was closing in on me. I was consumed by a deep sense of doom and despair, like nothing I had ever experienced before. As my vision continued to darken I reached a point of complete panic, where I thought that I was going to cease to exist. I felt a scream of terror welling up in my throat. It was from this state of sheer panic that the shift occurred.

Right at that moment I felt a strong pull to look up. As I did, I was suddenly engulfed in a brilliant white light, which came pouring down into me from above, filling my vision and entire body. This light filled every part of me, and all at once I experienced the most ecstatic feelings of unconditional love, bliss, connection, and peace. Amidst the white light there were swirls of gold, pink, and violet. There was a feeling of complete safety and protection within this light, but most of all, I felt like I was home.

I was consumed by the deepest feeling of connection, to what felt like the entire universe. I was suddenly aware of my place and purpose for existing, and in this state it seemed that all of my fears, doubts, and the confusion about life vanished, as though they had never even existed. Within the white light I was surrounded by loving beings, all of whom felt like old friends I hadn't seen in a long time. For the first time in my life I truly felt at home, where everything was right (a profound confirmation of some distant memory from deep within my Soul). I was so happy to be back home that I didn't ever want to leave again.

I'm not sure how long this state lasted, it could have only been a few seconds or a few minutes. As the feelings faded, and the white light disappeared, I began speaking gibberish. The words pouring out of my mouth sounded like some foreign language, one that I had never heard before. I could neither understand nor control what I was saying, and as I rambled, I began sobbing uncontrollably. I didn't know it at the time, but I later learned that speaking in "tongues" is a common occurrence following this kind of ecstatic experience.

The feelings of love and bliss that I had experienced moments earlier were now gone, having been replaced by complete numbness. I stayed in this state for hours, shaking and crying. Even after the tears were gone, my body continued to heave and tremble. I stayed awake through most of the night, periodically drifting in and out of sleep.

When I awoke in the morning everything seemed profoundly different. The room looked radiant and alive in the morning sun, and all of the colors in the room looked so vibrant. My faculties had returned, and I felt an abundance of energy and joy. I felt reborn in this awareness of an ever-present and unconditionally loving energy, and I wanted to tell everyone. I wanted to share with the world what had just happened to me, and to let everyone know that we are always surrounded by light, and that our true home is a place of unconditional love, bliss, and peace.

I called my friend from the party to explain why we had

unexpectedly left the gathering and what had happened to me. As I began to talk about my experience from the previous night, the words coming from my mouth sounded empty and meaningless compared to what I had been through. No words could accurately describe the unconditional love that had so profoundly shook me to my core. Everything I said seemed to fall to the floor like a dead weight. When I tried explaining the experience to another friend, the same thing happened, and I began to feel a panic arising within me that this experience would be lost forever.

Over and over again I tried to tell people of what had happened to me. I found it nearly impossible to describe the experience, and was often brought to tears by attempting to do so. It was heartbreaking to feel one of the most profound experiences of my life slipping from my grasp. Eventually I stopped trying to talk about it altogether, simply because it was too painful. And like many of the other spiritual openings I had been through, there was little context in my life for this experience, and so I felt no recourse but to let it slip from my mind and try to return to a "normal" life.

Over the next month I did my best to put it behind me and move on. Though I had begun my master's program in counseling, and found a job working at a restaurant, this profound experience stayed with me in the back of my awareness, serving as a reminder of a greater truth. I did my best, however, to focus on this new chapter of my life. I felt that I was going in the right direction by studying counseling, but I continued to feel a sense of doubt about my life, always aware that there was this greater reality present, even though I had no understanding of how to connect with it.

This incongruency between my everyday reality, and the greater reality which I was now aware of, eventually caught up with me, resulting in a deep state of depression. Looking back on it now I can see how after experiencing such bliss and unconditional love, to try and go back to my everyday life, filled with such anxiety, doubt, and uncertainty, only heightened my awareness of how disconnected I felt. The connection and love that I felt in my relationship with my girlfriend, friends, and family (although wonderful) paled in comparison to the feelings of unconditional love that I now knew was possible. It ate away at me to think that I could potentially be living in that state all the time, and yet to see that with my present trajectory I may never experience it again.

I did my best, however, to try and make it work. I believed that if I tried harder I could achieve a sense of well-being and happiness in my life, which perhaps would bring me closer to the feeling of deep connection I had experienced months earlier. The more I tried, however, the further I seemed to get from that feeling. My relationship with my girlfriend started to become stagnant, and we found ourselves stuck in patterns of watching television, buying things we didn't really need, and I started to become overly focused on food and sex as a way to appease my growing anxiety and depression.

Though I felt love and appreciation for my partner, I struggled in our relationship. I felt a nearly constant sense of dread and doom in my life that was subtly eroding my ability to function in the world. I began to look outside myself more and more to find relief from my depression. My girlfriend and I decided to try an open relationship, one that would allow us both more freedom to explore and have new experiences. This was the beginning of my downward tailspin.

The Dysfunction of Psychology

In addition to my relationship problems, I began having serious doubts about entering into the field of psychology. Looking around at my professors, my fellow students, and even the directors of the counseling program, everyone seemed to be suffering just as I was, if not more. I could sense the anxiety, doubt, and frustration that lay beneath many people's smiling faces. The theories we were learning in the program seemed overly intellectual, and aimed more towards helping people adjust to the disconnection they felt in their lives, rather than understanding the root cause. It was discouraging to feel that even my professors didn't really know what it was to be truly free of suffering, nor how to heal.

The longer I was in the program the more aware I became of how flimsy my education was. My professors were regurgitating theories that they had learned, while we memorized and regurgitated these same theories back, without actually experiencing their supposed healing effects firsthand. We seemed to mostly be learning how to categorize and conceptualize "mental illness," which I began to realize often only perpetuated the problem. It was disconcerting to see a lack of understanding (or even an acknowledgment) regarding the power of love to heal.

I also began to notice that, according to the text books we were reading, most everyone in my program seemed to be suffering from some form of mental illness to varying degrees. I saw the same power and control issues arise again and again between students and professors, between members of the faculty, and between clients and counselors. I noticed that the inherent power differential in a traditional counseling relationship lends itself to subtly reinforcing disempowerment among those being counseled.

It seemed to me that the entire concept of implementing calculated and strategic treatment plans for clients seemed like a head-trip, and somewhat manipulative. I could see how students and professors alike were attached to the the role "professional psychologist," as a way to enhance their sense of identity. When underneath I could feel they were still suffering in some way, trying to organize their life in a way that would appease their own subtle feelings of anxiety and deep-seated fears.

Ironically, the very text we were using to study mental illness, the Diagnostic and Statistical Manual (DSM), was an example of some form of insanity by those in power. The DSM is a comprehensive manual of all psychological dysfunctions, and is the foundational text used for diagnosing mental illness and prescribing medication. The ongoing joke in the counseling program was how it was well known that the DSM is sponsored, in part, by the same people who run some of the largest and most influential pharmaceutical companies in the U.S. It is no coincidence that the number of mental illness diagnosis in the DSM has significantly increased over the last few decades in direct proportion to the development of new medications to treat those very same dysfunctions. The more diagnoses that can be made for various conditions, the more medications can be sold to treat these "mental illnesses." This greed and manipulation by those at the top of the mental health field is an example of how the system itself has gone mad.

As I continued to struggle through school, I began reflecting on my life, wondering how I had become so disconnected from the happy child that I remembered myself to be. It was during this time that I returned to the teachings of Emmanuel that I had discovered as an adolescent, and began to remember these greater spiritual truths. One afternoon I found myself on a website devoted to the teachings of Emmanuel. In the footer of the website I noticed a lone phone number with no description. I had a question about an upcoming workshop and decided to call the number, assuming it would connect me with an automated recording, or perhaps to the web host who updated the site. To my surprise an older woman picked up the phone and greeted me. She introduced herself as Pat, and I was surprised to discover that it was Pat Rodegast (the woman who channeled Emmanuel).

Now in her late 70's, Pat was still channeling Emmanuel, and I immediately noticed her eccentric and quirky personality. She laughed loudly, was playful, and not at all what I expected a spiritual channel to be. She also offered to give me a channeling session. When I admitted that I could not afford the session, she offered to do it for free, saying there was a reason why I had called her. She told me to call her back the following Sunday for a session. I gave her no information about myself apart from my phone number—she didn't even know my last name.

The following Sunday, however, I couldn't bring myself to call her. I was anxious about what I might find out, as well as a bit put off by Pat's eccentric and wild energy. I was afraid I might find out that Pat was a little loopy, or that the teachings of Emmanuel weren't what I thought they were. It didn't matter because Pat called me. She then began channeling Emmanuel, and the session that followed was incredible.

Emmanuel told me things about myself that Pat could have had no way of knowing. The information that came through was amazing, and as specific as describing the color combinations I had been using in my recent paintings. One thing in particular that Emmanuel said, was that there would come a time when I would heal myself from a disease relating to digestion. I had not told Pat about my disease, nor given any indication that I was ill. Emmanuel said that I would heal myself from this intestinal disease, and go on to be a teacher and counselor for others who were healing.

To hear this information brought incredible joy and happiness into my heart, and I was in awe at the accuracy and poignancy of Emmanuel's words. By the end of the session I was in tears, overwhelmed, and left in a state of disbelief. Again, I didn't know what to do with this experience, and as exciting as it was, I was still feeling confused and hopeless about my life. One thing I knew for sure was that if I was going to become a counselor I had to finish my master's program, and so my resolve strengthened to focus on school.

This proved to be easier said than done, however. By my last year of graduate school my anxiety and depression had grown in intensity, to the point where I had resigned myself to seeing a psychiatrist, despite my awareness of the dysfunctional state of psychiatry and psychology. I remember the surreal experience of visiting the psychiatrist. It was a brief meeting that lasted roughly 20 minutes. Sitting in his sterile office under bright fluorescent lights, the psychiatrist asked me a few questions about my mental health, which seemed pointed at determining whether or not I was either suicidal, or a danger to others. When he seemed satisfied that I was more or less docile, he prescribed me medication for anxiety.

Within a week of beginning the medication I noticed some unsettling changes. Though it elevated my mood, it also created a manic effect, causing me to become overly excited, and even aggressive. I felt a new confidence, and found myself being more social and outgoing, yet in a less than peaceful way. My anxiety had lessened, but I also felt more reckless, not seeming to care as much about myself or others.

With this new found attitude, I started to break the agreements that my girlfriend and I had created regarding our open relationship, and I had sexual encounters with other women without informing her. This proved to be the final straw in our relationship. We decided to end our eight year relationship, a decision that was heartbreaking for both of us. And once our relationship ended, I became even more careless.

In addition, I had just graduated school, and felt such disillusionment with the field of psychology that I had little interest in pursuing the 3000 intern hours required in order to get licensed as a professional therapist. I was left feeling that I had wasted 3 years of my life, and in the wake of my breakup with my girlfriend and disappointment with school, I started to become increasingly self-destructive. Despite regular flare-ups of the symptoms from ulcerative colitis, I started drinking heavily, making myself even sicker on a regular basis.

In the absence of any direction, the focus of my life became pursuing women and sex, drinking with friends, and fitting in with the hip culture of San Francisco. My mental, emotional, and physical health began deteriorating quickly, and I found myself once again feeling isolated, hopeless, and desperate for something to wake me from this bad dream. The medication that I had been taking for ulcerative colitis was increasingly making me sick, causing my hair to fall out, and often left me feeling nauseous and fatigued. After a series of short term relationships and one night stands, I began to feel a new level of self loathing, knowing that I was not honoring myself or my Soul's purpose for this lifetime. And again, the Universe sent me another much needed wake-up call.

Kundalini Awakening

The experience occurred one night while I was sitting in the passenger side of my friend's car, waiting for her return from the store. We had just attended a lecture on the White Tara, an avatar of healing and compassion in the Tibetan Buddhist tradition. The talk seemed overly intellectual and a bit creepy, and I was happy that it was over. As I waited in the car I was meditating on my breath. I had also been juice-fasting the entire day—a practice that I had recently started as a way to give my intestines time to recover between flare-ups. I was feeling surprisingly peaceful, light, and relaxed as I waited for my friend.

Just as my friend was returning to the car, something strange began to happen. I felt a vibration in the base of my spine that felt like an intense tingling sensation. I paused and looked over at my friend. As we stared at one another, the last words I was able to speak were, "something's happening," at which point my body began to freeze up. My legs and arms stiffened out in front of me, and my head pushed hard back into the headrest. The vibration at the base of my spine began to grow in intensity as it slowly moved up my body. My hands clenched into fists that I couldn't open, and I started making uncontrollable wailing sounds, rocking my body forward and backward. I was barely able to turn my head towards my friend, who I saw out of the corner of my eye, looking shocked as she braced herself between the steering column and her seat.

The vibration grew in intensity and continued to rise up my body. When it got to my heart I felt a burst of energy in my chest, and experienced something that I can only describe as intense grief and intense ecstasy occurring simultaneously. My body began convulsing and shaking. The vibration continued to rise up into my throat and head. When it got to the top of my head it became even more vivid, feeling like a thousand tiny needles prickling my scalp. My vision began to get dark, and even though I had lost control of my body and was in this strange state, some part of me knew it was okay, and I heard a voice in the back of my mind say, "let go," at which point I released the remaining resistance I was holding. When I did, I suddenly felt the wave of energy shoot up through the crown of my head and out of my body.

My body went limp, and I was left weeping and trembling. My friend quickly drove me to her house and helped me to lie down on the sofa. While lying down I had alternating sensations of complete exhaustion mixed with powerful bursts of energy. One minute I wanted to jump up and celebrate, but as soon as I went to move, I realized I barely had the energy to lift my body. I felt like a train had passed directly through me. I spent the next few days recovering, trying to make sense of what had happened to me. A week later my friend sent me a text message that read, "you might want to research kundalini awakening."

I had heard the term before, but didn't know anything about

22

what a kundalini awakening was, nor the implications involved in having one. After reading up on the "symptoms" of a kundalini awakening, such as a loss of control of the body, uncontrollable wailing sounds, energy moving up through the body that originates from the base of the spine, I realized that this description fit my experience almost perfectly. The more I read up on it, the more I began to understand why it had happened to me.

The energy that I was repressing from earlier trauma in my life had created energetic blockages in my body, specifically in my intestines (according to Chinese medicine, each area of the body is responsible for governing certain emotions, with the intestines governing grief and sadness). A kundalini awakening often occurs when a person's energy system becomes blocked, and a sudden release of energy is required to clear the blockage. Looking back on this event, my physical disease seemed like a clear reflection of this energetic blockage in my body, and this release of energy was apparently necessary to initiate my healing.

What typically follows a kundalini experience is a period of months to years when parts of the self (parts that were previously being repressed in the unconscious layers of mind) come to the surface of one's awareness for a process of integration. This experience of integration can cause much inner turmoil, chaos, and intense mental anguish. This is described in numerous texts about kundalini awakenings, and it is said that in India there are mental institutions solely devoted to those individuals who have gone "crazy" following a kundalini awakening. I avoided reading about this aspect of the awakening process, perhaps because some part of me knew that I was about to go through it, and I didn't want to have someone else's ideas fueling the potential drama that my mind might create around the experience. I was feeling anxious and confused following the episode, and I tried to put the experience behind me.

Though the full effects of the kundalini awakening wouldn't be known to me for a few months, I quickly found that returning to my everyday life was nearly impossible, as I now had an increased awareness of the remaining energy blockages within me waiting to be released. My awareness of my body had intensified following the awakening experience, and I could now feel a quality of subtle spiritual energy within me as it flowed through my mind, emotions, and body. I could also feel when this energy was becoming stuck. With limited tools to move and release this stuck energy, however, I felt increasingly overwhelmed and vulnerable.

During this time my life in San Francisco continued to become more surreal and transparent. Everything I was doing felt like I was just going through the motions. I had begun experiencing life in a new way, with greater energetic sensitivity within myself and to the energy within others. I realized that life in the city was not supporting my overall health and well-being, and I knew I had to get away if I was going to keep my sanity.

Being in nature felt like a healing direction, and I decided to take a month off to work on an organic farm in Costa Rica. I figured this would allow me some time to process and integrate what had recently happened to me. I bought a plane ticket, packed my bags, and eagerly headed off for what I thought would be a relaxing break from the intensity of recent events.

The Power of Surrender

The farm in Costa Rica was in a remote part of the Cerro Chirripo Mountains, and getting there required a long bus ride up a winding dirt road, followed by a long hike up into the mountains. There was no road access to the farm, nor any hot water or electricity on site. I was committed to roughing it in the jungle to experience a life totally different from the one that I knew so well back in San Francisco. I was also taking a huge leap of faith by traveling to another undeveloped country, given my delicate state of health and vulnerability to intestinal infection. My need to make significant changes in my life was beginning to trump the fear of my disease and physical limitations.

The couple who owned the farm, Alex and Zina, were both Americans who had moved to Costa Rica to find a more meaningful way of life. Zina had two boys from a previous partner, and they all lived in a small house perched on a mountain overlooking the beautiful Cerro Chirripo valley. We all took turns cooking, and I worked in the jungle during the day with Alex, clearing, weeding, and helping to mill lumber from a giant felled tree near their house.

I had only been there for two weeks, and had been enjoying myself, when I became intensely ill. After eating some homemade cheese that was given to Alex and Zina by a local woman, I came down with a very bad stomachache. The pain worsened throughout the day, and that night I began having incredibly painful stabbing sensations in my stomach. The pain got so bad that simply having a sip of water felt like shards of glass rolling around in my insides. I was unable to eat or even drink water due to the pain. By the third day I began to become concerned. I was aware of our remote location, and how difficult it would be to get to a hospital if my condition worsened. I asked Alex if he might assist me down the mountain to the bus stop so I could go to a hospital. Alex, however, believed that my illness was on account of detoxifying from the chemicals in my body from life in the U.S., and that it would all resolve itself in good time. The lack of receptivity to what I felt was a legitimate concern only increased my anxiety.

By the fourth day I was so weak that I could barely move. Alex and Zina moved me into the main house and put me on a mat in the living room. They decided to do energy healing work on me that night. As they both sat around me by candlelight, sending healing energy into my body, all I could think of was how I had hooked up with two "crazy hippies" that didn't seem very concerned with my well-being. It seemed so clear to me that they were both lost in their fantasy of living off the grid, in a make-believe world where their energy could heal people.

My mind began to create all sorts of negative ideas and scenarios, reviewing the last few weeks for evidence proving that these two people were out of touch with reality, and that I was in real danger of dying atop this remote mountain. At one point during their energy healing the pains got even more intense, and I was moaning aloud from the stabbing sensations in my stomach. It was at this moment that Alex leaned in and whispered something in my ear that I will never forget; "have you ever thought about surrendering to

Jesus?" This phrase had a particular potent effect on me, and his words couldn't have been phrased any more perfectly.

Most of my life I had been very prejudiced against organized religion, particularly Christianity. This resistance was formed early in childhood, partly on account of my parent's reaction to mainstream organized religion, and also because I had had many experiences with religious folks over the years who seemed to be pushing their will onto me, never seeming to be that interested in getting to know me, or hear my point of view. From very early in my life I felt resentment towards those who spoke of Jesus and God with authority, when I could feel how their energy was less than totally loving and accepting, but rather rooted in some expression of anxiety or fear.

This form of subtle manipulation, with the aim of coercing someone into believing in a specific religious path, had always seemed particularly offensive to me. I had a history of bashing religion during my adolescence, believing that I knew a greater truth; that we all were connected by the same divine energy. Despite this intellectual understanding, however, I still hadn't felt this Higher Love very deeply in my life at that time.

So when Alex leaned in and whispered, "have you ever thought about surrendering to Jesus?" it triggered something deep within me. I felt a flash of anger, followed by a flurry of mental activity and accusations of these people taking care of me. It was suddenly so clear that these "crazy religious nuts" never really cared about me, and were happy to let me die, believing that I was simply detoxifying. In a matter of a few seconds I went even deeper into this extremely negative place of anger and fear. I wanted to scream and physically hurt Alex I was so angry.

And then in an instant a switch flipped within me. I suddenly saw how my mind was creating all of my suffering in the form of resistance to my situation. I saw that I didn't really know anything about Jesus because I had always been so focused on resisting Christianity. And in the midst of my intense physical suffering it occurred to me that I was willing to do anything to find relief, even willing to let go of my resistance to Jesus. In a moment of sheer desperation I yelled out, "Jesus, I surrender!"

The next moment I began vomiting in such a way that I had

never experienced before, nor since. I vomited what seemed like the entire contents of my body. It was a putrid bright orange liquid that came out of me, and I remember watching Zina back out of the room on account of the acrid smell. The bowl that Alex had brought me, in the event that I did vomit, filled and overflowed onto the floor. It felt like some sort of exorcism, and I was letting go of some deeply held "demons" in the form of a strong resistance to life. Even after my stomach had emptied, I continued to dry heave for some time. Within an hour of the purge I felt dramatically better. By the next morning the pain was gone, and I spent the next two days recovering.

This experience left a strong impression on me, highlighting the dysfunctional aspects of my own mind. I saw that I had created much of the psychological suffering of that experience through resistance and my own negative self-talk. I had created these stories in my mind about my circumstances, and about Alex and Zina, which ultimately proved to be false. If I had truly been interested in healing, it seems that I would have focused on healing thoughts and feelings, rather than the potential negative aspects of my situation. Feeling weak and shaken I decided it would be best to leave the farm and move on.

I said my goodbyes to Alex and Zina, and continued the next leg of my journey; a nine-hour bus ride up the coast. Exhausted, I could barely keep my head up, and quickly fell asleep on the bus. When I awoke, my bag with all of my personal belongings was gone from the overhead compartment. In my sleep deprived state I had made a critical error; leaving my bag unattended and vulnerable to theft. I was left only with my bag of clothes and sleeping bag, yet with no money, credit cards, nor even my passport. I was penniless, without identification, and alone in a foreign country. I began to panic, frantically searching for my bag. It seemed that my worst fear was coming true, and I did my best to calm myself down despite my situation.

Luckily, a women whom I had been volunteering with at the farm was on the same bus, and overheard the commotion. She offered to lend me some money, and amazingly another woman who owned a nearby hotel offered me a room at a significantly discounted rate, with the option of paying once I had secured some funds. I felt incredibly grateful to have received this support, and my spirits were immediately lifted by this stroke of good fortune. I accompanied the woman to her hotel, where she went out of her way to help in any way that she could. I was deeply touched at the kindness of strangers to help a person in need.

That night as I sat out on the veranda of the hotel, enjoying my dinner under the darkening sky, I felt a tremendous peace wash over me. Surprisingly, I felt a surge of joy at having lost all of my valuables, and began laughing at this new found sense of freedom. In that moment I clearly saw how ridiculous the whole drama was—it seemed absurd that anyone should feel so much angst over losing such small pieces of paper. In addition, I suddenly felt the weight of my personal identity being lifted. Having been relieved of my passport, somehow my beingness no longer felt reduced to a social security number, a name, or a country of origin—as though any of those superficial descriptors had anything to do with who I was. I was now simply a human being on the earth, enjoying a meal out under the stars.

And with this new sense of freedom came an inexplicable sense of joy, happiness, and aliveness. There was no logical reason to feel so happy given my circumstances. How could my feelings about the situation be so at odds with the reality of my circumstances? This experience seemed to further highlight just how irrational my mind was. As joyful as I felt, it was also unsettling to realize that I wasn't really in control of my own mind. My reactions in both of these situations; joy from losing all of my valuables; and extreme negativity while becoming sick at the farm, seemed to be occurring beyond my control. I remember thinking, "well if I am not in control of my mind, then who is?"

Discovering the Ego

The awareness of the dysfunction of my own mind stayed with me upon my return to San Francisco, and I began actively seeking out

28

answers. The answer came more quickly than I anticipated, in the form of the contemporary spiritual teachings of Eckhart Tolle. My friend gave me the book, "A New Earth," and I began reading and rereading the chapters on the ego. Tolle's teachings focus on understanding and dissolving the ego, which, as Tolle points out, is not personal, but rather a universal phenomenon occurring within most everyone.

For so long I had been carrying the dysfunction of my own mind around like a cross on my back, feeling that something was wrong with me for having negative and fearful thoughts, and for not being in control of my own mind. It was so liberating to see that the dysfunctional mind was not a reflection of who I was in my essence, but rather a psychological survival mechanism that is inherently part of the human condition, existing within almost everyone in varying degree. I was primed for these teachings about the ego, and readily absorbed the information. As I began understanding the mechanisms of the ego, I was amazed to see that much of my life I had been following this unconscious stream of thoughts in my mind (the ego), and consequently, causing myself so much suffering.

I had heard of the ego previously in my life, but never thought of myself as having an ego. When I thought of people with big egos, I thought of the greedy business person, or an overly confident and cocky person, but hadn't really considered my own ego that much before. I didn't truly understand what the ego was. As I continued listening to Tolle's teachings, I began to understand that the ego is literally the incessant voice in the mind that constantly hypnotizes one's attention with both positive and negative thoughts about oneself, others, and the world.

The ego is the voice in the mind that so many people mistakenly believe is who they are, and believe the voice to be an accurate interpretation of reality. To suddenly become aware that I am not the thoughts in my mind, but rather, that which is aware of the thoughts—the field of consciousness itself—was like opening a huge creaky gate that had been locked for so long. And now a sliver of light was beginning to shine into my life, and I began to notice a new vitality and aliveness that I had not felt in a long time.

During the two weeks that I studied these teachings, it seemed that everyday I was having new revelations as to how my ego had been running my life. I saw how the negative thoughts and beliefs in my mind were keeping my energy restricted, limiting my experience of love, joy, and connection. I saw how the way I related to people, the types of things I talked about, the activities that I thought were important, the foods that I ate, the goals in my life, and even the way that I breathed, were all influenced by the incessant voice in my mind. It seemed that almost every aspect of my life was in some way influenced by the ego. During those two weeks I withdrew socially, and became like a scientist of the self, observing my every thought, feeling, and action. I could feel that I was on the cusp of some major breakthrough, and yet nothing could have prepared me for how this opening would unfold.

The shift occurred during a meeting for an internship I was about to begin. The internship was for a position as a counselor for troubled youth with developmental disabilities at a counseling center in South San Francisco. The population was one of the most challenging to work with, and required a tough exterior and great focus. Looking back on it now, I can see that I was in no state to be starting such a position. Attempting to begin this position was my last-ditch effort to try and make life in the city work. The meeting began with each person introducing themselves, discussing their educational experiences, as well as their role at the center. The group included the principle of the school where the center was located, the head of the counseling program, other counseling faculty, and the new interns (myself and two other women).

When I arrived at the meeting I was continuing to practice what I had been practicing for the past two weeks; letting go of the thoughts in my mind, letting go of the need to control life, and instead, just staying present with my breath. From this commitment to stay present, something unexpected began to happen during the meeting. What I believe was partly due to my mild state of anxiety during the meeting, as well as the dissolution of the filters of my mind and ego that had been taking place over the last two weeks, I began to notice what might best be described as a heightened state of perceptual awareness. I began to see colors emanating from people as they spoke, as well as feel their energy very strongly in my own body.

As the principle began speaking about his love for his work, I saw light blues and purples swirling around him, and felt waves of loving energy flowing from his body. When the head of the counseling center introduced herself, I saw swirls of pink and violet moving around her, and felt waves of positive energy flowing from her body. It was so beautiful, and I was captivated by this new experience. When one of the counseling faculty spoke, on the other hand, there were no colors, but rather what felt like a vacuum, pulling energy from the room. It was uncomfortable to look at him, and I found myself wanting to turn away. When the interns spoke I saw small bursts of color and energy, but nothing like what I felt coming from the principle or the head of the counseling program.

When it was my turn to speak I was at a loss for words. I knew I was meant to say something about myself, and yet in this heightened state I was so overwhelmed and captivated by this new experience of seeing colors and feeling energy, that the normal function of my mind that usually kept tabs on appropriate social behavior had been switched off. I was truly being present, and in this presence I was experiencing a whole new dimension to life, with much less filter from my mind.

As I opened my mouth to speak, I paused. I realized that none of the thoughts running through my mind regarding what I could say about myself had anything to do with the truth of who I was. My education, where I came from, my hobbies, even my name, had nothing to do with who I was in my essence. I asked myself the question, "what is one thing that I know is true in this moment?" As I glanced around the room for inspiration, my eyes landed on a small bowl of fruit placed near the center of the table, and I heard myself say, "I like fruit," at which point I began to cry. The tears came unexpectedly, and I remember glancing up to see a look of confusion on the faces of the people at the table. I looked to the woman who had hired me and saw an expression that reflected a combination of confusion mixed with horror. She clearly was having second thoughts about choosing me for the position.

The group decided to take a little break, and the woman pulled me into her office to see what was going on. I explained that I had been reading Eckhart Tolle, and surprisingly, she understood. We both agreed that it would be best if I left the meeting. I remember walking out of the building and feeling this energetic heaviness moving up through my body and being released through my shoulders. I was letting go of something that had been restricting my energy for a long time, and this release allowed me to continue experiencing this heightened state of awareness.

As I walked out of the building I was shocked to see that the trees and buildings were also emanating bright and beautiful colors. I suddenly felt such indescribable joy and happiness. Driving home in this state was incredible, as everything (particularly the trees and sky) were infused with beautiful swirling colors and light. But most of all, I was remarkably happy. By the time I arrived home my perceptions had more or less returned to "normal," and feeling exhausted, I fell asleep.

Awakening the Heart

The next morning when I awoke, the first thing I noticed was an intense stillness. Though there were sounds of birds chirping and neighborhood noises, there was a palpable sense of stillness that felt profound. As I went downstairs everything felt and looked different. Nothing had been physically changed in the house, yet somehow it all looked slightly brighter, more colorful, and more alive. I also noticed a deep feeling of happiness for what seemed like no reason at all.

Over the next few weeks I experienced such deep levels of bliss and joy, and spent most days walking the streets of San Francisco so incredibly happy to be alive. I sat on a bench and marveled at how beautiful the trees were. I sat on the sidewalk and would laugh for no reason other than feeling so happy. Walking down the street I felt great love and gratitude for all of the people passing me by.

One older woman, in particular, stands out in my memory. I was sitting on the sidewalk watching the people pass by, when I saw her face. She was glowing with a golden light much brighter than what I was seeing in most people passing by, and her smile brought a powerful burst of love into my heart. She appeared to me to be an angel. I held my hands to my heart and cried in joy as she passed by.

For weeks I walked and just appreciated being alive. At night I enjoyed laying out under the evening sky, feeling an immense connection to what felt like every star in the universe. I would often alternate between tears and laughter, as my whole reality seemed to now encompass the most beautiful and heavenly realms. My mind was incredibly still during this time, and my body felt so good, so alive, and radiant with energy.

After a few weeks these effects began to lessen, and I noticed that my mind was once again becoming active. I began to have thoughts that these feelings of bliss would go away, and I really didn't want that to happen. Ironically, as my desire to hold onto this state increased, the more it slipped from my grasp. I found myself wanting to tell people about what I was experiencing, perhaps as a way to keep it alive.

I reached out to my uncle, who was a therapist. We went out to breakfast one morning, and while recounting my experience to him with enthusiasm and joy, I sensed that he wasn't really hearing me. I could almost see him filtering my words through his mind, trying to categorize and make sense of what I was saying based on what he had been taught was normal and healthy. I felt like shaking him and telling him to just listen to what I was saying. I found out later that he thought it would be good if I saw a psychiatrist, and possibly be put on medication.

In fact, the reactions that I was getting from most of the people around me began to have an effect on me. I noticed how uncomfortable it made most people when I talked about my feelings of unconditional love, bliss, and happiness. I noticed how people were reacting to me as if they thought something was wrong with me. Even though I was happier than I had ever been in my life, I began to question my own sanity.

One reason for my concern was that, because everything was so new, it was like relearning how to do everyday tasks. I remember the first time I used the stove to cook some eggs following my awakening, and it was like re-learning this simple task all over again.

The automatic behaviors of quickly grabbing a pan, turning on the flame, and cracking the eggs had been dissolved, and now every step of the process seemed fresh and joyous. I remember just laughing in amazement at the beauty of the hot pan melting the oil, and seeing the runny part of the eggs turn from clear to white. It was all so beautiful. I felt like a child again, experiencing everything as though for the first time.

When I invited my mother and sister over for breakfast one morning to share my new experiences, they came in the kitchen to find me standing over my pan of eggs, laughing, with tears in my eyes. They couldn't understand why I would be so happy to make eggs. I began to feel like I had departed from the "reality" that the majority of people were living, and it was making others uneasy. Most people feel they have to work for their happiness by doing something right, achieving their goals, or being good at something. You can't just be happy for no reason. And here I was, experiencing incredible joy from the simple task of cooking eggs.

Throughout all of these changes I was having an increasingly difficult time relating to my friends and family, and I realized there was no way I could go back to my old way of life. I now had the understanding of the limitations of the mind, and instead of trying to think about what to do, I started more fully feeling into what wanted to happen through me. I had gained the understanding that being in connection with the energy of the Universe meant letting go of the ego, letting go of personal desires, and aligning myself with the subtle spiritual energy I could now feel pulsing through my body.

This is when life really started to become interesting, as I was about to embark on a journey of deep personal transformation and healing. During this process I would begin to connect more fully to my heart, as well as understand firsthand the law of attraction, seeing just how powerful our thoughts are in shaping our experience of reality. Though the challenges I would face in the coming time would be more intense, in many ways, than what I had previously experienced, my perspective on life had been profoundly shifted for the better. I now had a higher perspective on the nature of reality, and greater tools for navigating life's challenges with loving awareness, rather than from the limitations of the mind.

A New World

The internal shift I had gone through seemed to open up a whole new world for me. Though the intense bliss and ecstasy faded after those initial weeks, I continued to feel incredibly happy. I no longer felt that background anxiety or dread in my life, but instead I mostly felt relaxed, joyful, and peaceful. The pressure I had previously felt to be successful, or to "make something of myself," had all but disappeared from my life, and I was left asking myself the question, "what do I want to do today?" The possibilities seemed endless now that fear was not such a factor in my life. I decided to quit my job, and instead just walk around. I would put my shoes on in the morning and head out the door to enjoy my life.

While walking the streets of San Francisco one day I noticed a flyer mentioning that the same hugging saint I had visited a decade earlier, Amachi, was going to be at her ashram outside of the city in the coming weeks. My previous experience at her ashram had had a profound effect on me, and visiting her again had often come into my mind since that time. It seemed like a sign, and I felt strongly guided to see her again after so many years.

It was a beautiful and sunny morning as I left my house for the ashram. I took the train out of the city, and then a shuttle, which was delivering people to the ashram. I immediately noticed a woman on the shuttle, on account of her peaceful energy, and I felt compelled to connect with her. But by the time we had arrived at the ashram, however, she had become lost in the shuffle, and I didn't see her again for the duration of my visit.

The day I spent at Amachi's ashram was wonderful. There were so many nice people there, and lots of excitement and commotion. Surprisingly, I didn't feel particularly compelled to receive my holy hug, but rather felt a desire to leave early. On the train back to the city I was wondering why I had felt drawn to leave early, when I noticed the same woman from the shuttle that I had seen earlier was now sitting only a few seats down from me. We began a conversation and immediately I felt a strong connection with her. Within minutes I began to feel something that I hadn't experienced before. It didn't feel like a sexual or romantic attraction, but it was a very strong attraction, stronger than any friendship that I had ever experienced. It felt as though I had known and loved her like a sister from another lifetime. She felt it too, and within a few minutes we were talking about it.

The woman's name was Ashana, and she had a very loving energy that sparkled in her eyes. We spent the next few weeks together just talking, hanging out, and meditating. I felt so safe and comfortable in her presence, and our time together seemed like magic. We would often just sit and laugh at nothing, being playful like children, taking naps in the park, or making food for each other. It felt like time disappeared when we were together. I could talk to her about my awakening experience of feeling joy and bliss, feeling a deep connection to the Universe, and I knew that she understood.

Ashana had also recently gone through her own awakening experience, and was preparing to move out of the city. During one conversation we talked about how exciting it would be to live in Hawaii. As we talked we both had a strong feeling that this would be a really good thing for us to do. In our excitement and joy we decided that we would travel to Hawaii together in a few weeks. I could hardly believe how quickly things were changing in my life. I had met an amazing new friend, felt extremely happy, and I was going to live in Hawaii. I was inspired, hopeful, and full of life.

In the past I would have been somewhat nervous about traveling with such abandon, on account of my digestive illness. But that fear was no longer with me, and I suddenly knew that I was healed. The miraculous healing had occurred quietly and simply. I awoke one morning (about a month after my awakening experience) and suddenly realized that I didn't need to take my medication anymore. So I stopped. I had been on medication for so long, taking 16 pills a day for eight years. In the past, had I missed a few doses, I would have been sick with pain, bloating, and diarrhea.

Amazingly, I stopped my medication and my symptoms were gone. Two days passed, four days, a week, two weeks, and still no symptoms. This confirmed what I already knew in my heart; that my disease had been healed through the release of blocked emotional energy in my body. The gratitude I felt for this healing was beyond words. It was like being let out of prison after eight years. I was so grateful to be healed, and wanted to share this experience with others.

It is important to mention, however, that in addition to the spiritual transformation that I had gone through, I had also begun intuitively changing my diet, removing many inflammation causing foods (such as gluten, sugar, and dairy), doing juice fasting, and taking specific supplements. Though I had done many of these things in the past, it was the dissolution of my ego which provided the big breakthrough, and which seemed to crystallize my healing process. But I do not discount the dietary and lifestyle choices that I was making, which is why I emphasize the importance of a holistic approach for the healing journey. This is what prompted me to create the last chapter of this book, entitled, "The Holistic Healing Process," which outlines all of the dietary and lifestyle practices that I regard as the most powerful tools for healing the mind, body, and spirit.

Though my body healed within the first month of my awakening, there was one incident where my symptoms briefly returned, and it felt like a test I knew I had to face. It was during a meditation one night that I was faced with some final aspect of my disease that I was ready to address. It first began as a sharp stabbing pain in my stomach, which jarred me from my meditation. It seemed to come out of nowhere, and although I had been accustomed to stomach and intestinal pain in the past, it had been over a month since I had experienced any symptoms from ulcerative colitis.

The sensations grew in intensity, to the point of becoming excruciatingly painful. I was confused as to where this pain could be coming from, and I watched as thoughts ran through my mind telling me to jump up and go to the emergency room, to call for help, and essentially to panic. It suddenly became clear to me what I knew I needed to do. Instead of acting on any of those thoughts, I made a conscious decision to sit there and feel the pain until I understood what it was.

As the pain intensified it felt as though my whole body was on fire. My mind was screaming at me to move, to do something, to react, but instead I just kept my attention on the center of the pain in my stomach as it roiled around inside me. As dramatic as it may sound, I remember having the thought "I will either die now, or understand what this pain is." Again and again my mind created thoughts to try and distract my attention away from the pain, and again and again I brought my attention back to the center of the pain. It was extremely challenging at first to go against all of my conditioning around what one should do when in this kind of pain, but then something wonderful happened.

There came a point where the ball of pain in my stomach stopped moving, and instead stayed in one spot. As I kept my focused attention on the ball of pain it began to vibrate very intensely, seeming to expand to fill my whole stomach. My mind threw one more thought at me, telling me I was going to die if I didn't do something. I was in a cold sweat, and I remember feeling tears flowing down my cheeks from the pain.

Right at that moment the vibrating ball in my stomach burst into a shock wave of energy that rippled through my entire body. It felt like a tremendous wave passing through every cell inside of me. The explosion of energy was not painful, however, but rather felt like a burst of very pleasant and almost ecstatic energy. It was a complete surprise to feel this painful energy instantly turn into something that felt good. Within a few seconds the pain was completely gone, and I was left laughing and crying.

It was from this initial experience of transmuting the energy of pain that I began to understand the power that we all possess to shape our experiences in life. Through meditation and focus we can each change the experience and quality of energy as it moves through us, transmuting all energy back into the experience of loving life energy. It takes practice and awareness, but I know that this ability can be cultivated within everyone.

To say that transmuting energy is an "ability," is not entirely accurate. When you drop thoughts that label life experiences as either desirable or undesirable, then the energy naturally flows and changes without effort. It is through resistance to sensation and life experience (in the form of labeling and judging) that we experience suffering. So it could be said that transmuting energy is a natural phenomenon that is always occurring, and it is only the process of remembering this natural way of being that needs to be cultivated.

Another interesting phenomenon occurring for me at the time, was that for roughly four months following my awakening experience, my sexual thoughts and desires completely disappeared. Whereas before I would have occasional thoughts throughout the day of a romantic or sexual nature, these thoughts were no longer present in my mind. Nor did I get sexually aroused during this time. I was so happy to be free from the burden of sexual desire, which had often weighed heavily on me previously in my life.

It seemed ironic that I should find myself headed for a community in Hawaii focused on sensuality and sexuality during this time of celibacy. The Universe works in mysterious ways, and in retrospect I can clearly see the benefits of this situation for my healing and process of learning. By entering into a community where sex and sensuality was the focus, it provided me an opportunity to observe and understand with greater clarity the nature of sexual energy, without being drawn into the unconscious behaviors that often accompany sexual expression. Spending time in this community proved instrumental for a deeper healing to occur within my unconscious, allowing me to address some deeply held wounds within myself.

For the majority of my adolescence and early twenties I had been very focused on sex. When my father passed away during my adolescence I had learned to sooth my inner wounds using relationships, intimacy, and sex. Though my sexual desires were likely no greater than most other men, it was my acute awareness of how I was misusing this energy that caused me internal distress. I had always been aware, on some level, that I was misusing the sacred experience of sexual union for selfish purposes of physical pleasure. This caused me to feel guilt and shame about my sexual expression, which only perpetuated my sexual misconduct. A few times in my past I had not been completely honest with women about my feelings, and I knew I had hurt more than a few people through this process.

When Ashana and I arrived at the community in Hawaii we were both overflowing with excitement to begin this next chapter of our lives. The property was beautiful, filled with coconut trees, an organic garden, and plenty of space for yoga and meditation. Everyone seemed so nice, the community was within walking distance to the beach, and the remote location provided amazing natural beauty all around. For the first few days we believed that we had found paradise.

Ashana and I quickly realized, however, the intense challenges of living in a communal setting. Though our days were filled with joyful times at the beach, preparing food, and working in the garden, we also got to see the inner workings of a highly emotional and sexually charged community in action. It was clear to see that many people within the community were actively involved in their own process of healing and growth. And I began to realize that I was still integrating the new perceptual capacities I had developed following my recent spiritual awakening, which was bringing up some rich and challenging material to work with.

Integration

What is commonly referred to as a "kundalini awakening" often brings to the surface layers of thought and emotion that had previously been contained within the subconscious part of the mind. For me, this took the form of sudden and inexplicable "dark" thoughts, violent imagery in my mind, and intense feelings and emotions. Sitting and watching the sunset at the beach, and then suddenly having a memory of being in a war and shooting someone, was confusing and scary. I didn't understand if these memories were real or imagined. This process occurred in varying degrees of intensity over the period of a few years, and it took me a while to understand what was happening. Looking back on it now, I can see that I was cleaning house at a very deep level, letting go of trauma experienced from this life, as well as past lives, dissolving many basal instinctual drives.

I was also continuing to integrate the effects of the empathic awakening that I experienced in San Francisco months prior. An empathic awakening opens a person up to the ability to sense and perceive beyond what is normally perceived with the five senses (seeing auras, feeling energy emanating from people, and even hearing other people's thoughts). Generally, the mind acts as a filter for how much sensory information we perceive. As the ego becomes dissolved through spiritual practice, however, greater sensitivity occurs, and more information can be perceived. The more sensitive you are, the more you can deeply feel what is occurring in other people without them saying a word, or even changing their expression or body language.

The initial experience of physically seeing vivid colors and energy in people faded following the first few weeks of my awakening, but I was left with an uncanny perception of the energy emanating from the people around me. This took the form of looking at a person's body or face and receiving a download of information about what emotional energy was flowing through them. It's as if there are very subtle swirls of energy moving around a person, giving off information about their inner experience. I also feel sensations in my body that give me this same information. It took me a few years to learn how to use this ability towards the healing of others, and the learning curve was steep.

Not fully understanding the process that I was going through, I often felt as though something was wrong with me, or that I was going crazy. I felt at the whim of the people around me, somewhat helpless to my environment and circumstances. It was a crash course in energy awareness, and it provided the motivation to understand how to transmute energy, learning how to focus and direct my energy in a loving way.

At the community in Hawaii I would be sitting next to someone, and suddenly feel a sense of dread. Looking over at the person beside me and seeing a furrowed brow, or a look of anxiety, provided me clues that this energy was likely originating from them. By moving away and sitting outside for a while, I discovered that the feeling would go away. It was through this process of trial and error I began to understand what energy was being created by me, and what energy was being caused by others.

To say that energy is ever being "caused" by others is not wholly accurate, however. Energy flow is a two way street. As soon as I begin to feel the energy of another person, it then becomes my energy, and what I do with it is my responsibility. If I choose to continue feeling negative energy, then it could be said that I am also creating it. What I have learned since this awakening is that energy is not personal, nor does it ever fully belong to anyone.

Life energy is flowing through everything all the time, being shared (consciously and unconsciously) with other forms of life, and we are each responsible for how we direct the energy that moves through us. When you either resist or become attached to the energy of others, then it stays within you too. When you remain open and with a quiet mind, the energy just moves straight through. We are each, in our own time, learning the art of self-mastery; that of becoming conscious creators in how we use our energy.

For the few months I lived at the community in Hawaii I had many wonderful experiences, and met many nice people. Ashana and I continued to deepen our connection, but it was also becoming apparent that our time together was nearing an end, and she had made plans to travel to another island. Near the end of my stay at the community I found myself connecting romantically with a woman in the community. During this time my sexual energy had reawakened, yet now I had a higher perspective on the experience of sexual union, and how I could potentially use my energy in a more heart centered way.

As my new partner and I began to be physical one night, I noticed that something didn't quite feel right. Though I had become physically aroused, I remained ambivalent about having sex. It suddenly didn't seem very interesting to simply enjoy pleasant physical sensations when I knew there was a world of unconditional loving energy that could be experienced. I just didn't know what that might entail, or how that might look.

I shared with her my story of energetic awakenings, and she was open to investigating how our sexual energy might be experienced in a more expansive way. We closed our eyes and intuitively began breathing together. With every inhalation I allowed the energy within the lower part of my body to move up into my heart. On the exhalation I gently guided the energy back down towards the base of my spine. We continued to breathe as we lay side by side on the bed, and I began to feel an energy (similar to the kundalini energy I had experienced before, yet much less intense), rising up my spine. I could feel the energy building and rising slowly with each breath.

At a certain point this energy reached my heart, and I experienced an energetic climax. I felt an explosion of pleasure within my heart, and this feeling rippled through my entire body. It was something that I had never experienced before in this context. This experience felt so good in my heart, and gave me insight into the possibility for sharing sexual energy in a new way.

The contrast between this new form of sexual expression, versus the sexual behavior I was witnessing at the community was like a wake-up call for me, showing me how important it was to heal any remaining sexual wounding that I was still holding inside. I now had the awareness that sexual energy was no different than life energy, and it became so clear to me when I saw people misusing their life energy to get their own needs met, rather than as a shared and mutual celebration of love. This misuse of sexual energy often stems from a deep belief in unworthiness, a lack of self-love, and from fear, rather than as the gift of love between two people.

I was also learning to have compassion for myself and others, seeing how hurtful this misuse of energy could be. When a person is expressing their sexual energy from anxiety rather than love, this energy can spread to other people, contributing to jealousy, anger, and resentment. Watching people in the community subtly hurt themselves and each other in this way (mostly unconsciously) was instrumental in my growth, and provided me the opportunity to reflect on my own past behavior.

I spent the next few weeks with my new friend, traveling the island together, and enjoying our romantic connection. However, I could sense that my time in Hawaii was coming to a close, and I began to feel into where I was headed next. I found myself gravitating towards the energy of the redwood trees. It felt good to remember the rooted energy of the old growth redwood trees in the mountains of California, and I decided to follow the call. I said my goodbyes to Ashana and the other friends I had made while in Hawaii, and bought a plane ticket to California.

Once back in California I bought a car, loaded it up with a few of my possessions, and headed North. I landed at an intentional community among the redwood trees of California. There were many wonderful aspects about living in this community. I lived in a cozy trailer in the woods, and when not working, I spent my time painting, playing guitar, and watching over the community children. I spent countless hours with the children, jumping on the trampoline, making-up stories, and having adventures. It was a wonderful opportunity to continue reconnecting with my innocence and child-like nature.

My time here was also challenging, however, and any ideas of a communal utopia were quickly replaced by the realities of sharing the everyday tasks of living with a small group of people. Unlike the community in Hawaii, this community adhered to a fairly strict and structured schedule. Sharing meals together, working alongside the same group of people, and sharing in many different aspects of life, quickly began to feel oppressive and stifling.

I also began to notice many of the same ego patterns in the community that were present in the mainstream culture. Instead of people competing for money or material possessions, however, there was a subtle energy of competition for being the most environmentally conscious, or the hardest working. This took the form of people being stressed out or anxious about creating any waste, or one-upping each other as to who was more hard working towards sustainable ways of living. It was fascinating to see how the ego could really attach itself to any concept or identity, even that of being sustainable and living in harmony.

It was a great reminder for me that the shift in consciousness must take place internally first, which then naturally manifests outwardly. Without the initial inward shift that takes place when you dissolve the ego, no matter where you live, or what you create in your life, the outcome will always be influenced to some degree by the ego. The thought, "If I can only move to the woods and live off the land in a community, then I will be happy and finally be able to live in harmony," had popped up in my mind more than once, and I often found myself believing it was a true requirement for my happiness. I was continually being reminded, however, that no future requirement is ever necessary for happiness.

Inner peace is always an option in each moment, regardless of your circumstances. As soon as you say "yes" to life, deeply accepting what is, suffering disappears. The key to remember is that peace can only ever be found in the present moment, not in some potential future destination. This shift in focus from future to present is what allows heaven to be created on earth now, and you don't necessarily have be living in an eco-village to experience it.

Heart Versus Head

Six months after leaving the intentional community in northern California I found myself living back in the city. I had been drawn there by a woman whom I had met at an ecstatic dance in San Francisco. Our connection was strong, and after a few months of seeing each other we moved in together. Although I was happy to be in a heart opening relationship, it was a challenge to reconcile my deepening spiritual path with returning to life in the city, and doing work that didn't truly fulfill my heart (I had taken a part-time job working at a restaurant in order to pay the bills). I was feeling a growing desire to share what I had been learning throughout my awakening journey, and I wanted to reach out to more people.

I decided to create a website and begin offering counseling based on what I was learning about the ego, energy and healing. This was something that in the past I would likely have felt too intimidated to attempt. I had never considered myself computer savvy, nor particularly that good with technical processes. However, with my new awareness of the ego, I now saw these thoughts of limitation more as a product of my conditioning, rather than based on any truth about what I was capable of. This higher perspective has allowed me to begin many ventures that in the past I would have thought impossible.

Starting my own holistic and spiritual counseling practice was a wonderful time of trial and error, and the learning curve was steep. As I found myself continually challenged with the complex processes of web design and marketing myself online, I was constantly coming back to my breath, and releasing attachment to the outcome of my project. Amazingly, it is by letting go of attachment to attaining that which you desire, that it can manifest more easily into your life.

On the other hand, without any form of desire or intention, not much happens in life, which after a while becomes uninteresting. So to be an effective co-creator with life, one must hold some desire, while simultaneously letting go of attachment to outcome. This is a profound paradox of creation that the mind generally has a hard time accepting. I have found that striking a balance between following desires of the heart, versus letting go of desires born of the ego, is necessary in order to live in balance and harmony.

Initially during my awakening process I assumed that every desire I had was coming from the ego. I would wake up in the morning and have a thought about putting on my pants (which seemed like a form of desire), so I wouldn't take any action because I was practicing dropping desires, assuming every thought was of the ego. So I sat there without any pants, until I figured I should just put my pants on regardless of where the thought was coming from.

Though this may seem like a silly example, it reflects a common theme among many folks going through the awakening process. As you unravel the ego you suddenly become aware of the infinite possibilities in your life, and it can become very confusing as to which line of thinking to follow. What I began to understand was that empowering certain thoughts and desires was absolutely in alignment with the Higher Intelligence and my Soul's purpose, while empowering other desires were not. In this sense, some desires could be considered helpful, and others a hindrance. After all, how effective can a person be out in the world if they're not wearing any pants?

Even those beings who are referred to as enlightened masters must have held strong desires in order to progress along their spiritual path. One has to desire to practice meditation, one has to desire to let go of the ego, one has to desire to know the Truth of who they are. These moment-by-moment decisions are spurred by desire. The difference between desires of the ego versus desires of the heart, however, comes down to motivation. The motivation of the heart is to allow for greater freedom, happiness, joy, and connectivity, whereas the motivation of the ego is to have more for oneself, to stand out, or to feel special and separate from others.

And so the process of distinguishing between desires involves honestly observing your motivations in any given moment. Instead of

46

letting go of every desire, learn to differentiate between the desires of the ego, and the desires of the heart. This can take some investigation, as there is much subtle gradation in the experience of desire. Noticing how the desire feels is the key. Does it feel expansive, open, and inclusive, or does it feel restrictive, selfish, and separatist? As you begin to clear away the confusion around where a desire is coming from, you can then move out into the world, following the desires of your heart with greater confidence.

This kind of subtlety aggravates the mind, which would much rather rely on a formula for what line of thinking, feeling, and action to follow. Historically, the role of organized religion served this purpose by offering moral and ethical codes of conduct for people to live by. But as we have seen throughout history, a set of rules is not effective in place of the intuitive heart. To know what behavior is in alignment with the Universe is to be connected strongly to your feelings and your heart, allowing you to receive guidance directly from the Higher Intelligence. In order to do that the ego must become dissolved, and the mind quieted. A quiet mind will allow you to deeply feel the energetic difference between choosing love versus choosing fear, and allow you to make the choice for love.

I initially assumed my desire to start my own business must be coming from my ego (the need to have money, security, or some kind of status in society), but the more I felt into it, the more I realized that my heart really wanted the experience of helping people, and bringing more peace and joy into the world. In order to do that I needed to advertise my services, and so it was a logical progression to take steps to create a website. This led to a desire to learn web programming, something I never would have thought my intuition would be guiding me to do. These thoughts about learning web design, which I knew would be challenging, also felt expansive, exciting, and inspiring.

I began to notice the difference in thoughts of this nature, versus the thoughts telling me that I "should" do a certain task, or I "should" learn this new skill, which often feel oppressive and controlling. The desires that arise from the heart feel significantly different—more uplifting and exciting in general. It can take some time and energy to investigate and uncover the difference between the two. The biggest difference in heart desires and ego desires is that the heart is not interested in the goal, but rather the growth and learning that takes place along the journey.

Often when starting a new venture that I feel intuitively guided towards, a thought might pop up that would say, "What's the point, why bother? The focus of my life is spiritual growth now, so there is no use for goals in the physical world." This line of thinking might make sense to the rational mind; if there is no attachment to the final destination, then why even take the journey in the first place? But when I notice how these thoughts feel (restrictive and uninspired), it lets me know that they are coming from the ego, rather than the heart.

Though the final destination in life is not of any real significance, the journey is. Things really gets turned upside down the more you realize that the whole purpose of life is the journey. The heart delights in the journey, appreciating every experience along the way, bringing more loving energy into the world all the while. And it is through our feelings that we know if we are following the correct path for ourselves in the moment. Putting my energy into building my counseling practice felt good, and brought new inspiration into my life, and so it was an easy call to follow.

Movement and Visualization

Though I had dissolved much of my ego, I began to notice that my awakening process was very much like a swinging pendulum; some moments I would experience profound feelings of connection, while other moments I would revert back to old patterns, experiencing limitation or fear. I could feel that there was still stuck emotional energy within me that needed to be released, and so I continued to search for ways to allow this healing to occur. Two powerful techniques I discovered for this purpose were movement and visualization.

I joined a group called "Authentic Movement," a somatic practice created by Mary Starks Whitehouse in the 1950s. The practice involves sitting in a room with a handful of other people in silence. As the participants stay aware of their inner mind-body connection, they begin to move spontaneously, based on intuitive guidance from within. The participants move freely through the space without guidance or facilitation, expressing sounds and movements as they arise. The format is incredibly simple, but allows for powerful emotional releases to occur. By tuning into your body, and physically moving the body in a meditative state, it becomes easier to drop the analytical mind, and can allow for repressed emotional energy being held in the body to begin surfacing.

Within the first hour of my first session I spontaneously began crying, feeling a deep sadness and grief that seemed to come out of nowhere. The quality of the sadness often did not seem connected to my life, but rather, felt as though I was tuning into the greater collective unconsciousness, allowing myself the opportunity to process some of the pain for all of humanity. The process felt tremendously cathartic and healing.

Additionally, I would have images arise that seemed like they were from other lifetimes. A powerful sensation that continued to arise during my practice was that of being stabbed in my intestines by a spear, and even an image of looking down and seeing blood pouring from my abdomen. It did not seem like a coincidence that the disease I suffered from in this lifetime was related to intestinal distress, and that it often had felt like I was being stabbed in my gut when my symptoms flared up. It occurred to me that this process of intuitive movement was helping me continue to heal remnants of the disease by healing deeply stored trauma from previous lifetimes.

One of the most healing movements that I often found myself repeating was the act of crumpling up into a ball on the floor, sobbing and feeling intense grief, and then rising up to my feet, extending my arms up towards the sky, feeling relief, joy, and lightness. It was such an amazing contrasting experience that seemed to mirror the cycles of death and rebirth. Over the course of the months that I participated in this weekly group, I would often repeat this movement, among others, sobbing and experiencing alternating feelings of grief and joy.

Another powerfully healing movement modality is free-form dance. This style of movement is more than just dancing, it's a way of relearning how to be in your body, giving yourself permission to really be you. There are many different names for free-form dance: Ecstatic Dance, 5 Rhythms, and Soul Motion, to name a few. Free-form dance has been a significant part of my healing journey, allowing me to reclaim much of my life energy and inner fire.

Earlier in my life I had often felt restricted in my own body, and dancing was never something that I enjoyed. To finally allow myself to really move my body in a beautiful and fluid way was like being reborn in a new skin. The first few times I truly let myself freely move my body, letting go of the analytical and self-conscious mind, I shed tears of grief (and joy) from having repressed myself for so long. Dancing is a wonderful way to clear stagnant energy and open new doors of creative expression in your life.

Another powerful way to move energy is through the process of visualization. During my healing process I intuitively knew that I wanted to explore visualizations, and so I sought out a counselor to guide me through my process. I found a counselor-in-training through a university master's program for counseling. It seemed to suite my purposes to actually find someone with limited experience, which provided a level of openness and spontaneity on the part of my counselor. I was feeling guided to go back into my past and heal emotional wounds that I felt were still present within me. The first visualization I underwent involved going back to visit myself as a child in the front yard of the house where I grew up. The memory was from the day I found out that my father had died in a car accident.

In my visualization I approached this child version of myself and picked him up, giving him a hug and feeling compassion and love for this part of myself. As I did, my child self dissolved into my heart, and I stood there in the visualization holding myself. Then something unexpected began to happen that I hadn't planned on for the visualization. I started sinking into the sidewalk, and as I did I was enveloped in a womb of earth, and continued to sink down into a huge underground cavern filled with turquoise water. As I lowered into the water I felt my body beginning to vibrate very strongly. The vibration continued to grow in intensity, and my body began shaking and trembling. The vibration felt immensely good, but also somewhat frightening and overwhelming, as in the back of my mind I had the awareness that I was tapping into some powerful energy source that I

50

didn't yet understand (which felt similar to the kundalini energy that had arisen in my body a year earlier).

I began to moan and sob as the energy moved through me. Though I was crying, the energy also felt deeply purifying and healing. It was at this moment when my counselor interrupted the session due to his own discomfort. Upon coming out of the visualization I saw a look of concern on his face, and with a shaky voice he expressed to me that he had started to feel strange during the visualization. He described feeling a vibration in his body, starting in his feet, and then moving up his spine. He said it got so strong that he had to interrupt the session.

When we hugged goodbye, I noticed that the back of his shirt was drenched in sweat. It seemed that during the session we had tapped into a form of energy that had begun flowing into the surrounding environment, as well as into my counselor. In our following sessions together we continued to explore the power of intuitively guided visualizations, yet I never fully allowed myself to go as deep as I had the first time, due to my awareness of my counselor's anxiety about the process.

This led me to exploring the process on my own. I would often sit in a meditative state alone in my room, allowing myself to go deep into my imagination, following the flow of the visualization process. It was an incredible process that lead me into the most beautiful and vivid imagery in my mind. I was able to connect with spirit-guides, angels, and receive information about my Soul's journey. These visualizations often ended in a specific environment (similar to the cavern with the turquoise water) where I would become filled with energy, and once again feel that intense vibration in my body. This energy seemed to be harmonizing my mind, emotions, and body, bringing healing into my being at a deep level.

The experience I just described was my first foray into consciously channeling energy. I also began noticing a similar phenomenon during my counseling sessions, and in conversations with people (particularly when talking about spirituality). I would often enter into the most beautiful lucid state of flow, where my body would also fill with the same vibrating energy that I experienced in the visualization process (to a lesser degree, however). My mind would become very still, and I would find myself just speaking without thinking at all. Information would come through that often surprised me, hearing myself say things in a way so that I was also learning during the process.

I understand this to be what Eckhart Tolle describes as becoming a channel for divine energy, a process that happens the more one drops the ego and stays connected to the present moment. This divine energy is flowing through each one of us in every moment. Yet, for many people this energy is still being distorted and restricted by the thinking mind and ego. As the ego becomes dissolved through spiritual practice, the desires of the heart and mind align, and the Universal energy is able to flow through with greater grace and ease.

I've found that I have abundant energy in the channeling state, and feel such a deep sense of purpose and meaning while engaging in this form of connection with others. Opening yourself up to becoming a channel also increases your sensitivity to the thoughts and emotions of others. One counseling session with a client, in particular, stands out in my memory as a moment where I realized just how powerful this transference of energy could be.

Transmuting Energy

I had been counseling a woman for about a month regarding a traumatic event that she had experienced earlier in her life. The event had involved watching one of her family members kill another family member, and had caused her to develop overwhelming anxiety and depression. She had begun the sessions not wanting to talk about the trauma, but rather, focus on other aspects of her life. We had four sessions together, during which I could sense that she was not yet comfortable talking about her traumatic experience.

By the fifth session, however, something had shifted, and I felt an opening to ask her about the event in her life. As soon as I did she became quiet. Though she continued to look at me with her familiar smile (she was always very pleasant during the sessions, and often smiled), I could sense her energy changing to that of fear, and I started to sense a change in my energy field as well. And then suddenly the energy within me became very strong. I felt a surge of panic and terror. My heart began pounding, and adrenaline flowing. For a split second I wanted to scream and run out of the room it was so intense. But I caught it very quickly, realizing that it was not my energy, but rather the energy coming from my client. I relaxed my body, focused on my breath, and allowed the strong energy current to flow through me.

Within a minute or two much of the energy had dissipated, and I was left in a state of intense presence and stillness. In order to transmute the energy I had closed my eyes, and when I opened them, I saw that my client had begun crying, something that she later told me she had not been able to do in years. She was then able to relate to me her experience of the traumatic event, which marked a turning point in her journey of healing.

This session was instrumental in my learning process about how to transmute energy. By staying present, allowing the energy to move through me (without reacting to it or resisting against it), an opening was created for the energy to move and dissipate. Perhaps it was my willingness to transmute this intense energy that had helped lightened the load for her, allowing her to finally let go of that significant emotional blockage. It seems that the more empathic we are, the more energy can be transmuted through us, and the more helpful we can be in dissolving trauma in others.

Having gone through my own emotional healing it has become like second nature for me to offer a safe container to help lighten the load for others. It was not so much a decision on my part, but rather, it just began to happen. Whereas before in my life, feeling someone's heavy emotional energy was unpleasant, now it felt like some kind of gift to transmute the denser energies of fear and grief back into loving presence. I experience it as a deepening of my connection to Source, as well as an influx of life energy. It seems to serve the highest good of all involved, and bring more peace and light into the world.

And so continued my journey of learning how to be more responsible with my energy, as well as learning how to transmute the energy coming from others. There is much to understand about this process, and it is an experiential journey of exploration and investigation. Learning to differentiate between what energy another is creating, and what you are creating can be helpful, but is not necessary. To understand that energy is impersonal means to let go of ideas of separation, to drop blame, and to surrender the idea that you need to protect yourself from other people's energy. The energy of the Universe is the energy of love, being expressed in a myriad of ways (even fear, grief, and anger), and there is no point in judging or resisting any of it. This remembrance of loving unity allows freedom, openness, compassion, and more love to flow into your life and the lives of others.

As each one of us develops the ability to remain in control of our reactions, choosing to accept life as it comes, then we can easily maintain energetic autonomy without being so affected by others. In fact, the more we learn to stay in a state of acceptance and allowance (no matter what is occurring around us), the energy of love and peace naturally flows out from within. Instead of absorbing other people's energy, we become a channel for deeply positive energy to help heal others.

Paradoxically, it is through letting go, relaxing, and being at peace with whatever is, that you develop this control over your own state of being, and can bring healing energy to others. While the mind would rather come up with a strategy for controlling and transmuting energy, love naturally returns when you let go and surrender your personal desires, dropping the belief that you are separate from others, or that you need to fix, control, or change life situations.

What happens as you practice surrendering the need to control or fix the "problem," is that over time you will find yourself naturally and effortlessly speaking healing words, or offering your energy in a healing way. And most importantly, peaceful energy will naturally be emanating from within you. The difference now is that your words or actions are no longer coming from your mind and your own selfish desires, but rather from a higher place within you; from your heart and Higher Self.

Divine Synchronicity

The more I let go of needing to be in control of life, the more magic seemed to infuse my day-to-day experiences. This took the form of feeling a deepening connection with the Universe, and experiencing amazing synchronicity and opportunity arising for me. My understanding of the phenomenon of synchronicity is that as we begin to awaken to the greater reality of Oneness, the Universe reflects back to us our state of shared connection through synchronous experiences. A person begins to see signs everywhere of how deeply connected everything truly is.

Another way to look at it is this; as a person begins awakening to the greater connection, they begin to see what has been there all along, yet which they were previously unaware of. It's as if most people are living with blinders on, so consumed with the thoughts in their mind that they miss what is happening all around them. Living in this unconscious state prevents a person from feeling the guidance from within, which would naturally align them with the right people, situations, and experiences that would best serve their Soul's growth.

One of the most remarkable moments of synchronicity happened for me when I was hitchhiking through Northern California. I had gotten dropped off at a camping spot in the woods, and was planning on hitchhiking back to my mother's house in Palo Alto, California the following day. That night I had a dream that I was in a car with my longtime childhood friend, and we were about to embark on a journey, when the car wouldn't start. My friend was turning the ignition, but the car was just making that sound as though it were going to start, but wouldn't. In the dream my friend and I looked at one another, and it seemed like a significant moment, because it was the first things I remembered when I woke up.

The next morning I was offered a ride by a woman who had been camping next to my site. As we got into her car, she inserted the keys into the ignition and tried to start the car. The engine just kept turning, but would not start. Eventually she got it going, and I thought to myself, "that's strange, just like in my dream," but didn't think too much of it.

As we drove down the highway we struck up a conversation about middle names, and the name "Joy" popped into my mind. I mentioned that if I ever had a daughter, I would choose the middle name Joy for her. We both agreed it was a beautiful name. The woman dropped me off at the intersection (which was geographically isolated), and I stood on the side of the road with my thumb out.

After about an hour I began to notice how few cars were passing by, as well as how cold it was. It was the middle of February on an overcast day in the mountains of Northern California, and as it began to rain, I realized that I had no rain gear with me, nor did my phone get reception. I began to feel some anxiety about my predicament. I was in the middle of nowhere, without any visible shelter for miles, and had very little clothing to keep me warm.

My fingers and toes were numb, and as the rain continued to fall, I decided to listen to some music on my Mp3 player and dance on the side of the road to stay warm. The first song that came on was a spiritual song, and one of the lyrics struck a chord; "all I need for my protection is just faith to ride upon!" Hearing this part of the song suddenly lifted my spirits and I began laughing, singing aloud to the Universe while dancing, "all I need for my protection is just faith to ride upon!...all I need is faith!" The song reminded me that my thoughts were powerful, and that having faith was all I needed to see me through any situation. I delighted in this awareness, and continued to sing about having faith while dancing on the side of the road.

It was only a matter of minutes before I saw that an approaching car was slowing down for me. I grabbed my bag and ran over to the car, amazed at how quickly my luck had changed. The woman leaned over and opened the passenger side door with a big grin on her face. She stuck out her hand and introduced herself. "Hi, my name is Faith," the woman cheerfully announced. I was blown away. What were the chances that a few minutes after singing out that all I needed was some faith, that a woman named Faith would pick me up? I told her of the coincidence and we both laughed. She clearly understood this type of synchronicity. As we drove we talked about her name, and I inquired if she had a middle name. I could hardly believe it when she replied, "Joy." I explained how a few hours earlier I had been discussing the middle name "Joy," and how beautiful that name is. We both laughed at how incredible the coincidence was.

Faith told me that her roommate just happened to be driving down to Palo Alto later that day, and would likely give me a ride. After a quick phone call, my ride down south was confirmed. We had some time before her roommate would be ready to leave, and decided to stop for lunch. As we got back into her car after lunch, Faith put the keys in the ignition and tried to start the car. The engine just turned, but would not start. After a few tries she eventually got the engine going. I couldn't remember the last time I got into a car that wouldn't start, and here it had happened twice in one day, right after having a dream about that very same experience.

Having experienced countless other amazing synchronistic events similar to this one has served to reinforce my understanding of the greater reality; that everything is connected by a Higher Intelligence. This intelligence is not something outside of us, but rather, is a part of us. This intelligence is within all of creation, is a part of everything, and is an organizing principle in the Universe. To have this kind of knowing has dissolved so much of the fear and resistance within me, making it easier to trust the flow of life.

The Highest Excitement

Noticing so much synchronicity in my life, I began studying the law of attraction. The law of attraction points to the connection that each one of us shares with Life itself, and to the greater whole. We are always in communication with the Universe, creating our experience of reality based on what thoughts and emotions we empower with our attention. Every thought that you think is felt by the greater Universal Energy within you and around you, and consequently, energizes more of that experience in your life. As your perceptions of reality shift with each thought and emotion, you attract people and circumstances into your life that reflect back to you the energetic "signal" you are sending out. This takes the form of synchronicity and opportunity arising in your life that allow you to continue creating your reality in whatever manner you choose.

Many law of attraction teachings focus on following your highest excitement as a way to raise your emotional vibration in order to manifest the things that you want in life. The idea is to mainly focus on aspects of life that inspire and excite you as much as possible. Joy and excitement just happen to be very effective emotions for manifesting what you desire, which is why these emotions are emphasized in the practice.

While following your highest excitement can definitely spur growth and deepen self awareness, I have found that they are only partial spiritual truths, merely one facet of self-mastery. These teachings do not necessarily help a person dissolve the ego, or create a lasting connection to the Source of love within. Often times these teachings appeal to folks who are still trying to push away some part of themselves which they have yet to accept, or to escape from pain they are still holding within. I learned this lesson firsthand while practicing the technique of following my highest excitement.

Looking back I can see that part of my motivation to deepen my understanding of the law of attraction was due to some anxiety I was feeling about the non-physical beings I was connecting with. By opening myself up to become a channel for energy, it also opened me up for communication with non-physical beings, and I found myself contacted psychically and emotionally by a variety of different energies. I don't believe this occurs for everyone on the the spiritual path, but it has been a part of my journey, and also a wonderful blessing in disguise.

I experienced this in different ways. Sometimes I would just have the sense of a non-physical being in the same room as myself, or sometimes I felt the heavy emotional energy of an environment (as though some trauma had taken place there), and I could feel the presence of beings who were still attached to the negative energy in that environment. Other times I've seen visual images of spirits. On occasion I have had what felt like the presence of beings from other planets reaching out to make contact with me.

It takes a high level of discernment, however, to differentiate reality from fantasy, and ultimately, it has served me best to let go of any thoughts or stories I've had about what I was experiencing.

Regardless of whether it was real or imagined, I have since learned to refocus my attention inward in times of distraction, to the point where I seldom experience this phenomenon anymore.

One of the most pleasant non-physical relationships to foster is with those sweet Souls commonly referred to as angels. One way to describe an angel would be as a Soul who has worked through their human karma, and now serves as a guide for those of us still in our process. Connecting with an angel is a very uplifting experience. It feels as though you are surrounded by an invisible energy field, and that you are being showered with unconditional love for no reason other than that you exist. It is wonderful, and always a blessing when it occurs. Simply by holding the intention to connect with your angel guides, you can begin to strengthen your relationship with loving non-physical light beings.

These new connections lead me to notice how my personal vibration was effecting what energy I was connecting with. I noticed that when I felt filled with joy I didn't sense these "unfriendly" beings, whereas when I felt some form of negativity within myself, these energies seemed to be more attracted to me. This is what led me to start focusing on my highest excitement most of the time, focusing only on positive and uplifting thoughts. And though my intentions at the time seemed to be pure, the underlying motive was still to escape some anxiety and fear that I was experiencing. Regardless, it lead me on an amazing journey, one that revealed to me a lot about myself and the subtler layers of the ego.

Following your highest excitement is a distinctly different process than the mindful awareness practice of accepting whatever thoughts and feelings arise, without labeling or judging what you are experiencing (a process which naturally transmutes all energy back to a peaceful vibration). Ultimately, I would return to this mindful awareness practice, but for the time being I was experimenting with manipulating my own emotional state, for what seemed at the time to be for my highest good.

As I continued the practice I noticed that I was gravitating towards ideas about human potential that I might not have believed in otherwise. The breatharian lifestyle, in particular, really grabbed my attention, and I spent hours watching videos of people who claimed to live solely on their breath, needing neither food nor water for their survival. The theory is that by purifying oneself sufficiently, it allows a person to take their nourishment directly from a higher source, from God. In order to get to the breatharian state, one needed to go through an intense process of fasting and purification.

My thought process at the time was that if I believed in something strongly enough, and raised my vibration adequately, that I could achieve anything I desired, and manifest any experience into my life. I still believe this to be true to a certain extent, but I also have a deeper understanding of the difference between fantasy, versus what is truly possible through a deep commitment to one's spiritual growth and evolution.

The possibilities of breatharianism inspired me endlessly. I continued researching the topic, seeking out any information I could find. In my research I came across a breatharian couple that claimed to have raised a child without food. The mother claimed not to have eaten during her pregnancy, a feat that should have killed her and the child, and yet miraculously in the videos they both appeared to be in radiant health. This idea may sound crazy to many people, and yet the energy of the couple was so vibrant and loving, and their words felt so honest and true, that it awakened some memory deep within my heart the possibility of it.

In an incredible synchronicity, I happened to randomly meet the couple at a gathering a few days after first watching their videos on breatharianism. I had no idea they were even in the U.S., let alone the same city as me. The couple, Akahi and Camila (who now travel the world holding workshops on pranic nourishment), told me of their experience transitioning into the breatharian lifestyle, having a child in the pranic state, and what it has been like for them since.

From watching their videos, and now meeting them in person, it confirmed for me just how bright and healthy their energy was. They were both glowing, filled with an abundance of energy, and I could feel that they were speaking from their hearts with honesty and integrity. They explained that there was an 8-day process that involved fasting and specific breathing practices for activating strands of DNA in the body, which allowed a person to take their nourishment directly from the energy in the air. They invited me to do the 8-day process with them, which I enthusiastically accepted.

While not needing to eat food or drink water may sound unbelievable to some, this felt very possible to me, and despite the fact that I am not currently a breatharian, I am certain that there are people on the planet that are living this way—Akahi and Camila being two examples. There are many documented cases of people going for extended periods of time without food or water with no negative health effects.

A well-known Indian breatharian, Prahalad Jani, underwent the scrutiny of study by British researchers, allowing himself to be confined in a room for 10 days under close observation and video surveillance. Researchers evaluated him for 10 days without food or water, and found that his body did not become depleted in any way during this time period. Not only that, but he appeared to be in incredible health for a man of his age.

My own experiences of fasting also reaffirmed the positive and amazing benefits of eliminating food from the body. There have been times during fasting where I felt so much joy and happiness, as well as felt a deep connection to the Universe. There were nights where I had so much energy during a fast that I could barely sleep, my body vibrating with vital life energy. It made no sense to my mind how I could feel this way without food (everything we have been taught about having energy is related to the types, and quantities of food we consume). But I had experienced it, so I knew how amazing it could feel. It was from my direct experience of fasting, as well as seeing others living without food, that I came to believe that I could also live in this state of pranic nourishment.

My excitement was continuing to grow, and after sharing all of the information about breatharianism with my partner, she made the decision to join me for the 8-day transition process. We spent countless hours talking about what it must be like not to eat food, and what effect that would have on our social lives, and the lives of our friends and our families. I was also feeling tempted to questioned the method for attaining this state of being. It seemed unbelievable that we could become breatharian after only eight days of fasting and breathing practices.

But I was committed to my practice of only thinking positive thoughts and following my highest excitement, and so every time a thought of doubt, worry, or "what if?" came into my mind, I would either refocus on a positive thought, or come back to stillness. I wasn't yet aware enough to clearly differentiate (in this situation, anyway) between the thought processes arising from the ego, versus the function of the mind to reasonably and logically evaluate the reality of the situation. Having become aware of the limitations of logical and rational thought processes, which can easily be usurped by the fearful calculations of the ego, I had become somewhat determined to resist that line of thinking, lest it restrict my ability to expand and grow in seemingly "miraculous" ways.

With more enthusiasm than hesitation, my partner and I decided to undergo the breatharian transition. The 8-day process was a wonderful, intense, and challenging experience, consisting of two days of juice fasting, followed by four days of dry fasting (no water and no food), followed by two more days of juice fasting. Each day was comprised of meditation, visualizations, and breathing exercises. Akahi led us through exercises using specific breathing techniques and visualizations in order to move the energy of the breath through the body and activate different energy centers in the body. The guided visualizations were also intended to activate additional strands of DNA, which Akahi believed could allow a person to receive energy directly from the prana in the air.

The first half of the 8-day process was rocky, and I felt sick, discouraged, and was having second thoughts about going through with the process. The challenges increased during the dry fast. Not eating is one thing, but not drinking liquid is a whole other challenge to overcome. The body goes through interesting changes when you stop drinking liquid. Your skin becomes very dry and leathery, you lose a lot of weight, and your thinking processes can alternate between significantly speeding up or slowing way down. I had moments during the fast where my mind was very still, while other moments my mind seemed to be racing a mile a minute.

Overall, it was an amazing experience, but the process also felt overwhelming. While my partner went back to eating food shortly after the end of the fast, I decided to continue on. After three weeks it became too much for me, and I decided to start eating food again.

Eating was a relief, and even though Akahi and Camila make it clear that the 8-day process is not necessarily about becoming a breatharian, but rather a process for reprogramming the body to take nourishment from a higher source, I felt confused and misguided about the process.

In the time since this experience I have researched breatharianism extensively to try and understand why some people seem to be able to live this way, while others cannot. Perhaps this is the process of evolution for the human species, and those living in the pranic state are showing us what is possible for the future of humanity. Or perhaps this phenomenon is occurring only in some individuals, and does not indicate the direction of our collective evolution. There is no way to know, nor any real reason to uncover this.

What was most startling to witness, however, was how I had become so consumed with my excitement for the breatharian lifestyle, that I forgot to listen to my own guidance, to my own inner compass. This was the big lesson for me. Just because something is exciting, doesn't necessarily mean it is in alignment with your highest good. After all, the ego can get excited about many things. I had been seduced by a fantasy of some "better" way to live, a way that would make me happier than I already was. To see this misstep was very humbling, and caused me to reflect on my process, and the events that unfolded following the eight day fast.

About a month after the 8-day process ended, my partner and I ended our relationship. This was not entirely on account of the breatharian process, but the fallout after the experience definitely contributed to misgivings that my partner was already feeling towards my seeming lack of connection to reality, as well as my ability to be a stable partner or potential father to a family.

Reflecting on my motivation for becoming a breatharian, I saw that I had been holding a desire to escape some aspects of the human experience and the physical world. This had been a common theme throughout my life, as I often turned to spirituality when I didn't want to deal with what life was presenting me. This experience served as a reminder that, ultimately, there is no need to push through anything, to try and escape from anything, nor any need to struggle towards a specific outcome. Life is simply happening, and it is up to each of us to relax into the flow, follow our hearts, but also use our heads to be reasonable and rational—a true melding of heart and mind. Effort is required to honestly look within and see what thoughts, beliefs, and emotional patterns one may still be holding onto that no longer serve the Soul's growth.

This time of self-reflection involved tuning into the greater themes and experiences within my Soul's purpose. As I let go of this last chapter of my life, I began meditating on how I truly wanted to live my life. Part of this reflection was doing research about alternative ways of living, and using creative writing as a tool for prayer. Over the course of a few weeks, a vision began to emerge within my heart that inspired me tremendously.

I saw myself living off-grid in an earthen structure made of strawbale and cob. I suddenly knew that I wanted to build a house in the woods for myself where I could one day have a family. It was a long lost dream from my childhood that I had locked away for many years. But now just the idea of it felt so inspiring and exciting. I knew that I would first have to find a suitable place to live, a location that would allow me to be close to nature, yet not too far removed from civilization. I resolved to set out on a road trip to find my future home, a place where I could start a family and live a natural life.

One obstacle, that in the past might have prevented me from following my intuition and embarking on this new chapter in my life, would have been the question, "but how will I support myself?" The energy of doubt that often accompanies this question is, perhaps, the most common obstacle preventing many people from following a dream. I know now that when you feel something strongly in your heart, and make the decision to follow the call, the Universe begins to arrange itself in your favor. When you let doubt creep in the Universe also listens, and responds in kind. Having gained a greater understanding of the law of attraction as a result of following my highest excitement, I began to utilize a process of visioning that I had recently begun studying (a more structured form of prayer).

The first part of the visioning process is to ask for inspiration and guidance about how to best move forward, which is done following meditation when the mind is quiet. The inspiration that came to me was writing—something that I have always loved to do. As part of my healing process I had researched and studied all things related to health and healing for over a decade, and so it seemed like a fitting choice. During my nightly prayer and visioning practice I began imagining myself acquiring a job writing on health topics, seeing myself living and working on the road. The next day I went online and applied for two writing positions in which health was the focus. A few days passed and I didn't hear back from either company, and soon it slipped from my mind.

Within two weeks I received an email from a woman who worked at a popular question and answer website. She wanted to offer me a job writing articles online about health and healing. Incredibly, the position was being offered to me from a company that I did not apply to. The woman had randomly come across my website and thought I would make a good fit as the health and healing expert for the newly forming health section of their website. I inquired if my resume had been forwarded to her by another company and she assured me it had not. Part of me was amazed, and part of me was becoming more accustomed to how the Universe seemed to continually support my ever-unfolding journey.

I now had a clear vision and means to support myself, and felt ready to take action. After living in the city, I was excited to travel and find a place that really felt like home. I traded my car in for a van, and created a very livable space inside for myself, complete with a bed, a pull out kitchenette, drawers for my clothes, a cooler for food, and a 5-gallon water jug so that I would always have purified water to drink. I explained my unfolding journey to my clients, and thankfully, they were on board to continue our sessions over the phone while I traveled.

Following My Heart

I set out on the road on a crisp February morning, letting my intuition be my compass. I had no notion of where I would be heading, but wanted to see what would happen if I simply followed my intuition and the inner guidance from my heart. If I had the option to go right or to go left at an intersection, I would take the direction that I felt more drawn towards in that moment. This was a distinctly different process than I had ever engaged in before when traveling. In my old life I would have had many preconceived ideas of places that I wanted to visit, or ideas of where I "should" visit, and stick closely to my itinerary. To live in this new spontaneous way felt liberating, inspiring, and tremendously exciting.

It was a wonderful year long journey that took me all throughout the western United States. I met many wonderful people and saw many amazing things as I traveled. Living on the road has its challenges, yet with my deepening self awareness and self-control, it had become so much easier to go with the flow, rather than try to hold on too tightly to the steering wheel of life.

One of the most memorable experiences of my trip took place at a Rainbow gathering in Montana. If you are unfamiliar with Rainbow gatherings, it is an annual festival that began in the 1970's, with the aim of promoting peace, self-expression, and freedom. The gatherings are not-for-profit, completely volunteer run, and usually take place out in nature for the duration of a week to a month. The festival is free to all who desire to attend, while most people who attend choose to volunteer in one of the many community-run kitchens associated with the different Rainbow "families." I was stunned to see the dedication and commitment that existed among the die-hard Rainbow community. At the gathering in Montana it was estimated that roughly 7000 people attended, all with the shared intention of celebrating life together in the wilderness.

The climax of the experience occurred on one of the last days of the gathering, where it is tradition for everyone to spend the first part of the day in silence. It was amazing to share space with 7000 people all being silent for a morning. In the early afternoon the rainbow tribe then congregated in the main meadow to hold hands in a circle and chant "Om" for five minutes. My eyes welled with tears of joy as I stood chanting in a circle of thousands of people, which spanned more than a mile in diameter. I have never seen such a large group of people holding hands and unified in such a way.

I remember looking out from the hillside I was standing on, peering across the expansive meadow to see the tiny dots of people lining the slopes of the adjacent mountainside. It was an incredible experience, and the vibration of peace that was collectively created through our chanting reverberated powerfully through the air, the earth, and through each one of us. This is an experience I will never forget, and has provided much inspiration for the very real possibility of a world population living in harmony and unity. I left the gathering feeling inspired and enlivened.

While living on the road I continued to feel an immense inner freedom and profound connection to all of life. Feeling one with the trees, plants, animals, and the earth, allowed me to feel at home most anywhere I went. There were days where I experienced near perpetual states of bliss. Meditating for hours in the woods, swimming in rivers and lakes, singing to the trees, and enjoying just being alive became my new everyday reality.

I noticed, too, that I was interacting with people in a new way, as though everyone was a friend. I now felt a strong brotherly or sisterly bond with many people I encountered, allowing strong connections to form almost instantly. Walking down the street and suddenly gravitating towards someone, sparking up a conversation with them, and within minutes feeling a deep Soul resonance, is a remarkable experience. There is nothing quite like looking into the eyes of a stranger, feeling an immediate outpouring of love, and then to suddenly find yourself communing with this dear Soul as though they were a long lost friend. Meeting my "Soul family" in this way has been very inspiring, and has allowed me to connect with other healers and spiritual seekers who generally share a similar desire; that of working towards the collective awakening and healing of the planet at this time.

It is such a beautiful experience to feel your part in the family of creation, rather than merely identifying with a particular group of friends, a particular culture, lifestyle, or even your family. During this time I had very little interest in connecting with friends from my past, or my blood family, as I was so immensely enjoying the deep freedom of simultaneously feeling connected to everything, and within that connection, feeling a profound autonomy. I had released myself from energetic codependency with friends and family from my past, and was now experiencing greater states of personal freedom to live my life the way that I had always wanted.

However, I also faced immense challenges and obstacles during this time. Some of these tests I passed, while others proved to be humbling experiences. At one point along my travels I found myself down in the jungles of Mexico, drawn there by a spiritual gathering. As beautiful as the gathering was, it was wrought with challenge. By day three I had become sick with an intestinal infection, had been stung by a scorpion, and the entire lower half of my body had become covered in a mysterious rash that burned and itched relentlessly.

As I lay in my tent in anguish, I couldn't help but laugh at the absurdity of my predicament. And even though I was in pain, I realized that I wouldn't have wanted my circumstances to be any different. I was learning so much from the situation. I felt really alive, activated, and deeply in the flow of life, with plenty of opportunity for the spiritual practice of acceptance and non-resistance. Through these types of experiences I began to see how every challenge truly is an opportunity to grow and gain greater mastery over our thoughts, emotions, and reactions. Without them we would not progress as quickly on the spiritual path.

Sexual Energy and Celibacy

While living on the road I inadvertently began one of the most powerful processes I have ever undergone; conscious celibacy. It was a natural progression, and I stayed in this practice for roughly a year. What I learned about myself and the nature of sexual energy during this time has had a profound effect on my life.

Sexual energy permeates every aspect of our lives, including the work that we do, our creative projects, our relationships with others, our relationship with food, money, material objects, and even the earth. Sexual energy is our life energy, the energy of creation itself, and I feel that it truly is the deepest desire of every human being to use their energy for the highest good of all.

My journey into celibacy began as I started living more fully in the present moment and from my heart. As I continued to feel into the nature of my thoughts, learning to empower thoughts that felt good in my heart, while dissolving the mental patterns responsible for creating negativity, what I noticed was that most sexual thoughts did not actually feel good. I began to see a pattern emerging around my sexual thoughts, and I observed how in moments of anxiety or boredom, I was more likely to have a sexual thought than when I was in a peaceful state.

It became clear to me that these thoughts were not in alignment with my highest good, but rather a mechanism of my ego for soothing anxiety, and tended to distract me from taking greater personal responsibility for myself in the present moment. Having sexual thoughts about another has often felt as though I were taking something from someone else that didn't belong to me, a form of disrespect, even if it was only in my mind. So in the moments when sexual thoughts arose, I practiced bringing my attention back to my heart, feeling my breath and inner energy field. Within a few weeks my sexual thoughts had mostly disappeared, and I neither felt the urge for self-pleasure, nor sexual experiences.

The transition into celibacy was quite natural, and did not take much effort initially. It felt like a lightening of a weight that had been on my shoulders for a long time, and I was happy to be letting go of these patterns within myself. It is important to note the difference between the process of repressing sexual thoughts out of fear or shame, versus allowing old patterns to be dissolved that no longer serve the heart. My intuition was guiding me to free myself from old programming, and so following this guidance from within was the most natural thing I could do.

Though my sexual desires had disappeared by the end of the first month, I did have a series of intense sexual dreams that took a bit more time to dissolve. Amazingly, I experienced intense sexual dreams on the first three full moons during my time of celibacy. This was the first time in my life that I really understood just how powerful an effect the moon has on our minds and bodies.

Though going into celibacy was relatively easy and natural, the challenges that arose in other areas of my life during this practice provided me with great material to learn more about how my mind and ego operated. I noticed that celibacy was similar to the fasting experiences I had gone through in the past. And just as I sometimes had an increase in sexual desire during fasting from food, conversely, I often experienced an increase in my cravings for food (as well as other stimulus) during my time practicing celibacy.

This reminded me again that the root of the ego is actually addiction itself. This energy of addiction can be for anything, and is felt as a compulsive desire to escape the present moment through the distraction of some form of stimulus. The addiction of the ego is generally most strongly experienced in the following areas; food, sex, money, and power, but can also be experienced in any activity where the objective is escape through pleasure, such as drugs, music, exercise, or entertainment. This does not mean that the motivation to engage in any of these activities is necessarily coming from the ego, but it is through these activities that the ego can potentially strengthen itself through addictive tendencies.

The compulsions that arose for me during this time could be quite strong, and it took a great deal of resolution not to react to them. Fearful thoughts regarding money, my health, or the state of the world would often pop into my mind, seemingly out of nowhere, and I had to continually practice coming back to my heart. My compulsion for food became very strong at times, to the point that I would find myself in the supermarket late at night looking for something to satisfy my cravings. More than a few times I gorged myself on ice cream, cookies, or chips, to the point that I made myself sick.

These were wonderfully humbling experiences for me, and allowed me to see just how powerful Life Energy becomes when it is diverted away from sexual thoughts and desires. It also helped strengthen my motivation to heal and move forward, letting go of compulsions, and being more present. As I continued staying present, the more I saw what was underlying the compulsions; repressed pain, fear, and sadness.

This unfolded in the most unexpected way. When I had the choice to follow the compulsion or return to the present moment, I made the choice to be present and feel what was within. In the next moment I would often feel a deep sadness for what seemed like no reason at all. By simply sitting with the sadness it began to lighten and dissolve. In other times I released this emotional energy through crying. It felt wonderfully cathartic to give myself time and space for this natural healing process.

In retrospect, I believe this sadness and emotional outpouring was due to repressed pain from sexual wounding that I had experienced in my past, which was coming to the surface for me to feel and consciously release. These sexual wounds were not necessarily inflicted on me, but rather, ways in which I had energetically hurt others and myself by misusing my own sexual energy. To witness this and let it go felt very healing and cathartic, as though I were touching the deepest portions of my heart where this sadness had been hidden for so long.

In addition to sadness around my own sexual experiences, there also arose a deep sadness within me for the sexual wounding that has occurred within the whole of humanity. A few times I experienced deep emotional releases, grieving for what felt like the pain that has occurred between people when we hurt and manipulate one another, particularly related to the issues of domination and control—one of the greatest misuses of sexual energy. By exerting domination and control over others, we feel a temporary relief from the anxiety of separation from our hearts and God, but ultimately, this need for control causes pain for others and for ourselves.

You can see this expression of control and domination in the way that many people relate to one another. Most people have had the experience throughout life of being controlled by parents, teachers, friends, romantic partners, employers, or co-workers, with this pain often becoming internalized and repressed, beginning at a very early age. Exerting a certain amount of control is necessary to provide a structured and safe experience for oneself and others, and yet many expressions of control are often coming from a deep seated fear and anxiety about life.

I didn't know it at the time, but my resistance towards those who tried to exert control over me lead me to strengthen that very same ego mechanism in myself, which I had played out in my relationships (romantic and platonic) many times throughout my life. I had done so as a way to feel some sense of power amidst my underlying feelings of powerlessness. True power, however, comes from knowing yourself; knowing what motivates you and why. When you know yourself, no one else can have power over you.

One of the most wonderful outcomes of celibacy was an increased awareness of the sacred aspects of all life. As I repeatedly redirected my attention within, my heart truly opened to greater depths of gratitude for the magic and mystery of life. Watching a ladybug crawl across a leaf, or the delicate flow of water in a stream, could easily bring me to tears of joy. Everything seemed to take on greater meaning and magic, as though I was witnessing the most beautiful dance of creation happening all around me. I began to feel on a deeper level just how blessed we are to be here having this incredible human experience. This phenomenon would come in varying waves of intensity, and seemed to increase the longer that I remained celibate.

Another wonderful effect that occurs when you retain your sexual energy is an increase in physical and mental energy. There were some nights when I only needed a few hours of sleep, and had so much creative energy that I would spend hours writing, painting, or playing music. I found that my mind became much sharper and more focused during this time, which spurred me to find new ways to use this increased mental energy in order to prevent stagnation. I found that an abundance of physical exercise, creative expression, deep breathing, and a balance of structure and spontaneity in my life, helped to keep this energy flowing in a positive and healthy way.

Through this process it became very clear just how strong Life Energy could flow when directed in such a focused way. As we become more discerning with what thoughts we empower with our attention, then each thought that is created has that much more energy and power. The more focused the mind becomes, the signal that we send out to the Universe is that much clearer and more energized.

This seems to be one reason there is still much fear around sexual energy. For the most part, we are still collectively afraid of our own power and creative potential. This is changing, however, as more and more people are awakening, and learning to become more responsible with their energy. The more energy that flows through us, the more responsibility we have to use this energy in positive and uplifting ways.

After roughly a year of practicing celibacy I began to feel that this cycle of healing in my life was coming to an end. There came a time when I intuitively knew that it would not serve my growth anymore to continue the practice. Remaining celibate began to feel more restrictive rather than expansive, and so my journey of celibacy gradually came to an end as naturally as it had begun. As I ended my journey of celibacy I was surprised to feel a very strong desire to have a family. I felt more clear and excited by the idea of being a father than ever before.

This new inspiration to have a family prompted me to create another vision board filled with some of the images that had come to me during my time in celibacy. I often had visions of myself living in the woods, building an earthen home, and raising my children alongside my loving partner. Though I didn't feel ready to begin creating a family just yet, I was ready to call in a partner to my life to share in the love that I had cultivated over the last year.

The image that I clipped from a magazine that seemed to embody the energy of my future partner was a painting of a dark haired woman with the words "I am enough," written across her shirt. This image popped out at me as soon as I saw it, and it felt in alignment with much of what I had learned through my time of celibacy over the last year; that by letting go of the need to control life, I'm continually brought back to that place of remembering that I am enough, just as I am. I pinned my vision board up in my van, and once again headed out on the road.

The Next Chapter

It was now late in the autumn season, and as I was traveling through the cooler region of the northwest United States, I found myself feeling drawn to Hawaii (which would be a nice place to spend the cold winter months). I set the intention for Hawaii, added a few inspiring tropical images to my vision board, and continued westward.

I made my way towards the coast, and landed in a charming town in Northern Washington. While there I connected with a woman on the dance floor at a local ecstatic dance, and we began spending time together. I was inspired by her gentle and peaceful energy, and over the coming weeks we shared many nice dances together. Soon we began seeing each other on a regular basis.

It was a wonderful heart opening experience to once again be in a relationship following my inner journey of celibacy. It was sweet and magical to feel that her energy so closely matched the vision that I had put out to the Universe when asking for a romantic partner. The energy that we shared grew stronger, and Mia and I began spending more time together, sharing meals, playing music, and dancing in her quaint and cozy Victorian home.

One day stands out in my memory as particularly magical. We had just spent the day together relaxing and playing. As daylight faded we moved indoors to warm up. The setting sun filtered in through the window, casting a soft golden light through the room. As we made ourselves comfortable amidst the pile of pillows on the living room floor, Mia casually mentioned that she owned a second home in Hawaii, and invited me to come stay with her there for the winter. I laughed in amazement and explained how I had recently set my sights on Hawaii for the winter. It was a wonderful synchronicity that felt very good in my heart, and I gratefully accepted the invitation.

To celebrate we put on some music for dancing. An appropriate choice seemed to be the popular Hawaiian musician, Israel kamakawiwo'ole's rendition of "Somewhere Over the Rainbow" (and one of my all time favorite songs). As I danced alongside my new friend and partner I was overcome with happiness and a tremendous feeling of freedom and magic that seemed to permeate the fabric of my life. Within those tender moments, surrounded by the soft glow of golden light from the setting sun, I suddenly felt as though the gates to some heavenly realm had opened up before me. For a moment I was brought back to the visceral feelings I had experienced during my awakening many years earlier of intense ecstasy and bliss, a tremendous love overflowing from within. As we danced I cried, holding my hand to my heart in deep gratitude. I felt so alive, so present, and joyful beyond words. "Somewhere Over the Rainbow" played on repeat as we swayed in unison to the sweet melody, before finally collapsing into the pile of pillows on the floor, smiling and laughing. Feeling tender and content we lay there, soaking up the beauty of the moment.

Soon Mia would be getting ready to meet her daughter for dinner, and I would find myself heading out for a stroll through the dusk hours along the Washington coastline. I wandered down the sidewalk, meandering through a few neighborhood streets, and arriving, by chance, at a nearby park. I plopped down on the grass with a gentle sigh, sitting within close proximity to a group of elderly folks arranged in a circle under a lit gazebo, preparing for what looked like a small and informal musical recital. There was no audience to speak of, expect for myself. Curious as to what they might be performing, I edged slightly closer and lay down in the grass to gaze up at the first stars of the night. Had I been sitting upright I might have seen them unpacking their ukuleles, and may have even guessed their song of choice.

As I lay in the grass, peering into the nighttime sky, I wasn't entirely surprised to hear the sweetest rendition of Israel kamakawiwo'ole's "Somewhere Over the Rainbow" wafting through the crisp autumn air. I couldn't help but smile, taking a deep breath in amazement at the perfection and synchronicity of this moment. What were the chances that this was merely coincidence? Though synchronicity has increasingly become a more normalized part of my day-to-day experience, I have yet to become so thoroughly accustomed to it that I don't still revel in the magic and mystery of these divinely orchestrated "cosmic tickles."

A few weeks later I made my way back to California to put most of my belongings into storage in preparation for my move to Hawaii. I parked my van at a friend's house, packed my things, and bought a one-way ticket to Hawaii to meet Mia. She picked me up at the airport, our reunion sweet and playful. That night we slept out under the stars on the beach, and the next day we made the short trip to the other side of the island to her house. Mia had never seen my vision board, nor had I mentioned anything about it to her, and yet upon entering her beach side house I was amazed to see a small poster hanging on the wall that simply read, "I Am Enough," the same phrase from the image of the woman I had posted on my vision board months earlier.

And this is where my story leaves off. The Universe never ceases to amaze me with its surprises, magic, and unfathomable beauty. I continue to explore and investigate more about myself and the nature of Creation everyday. With this new found wonder, joy, and excitement for life, I have grown to appreciate the journey that my Soul is on—a journey that far exceeds the struggles and triumphs of this one particular lifetime. It has become clear to me that we are each on a journey of self-expansion, one that extends for all eternity. There is no end to what we can discover, experience, and create. Though the mind may not be able to comprehend the beauty and magic of the path that we are on, the heart does. The heart knows, beyond a shadow of a doubt, who we are and why we have come here.

And while sometimes I do fall back into old patterns, every slip-up provides me with greater motivation and commitment to live in accordance with the highest good of all life. This is the Divine design, and it truly couldn't be any other way. I feel blessed, grateful, and joyful to be alive, and to be sharing the energy of wakefulness, joy, and peace with others along this truly sacred journey.

Part II
The Awakening

~*~

"Your own self-realization is the greatest service you can render the world." -Ramana Maharshi

Every person on the planet is on the path towards spiritual awakening, even if they don't yet know it. At the deepest level, every human desires to know peace, to know love, to know their eternal self beyond the limitations of fear and ego. And while the inner anguish and suffering that so many people experience is the result of denying our true nature, it is through this suffering that a person is propelled down the path of inward investigation and spiritual awakening. There comes a time along a Soul's journey when the question arises, "what is this all about...what is the reason for so much uncertainty and pain in my life?" It is at this point when a Soul begins to wake up from the illusion created by the world of form, consciously embarking upon the return journey home. Living unconsciously, then, is a necessary stepping stone on the path towards waking up and living more consciously.

Once the awakening has been initiated, it is only a matter of time before full self-realization occurs. It may take lifetimes, but once an opening is created, it is impossible to go back to living completely in the unawakened state. This process appears to be speeding up, however. As the drama and pain on the planet increases, it is causing many people to begin searching for deeper meaning and truth in their lives. And because you are reading this book, you too are likely seeking to know the depths of yourself more fully. By understanding how the mind and ego operate, you can free yourself from suffering and mind-made limitations in each moment, allowing yourself to live more fully from your heart.

The Ego and the Mind

You are not the voice inside your mind. You are not your emotions. You are not your body. Who you are is beyond any one of these temporary expressions. Who you are in your essence is the field of awareness that is experiencing it all. But even these words cannot accurately describe the Truth of who we are and what life is, because they are merely concepts, and the fullness of that which we are is beyond conceptual understanding. This Truth, however, can be recollected, not from within the mind, but rather, from within the depths of one's heart and Soul.

...In this moment are you able to feel your childlike nature; the feeling of wonder, magic, and natural peace and contentment just for the experience of being alive? Do you remember what it feels like to love all of life unconditionally from this state of innocence?...And can you remember at what point the voice inside your mind began to cover over your awareness of this natural way of being, and of who you truly are?

By quieting the mind and returning to the present moment we allow ourselves the opportunity to reconnect with who we truly are. From this deeply connected state we regain our child-like innocence, naturally going with the flow of life, and feeling a profound sense of peace, love, joy, and freedom. Many people, however, only experience fleeting moments of such freedom, and often feel confused about how to cultivate greater states of inner connection. "How do I get out of my head and into my heart? How do I learn to trust life and go with the flow, rather than needing to analyze, control, and obsess over the details of life?"

Understanding what the ego is, and learning to transcend beyond it, creates a foundation for having a more authentic experience of yourself and life. Dissolving the ego uncovers a deeper dimension within you, bringing a richness and depth into your life that is far greater than what can be experienced through the thinking mind. This section is entitled "the ego and the mind" because the two can be so intertwined that most people are unconsciously using their mind in service of the ego. I use the terms "ego" and "mind" interchangeably in this chapter as a reminder of this entangled connection. The mind is a powerful tool, but in order to use it in service of your heart, it's capacities must first be untangled from the mechanisms of the ego. So what is the ego?

The ego is a deeply rooted psychological adaptation that has developed over thousands of years to ensure the survival of the individual. The foundation of the ego is a belief in separation, a belief that you are alone in the world and must struggle for your protection and survival. The ego can be observed as the compulsive voice in the mind which is constantly interpreting and filtering the experiences of life through the intellect. This voice is constantly thinking about future events, obsessing over the past, commenting on everything that is happening around you, and making judgments of yourself, situations, and other people.

The ego is literally the voice inside your mind that has been talking to you, and commenting on life around you, for the majority of your life.

Many people are still predominately identified with the self talk in the mind, so much so, that this concept may seem foreign at first, and may spark the question, "well, if I'm not the voice in my mind, then who am I?" Beyond the voice in the mind you exist as a field of awareness, as consciousness itself. Who you are transcends all of the surface layer aspects of yourself; your name, your personality, your family history, your stories, your opinions, and all the accumulated mental constructs of who you think you are. Beyond these temporary expressions of yourself, you are the awareness that is experiencing it all. You can feel this state of awareness right here and now by bringing your attention to this moment, feeling the stillness that simultaneously exists within you and all around you...

In this state of presence an inner knowing arises that we are not separate, but rather a part of all creation. We are one with all that is, connected to something greater than our individual self. There is an intense joy and liberation in this feeling of connection. You may be able to feel this experience momentarily throughout your day, and as you do, watch what covers it up—it is likely either the thoughts within your mind, your emotional reactions, or distractions from the world around you.

At this stage of our collective evolution, however, most people are still hypnotized by the incessant voice of the ego, and do not feel their true essence very fully. And so the process of reconnecting to our natural state of awareness first involves learning how the ego operates, and then choosing to let it go. Through this process of understanding, you will naturally begin to cultivate greater inner silence, moving beyond the limitations of the ego.

The Origins of the Ego

The ego forms early in our lives as we learn to identify ourselves by mental concepts; a name, personality traits, likes and dislikes, opinions, and as the general stream of thoughts that arise in the mind, much of which is influenced by our family and the culture around us. We learn to mistake our sense of Being with mental concepts and thoughts about ourselves and the world. As the developing ego forms during childhood, the belief in separation begins to take root within the psyche. A label has been given to "me," thereby creating the "other" as that which is not "me."

This experience of separation and differentiation has been a natural part of human development, and has served our collective growth and evolution for thousands of years. Feeling deeply separate from other forms of life has created the rich experience of being alone in the world, and mastering the art of physical survival. This, perhaps, was a noble pursuit in the past, and must have served the desires of the collective consciousness throughout the history of humanity. But as with any experience, there comes a point where it is no longer interesting. When all that can be learned from the experience of separation and individuation has reached its peak, we begin moving back into the fullness of oneness, dissolving the illusion of separation. We now stand on the cusp of a new era in our collective human experience, an era of shared unity, unconditional love, and connection.

In order to move into this new era, however, the old ego structures must first be dissolved. The ego has become like an outdated software program, becoming so dysfunctional that it now threatens the survival of the human species, and all living creatures on the planet. Because many people are still unaware of the ego existing in their own minds, they continue to be motivated, to a large degree, by the fear for survival, and a belief in separation.

You can see this in the way that many people are motivated by selfish desires to have more for themselves, and to enhance their sense of self through possessions, money, accomplishments, or status. There is a profound shortsightedness that occurs through the ego, however, which places almost complete importance on individual needs, rather than the collective health and well-being of the whole. Ironically, it is this ignorance of our shared connection which has now become a threat to our individual survival on an increasingly fragile planet.

This is the turning point that humanity is experiencing right now, where the old ego structures are becoming increasingly dysfunctional, and people are beginning to wake up to the greater reality. Now, more so than ever before in the history of humanity, the veil of illusion and separation is falling away. And as the veil is lifted, powerful transformations are taking place, both individually and collectively. The experience of awakening to our true nature and shared connection is an immensely joyful celebration like no other, and expands the loving energy in the Universe through the process. I feel this to be the primary purpose for the existence of the ego; to serve as a catalyst for this divine remembrance of our true nature, and for the bliss, joy, and unconditional love that is amplified throughout the process of awakening.

For now, however, we are still collectively in the waking-up period. It is up to each one of us, if we so choose, to begin withdrawing our attention away from the thoughts, feelings, and actions that perpetuate the illusion of separation, and that strengthen the ego. These mental and emotional patterns of separation were formed early in life, and so it can take some time and commitment to dissolve them. Understanding how the ego operates is the first step towards spiritual liberation.

Mechanisms of the Ego

The ego behaves in a very systematic way, primarily strengthening itself through identification with form. Form, in this context, refers to physical forms such as material objects, other people, your own body, as well as mental and emotional forms (thoughts, concepts, beliefs, stories, and emotional patterns). The mind is looking for a self-identity through the world of form, thereby reinforcing the experience of separation, effectively creating a conceptual "you" that constantly needs defending in order to survive.

The ego searches for permanence in form, even though it is clear that nothing in this world is permanent, but rather, constantly changing, growing, and evolving. Because the ego seeks security in the world of form, the mind is constantly moving between the past and the future, trying to plan for the future, or obsessing over what went wrong in the past that threatened homeostasis. Even when the mind can control the circumstances of life, however, it never feels content for very long. The mind is always aware that something or someone may come along to threaten your sense of identity and safety.

The ego thrives as long as it feels separate from life around itself, and so it seeks to create an identity for itself that is different than others—that is either greater than, or less than others. The ego can either create a positive identity or a negative identity. The thought, "I am better than others," is the same ego mechanism that operates in the person who thinks, "I am worse than others." The more you observe the thoughts in your mind, you will see the subtle ways in which the ego reinforces a conceptual identity based on separation.

All of the mental constructs you have about yourself (what is generally referred to as the personality) are mostly a culmination of mental and emotional patterns that were formed throughout your life in response to the types of reactions you received from the world around you. In that sense, the personality is more a reflection of circumstances and the environment, rather than any inherent truth about who you are. This would become apparent if you were to observe the ever changing shifts in your self-image that occur over the course of a day. When people respond positively to you (your friends, partner, parents, or boss), you then feel good about yourself. When people respond negatively to you, you then feel poorly about yourself.

This continual shift in your self-identity highlights that the view of yourself through the lens of the ego is always a distorted and limited version of you. The mind then becomes attached to these ever changing self-concepts; "I am the victim, the unhealthy one, the worrier, the successful one, the strong one, the caretaker, the hard worker, the anxious one, or the helpless one." Whenever you see yourself as a certain type of person, it is the voice of the ego seeking to strengthen itself through a conceptual identity. The ego is not concerned with what you identify with, but merely that you have some form of identity.

Another way in which the ego strengthens the false sense of identity is by blaming, criticizing, and judging other people, or life situations. By making another person wrong, you are by default right, and in a place of superiority. When you are dissatisfied with what is happening around you, you are effectively saying, "I am better than this," reinforcing the experience of separation between you and life around you. You may temporarily feel good through this type of ego reaction, but very likely you will eventually feel the pain of loneliness and separation that occurs when the ego has been energized.

The more negatively charged your thoughts are, the better the ego can captivate your attention, and the more likely you are to identify with these thoughts. The more that the mind can find fault in other people, places, or situations, the more reason your ego has to react against them, perpetuating the experience of separation, and thereby strengthening the false sense of self.

The ego is generally concerned with the future and the past, keeping a person distracted from the present moment. The mind is concerned with getting more, achieving more, and being greater, while always reinforcing the belief that happiness and contentment exist somewhere outside the present moment. Even the desire to become spiritually enlightened can be a desire of the ego. If you are unconsciously seeking to find happiness somewhere in the future by becoming "enlightened," then it is the ego at work.

Notice, however, that even when you achieve what it is you think will make you happy, the mind will very quickly find another goal for happiness, one that can only be found in the future. Contentment and peace are perpetually a distant reality, only experienced in small bursts as a person temporarily gets what they want. The present moment is generally unacceptable from the perspective of the ego, and the mind will do whatever it can to preoccupy your attention with attaining some future goal, material possession, symbol of status, or position of power.

The ego seeks to use other people in order to strengthen it's own self image. In social interactions it is quite common for the ego to begin assessing the other person in order to determine how he or she may serve the ego's needs. The mind will create a story about the other person, and try to categorize this person based on assumptions and past experiences, rather than experiencing their essence directly. If the ego determines that the other will somehow enhance one's own image in some way, then an effort will be made to keep this person around. If, on the other hand, the ego cannot get it's needs met from another, then the ego quickly loses interest. The ego is drawn to others who have power, material possessions, or status as a way to enhance oneself through association with the other person. Conversely, the ego can also be drawn to those whom appear weak or suggestible, as a way to derive power and attention from others.

Listed below are some common ego thought patterns that you can begin to notice within yourself. Keep in mind that the ego is not personal. The ego is not who you are, but rather, a universal experience that every human being, in their own time, is learning to transcend beyond. There is no reason to beat yourself up when you catch the ego in action. In fact, it is actually a success, in that you are one step closer to living in Truth, to being more authentically you.

Ego Thought Patterns

-Any negative thought or emotion, such as annoyance, frustration, anger, jealousy, boredom, irritation, anxiety, or a feeling of dread or doom.
-Becoming defensive
-A compulsive need to be in control of your life, or a compulsive need to feel control over others.
-Compulsive thoughts, reactions, or behaviors.
-Dissatisfaction or resistance towards the present moment.
-Recurring thoughts about the future or past.
-Comparing yourself to others (feeling either superior or inferior to others).
-Over attachment to material possessions, people, or places.
-Stories in your mind about yourself or others that are not based on objective facts.
-Role identification where you slip into playing a role unconsciously (the caretaker, the assertive one, the shy one, the good friend, the rebel, etc).
-Being overly concerned with other people's personal affairs.
-Competitiveness and aggressiveness.
-Needing to stand out or feel special.
-Criticizing, blaming, or judging others or yourself.
-Possessiveness or jealousy.
-Random and aimless thoughts that distract you away from the present moment or leave you feeling drained.

Dissolving the Ego

All that is required to begin dissolving the ego is to become aware of the ego as it operates within you. When you notice the ego in action, simply drop the ego based thought and bring your attention back to the present moment. This may feel challenging at first, and it can be quite alarming to see how much of your life may have been influenced by the incessant voice in your mind.

Just begin by noticing the thoughts in your mind that lead to negative states such as anxiety, doubt, depression, dissatisfaction, jealousy, anger, or frustration. Notice how the thoughts, and the consequent negative emotional reactions that are created, energize your experience of separation, and ultimately cause you to suffer in some way. It is never the situation that causes you to suffer, but rather, your thoughts about the situation that creates suffering within.

Whenever you catch yourself lost in thought, simply bring your attention back to the present moment. Notice the sights, smells and physical sensations around you. Feel your breath and your inner energy field. Through this process you will begin dissolving your addiction to compulsive thinking, no longer allowing yourself to be hypnotized by thoughts, no longer allowing them to take you on a roller-coaster ride in your mind. You become the conscious observer, as though you are peacefully watching your mind from a distance.

By becoming a conscious witness to your own mind, you create space between yourself as awareness, and the stream of compulsive thinking in your mind. In this moment you have become free from the ego—you are aware of the thought, but you are no longer identified with the thought. In this moment a stillness arises within, and you feel a deepening connection to who you are in your essence. This process of dis-identifying with thoughts and continually coming back to the present moment takes practice, but over time will incrementally increase your presence power, and the quality of your life.

The Power of Non-Attachment

Practice non-attachment to your thoughts, dropping them one by one as they arise in your mind. When a label or judgment arises, let it go and come back to the present moment. You don't need the label or concept about reality when you can directly experience it for yourself. Judgments and labels only get in the way. Yes, you may need to give a label to something for practical purposes, but you can do so without attachment to it. Do not believe for a minute that the word you have used to describe something actually fully represents the greater reality of what that thing is. This goes for objects, places, experiences, as well as the nature of other people. Just because a person is exhibiting a personality trait in this moment, does not mean it is who they are.

Do not become attached to any thought that your mind creates. Instead, stay open, alert, and present, observing what is actually happening around you, without needing to conceptually understand or interpret life events. In order to move beyond the inherent limitations of the mind, stay connected to your own eternal nature, and choose to see beyond the ego patterns in yourself and others.

As you practice non-attachment to your own thoughts, you may notice that you begin to let go of attachment in the many areas of life; relationships, material possessions, and work and living situations. This doesn't mean that you necessarily let them go from your life, but rather, you let go of your attachment to them. The things of life come and go, and by practicing non-attachment you can enjoy the ride without obsessing over, holding onto, or pushing anything away.

Simply notice thoughts as they arise which relate to trying to hold onto something in your life; "I really want to say the right thing to my partner so he or she knows how much I love them;" "I need to make sure everything goes perfect at work today;" "I really hope I get that promotion at work." Really, why? Why not trust that everything in your life is playing out exactly as it should, and that there is a bigger picture of your life than your mind could ever understand? When one thing leaves your life (a relationship, job, or material possession, for instance) it creates space for something new to enter. And it is the Higher Intelligence of our Soul that guides us towards just what we need to experience for our growth. Without this natural flow of give and take we would never grow or evolve, and life would become pretty boring.

The Power of Non-Reaction

One of the most effective ways to dissolve the ego in yourself and others is through non-reaction. The ego is not who you are, and it is not who the other person is. When you see the ego operating in yourself or another, choose to look beyond it. Make the conscious choice not to react against the ego, and instead, hold compassion for the other person and yourself. This may take practice, but I have found no better way to transcend the ego than this method of non-reaction.

The ego is fear-based illusion, and any action taken against the ego only perpetuates the illusion of separation. Why push against something that is not real? The only motivation to "do something" about it comes from the belief that it is real and that you have to take action against it. All that is required is for you to become aware of the ego, and then refrain from energizing it through reaction. Simply stay in a non-reactive state. The voice in your mind may be running a mile a minute with thoughts about the situation, but you can simply keep returning your attention to the present moment, without buying into any of those thoughts.

Focus on the humanity that you feel in yourself and within others. Focus on the glimmer of light coming from others, even when the ego seems all-pervasive. Choose to remain present and neutral instead of believing any thoughts about yourself or the other person. In this way we each have the potential to be vehicles for transformation, allowing more conscious awareness into our own lives, and the lives of others.

The Power of Non-Judgment

The mind often identifies negative aspects about situations or people, and then goes about defending its position by looking for "evidence" that validates the judgment. This is the power of our thoughts in the process of shaping our perceptions of reality. Once we make a judgment, we set into motion a filtering of our own perceptions of reality based on what we expect to see. Our perceptions become focused on all the negative aspects associated with the judgmental thought, and so the mind undoubtedly finds the "evidence" it is looking for. Belief systems are like self-fulfilling prophecies in this way, and when you are attached to the thoughts in your mind, every judgment is accurate as far as the mind is concerned.

Underlying every judgment is non-acceptance in some form. When a person has yet to accept some aspect of themselves, this inner resistance is often projected outward in the form of judgments or negativity. A clear example of this would be the subjugation of women that has occurred over the last few thousand years in most cultures around the world. The reason for this repression is that many people have yet to fully accept and integrate their own feminine nature. If you've ever spent time with someone displaying misogynistic tendencies, you may have noticed a distinct lack of feminine qualities within them, such as empathy, receptivity, gentleness, or compassion. It would be clear to see that this person has yet to accept their own feminine energy due to fear or ignorance, projecting this lack of self love outward towards women through negativity or abuse. And collectively, most societies are still working towards bringing greater love and acceptance to the divine feminine aspects of creation, which is why we still see a predominately male dominated world (though this is now changing).

So whenever you find that you are either judging yourself, another person, or life circumstances, take the time to go within and notice where you may still be holding negativity or resistance towards yourself. Are there aspects of yourself that you are repressing or in denial of? Are there parts of yourself that you continue to withhold love and acceptance for? Take the time to investigate what core beliefs, thoughts and values may be reinforcing this state of non-acceptance, and be willing to let them go once you identify them.

By letting go of judgments we offer ourselves the opportunity to actually learn and grow from life situations, rather than become calcified in a rigid belief system. And when you let go of judgments of others, you hold them in a more loving light, allowing them to learn and grow as well. If your experience with another person has caused you heartache and suffering, be grateful for what you have learned

89

through your time with them. Your suffering has caused you to strengthen your commitment to create more uplifting and positive relationships in your life, to embody your power more fully, and to live in a generally more loving way.

The Present Moment

Present moment awareness is the foundation of spiritual liberation, and can free you from the grip of the ego. The more you remain present, the greater of a connection you will feel to life around you, and to your essential nature. As you are reading this, pause for a moment and look out into the room. Ask yourself, "what will be my next thought?" And as you wait, notice the stillness that exists in the gap of silence...

This presence, devoid of thought, is who you are. This pure consciousness, pure awareness, unattached to any thoughts or stories about yourself or life, is who you are in your essence. But the experience of your true nature can only be felt here and now. Once a thought about the future or past arises, you begin to lose awareness of your essential nature here and now. The practice is to continually loosen your attachment to your thoughts as a wholly accurate interpretation of reality, and instead, experience the truth of who you are in this moment.

This does not mean that you stop using your mind altogether. Instead, you (as conscious awareness) begin using your mind with greater discernment, choosing when and how to use your thoughts to create your experience. The first step, however, is to learn to quiet the mind and return to the present moment. Why is the present moment so important? Because this is where life is happening. Have you ever existed anywhere other than in the present moment? What you may realize is that every experience you have ever had has taken place in the present moment. And you may also notice that it is your level of presence that determines the quality of your moment to moment experience, which, in turn, creates the overall quality of your life.

The mind often becomes distracted by the future or past, believing that it can prepare for future events by thinking. And while some thinking and preparation may be required for planning a project, taking a trip, or working out the logistics of future events, the majority of thinking about the future or the past is not only pointless, but actually prevents you from taking appropriate action when it is necessary to do so. The psychological angst created by obsessing over the past or future drains your energy and causes confusion in the mind and energy field.

Let go of thinking about the future or the past, and instead, simply focus on what you can do here and now. Stay aware and alert of what is required of you in this present moment. All other steps will be made known to you in the appropriate time. It takes focus and discipline to continually bring your attention back to the present moment, and it will likely be a lifelong practice. The more you can remain present, however, the more you will witness profound shifts in the quality of your life.

Emotions Versus Feelings

What commonly draws a person out of the present moment are strong emotional reactions. What are generally referred to as "emotions," however, can be somewhat deceiving, and often actually distract a person away from what they are truly feeling inside. By understanding the difference between emotions and feelings, you can begin dissolving emotional drama that would otherwise hijack your attention away from the present moment.

I have found that feelings occur as actual sensations in the body or energy field, whereas emotions are what occur once the mind assigns a conceptual label to a feeling. For instance, pain or sadness can often be felt as an aching or dull sensation in the body, while fear, anger, or jealousy can often be felt as a rush of energy moving through the body. When you remove the labels of "pain, sadness, fear, or anger," however, these experiences remain neutral, and simply exist as sensations being experienced within you. If you remain neutral, simply observing whatever is happening in your body and energy field, emotional reaction does not exist.

Ironically, it is often emotional reaction that actually prevents a person from deeply feeling what is going on inside. Emotions act as a buffer between a person and their direct experience, with the ego attempting to protect the psyche through emotional reaction. Anger, for instance, always arises in response to feeling either pain, fear, or sadness. The ego defense mechanism of anger gets activated almost automatically in a moment of vulnerability, preventing a person from feeling the underlying pain, fear, or sadness.

In a much earlier time in our history this ego mechanism would have likely helped ensure the survival of the individual. A hunter or warrior pausing to feel sadness or pain would undoubtedly leave themselves vulnerable to attack from a predator or an enemy. Conversely, the ego reaction of intense anger might allow a person to do unspeakable actions necessary for survival, without feeling the consequent pain that their behavior caused for other forms of life and the greater whole.

In modern times, however, our day-to-day physical survival no longer requires the same kind of vigilance that was once required of our ancestors. Yet the ego still attempts to protect the psyche as though one's physical survival were at stake. It is quite common to see a person become angry in order to push the other person away so that their true feelings of pain or sadness will not be exposed—even though exposing one's true feelings would in no way jeopardize the person's actual physical survival in any way.

Not only has this ego mechanism become outdated, it is now actually threatening the survival of our species, as well as other forms of life on the planet. Being in touch with our feelings is what allow us to connect with other forms of life, receiving energetic information from others, as well as allowing us to consciously express our emotional energy to life around us. When the ego covers over our feelings, we lose our connection to the greater whole, allowing a person to do tremendously harmful things to other forms of life without feeling the repercussions.

In modern times this ego survival mechanism has caused many

people to cover over their own feelings so deeply that they have become almost completely numb to what is going on inside of themselves, and to the feelings of others. Because of this, their actions of greed and manipulation have wreaked havoc on the environment, and caused immeasurable suffering for other forms of life. We see evidence of this in the way that individuals, corporations, and governments have caused so much harm in the world without seeming to feel the effects of their actions.

Dissolving Emotional Reaction

Create space between what you are feeling, and your reactions towards what you are feeling (emotions), by coming back to your breath and the present moment. Bring as much peace and acceptance to what is happening within you, without reacting against it. This will begin dissolving the unconscious patterns of creating emotional states that cause suffering for yourself and others. By coming back to your breath you will naturally return to a place of centered peacefulness. As you master non-reaction you will notice that much of the drama and conflict naturally dissolves from your life. In the absence of negative emotional reaction, the experience of creating emotions becomes a conscious practice, where you allow for positive and uplifting expressions to move through you, while no longer fueling negative emotional experiences.

It is also helpful to really unravel any myths you may have about "positive" and "negative" feelings. What is a negative feeling, what is a positive feeling? I have found that sadness and grief, for instance, can sometimes be very positive, and are necessary to experience from time to time in order to maintain balance within my life. Sadness felt at the loss of a loved one, or the ending of a relationship is a natural part of the cycles of life. So sadness can be viewed as very "positive" in some circumstances. As we learn to stay present with our feelings without needing to label them, these experiences add to the richness and depth that we feel in our lives.

Again, it is only once the mind interprets these feeling as

negative that it causes suffering. When you resist the sensations of sadness, it then turns to anger, jealousy, resentment, anxiety, or depression, and can potentially become a destructive force in your life. And the only way that the pain of sadness could turn into a negative emotion is if you view it as a negative experience, and then react against it. Instead, choose to remain neutral and in a state of complete acceptance for what you are feeling. Over time, this will dissolve emotional patterns of the ego.

Dissolving Limiting Core Beliefs

Underlying the thoughts that we audibly hear in our thinking mind, exist layers of unconscious beliefs that have been so deeply programmed within us that we don't even experience them as thoughts, but rather, as automatic and immediate reactions. A belief, however, is simply a thought that you have thought enough times that it has now become automatic.

You can dissolve any limiting core belief by first seeing it, and then choosing to override it with a new belief, or simply by resting in the stillness of the present moment. Whenever you catch yourself in a state of negativity or ego reaction, take the opportunity to investigate your thought process to uncover the deeper unconscious belief that may be fueling your automatic reactions. Some common underlying core beliefs that may be shaping your moment-to-moment reactions are:

1. I am not good enough
2. I must prove myself worthy to receive love
3. I am not capable or competent enough
4. I do not have control over my reactions or thoughts
5. I must struggle in order to survive
6. The world is a dangerous place
7. Material possession, status and money equal happiness
8. I must fulfill other people's expectations

9. I must be perfect
10. Other people's perceptions of me define who I am
11. I must be logical and practical at all times
12. My feelings don't matter
13. I am responsible for other people's feelings
14. There is no order in the universe; life events are random
15. I must be in control of all aspects of my life
16. I don't deserve to feel good
17. I don't deserve to have abundance in my life
18. I am unable to change the circumstances of my life
19. I am powerless

Underneath most negative or limiting thoughts you will likely see one or more of these core beliefs. There are often multiple core beliefs operating simultaneously at the unconscious level within a person, which influence surface layer thoughts, and often create negativity and emotional turmoil. By identifying the core belief underlying the thought, you allow it to be witnessed and released from your subconscious mind, dissolving it's hold over you. Here are a few examples of common negative thought patterns, with the accompanying core belief.

Thought: "I can't change professions because my friends and family won't approve if I quite my job."
Core Beliefs: I must fulfill other people's expectations. I must be logical and practical at all times. Other people's perceptions of me define who I am.

Thought: "I don't know what I would do if my partner left me, I don't think I could handle it."
Core Beliefs: I do not have control over my reactions and thoughts. I am not capable or competent enough. I am powerless.

Thought: "My friends and family will think I'm strange if I start eating healthy and begin practicing meditation and yoga."
Core Belief: Other people's perceptions of me define who I am. I must prove myself worthy of other people's validation and love. My

feelings don't matter.

Thought: "I can't mess up this project at work—it has to be perfect."
Core Belief: I must be perfect. I must be in control of all aspects of my life. I must struggle in order to survive.

Thought: "Look at that person with so much wealth, I will never have what they have."
Core Beliefs: I am unable to change the circumstances of my life. I don't deserve to have abundance in my life. Material possession, status, and money equal happiness.

Thought: "I better say something nice to this person. I don't want to hurt their feelings, or to appear rude."
Core Beliefs: I am responsible for other people's feelings. I must fulfill other people's expectations.

Thought: "What if the plane goes down during the flight—who will take care of my family?"
Core Belief: There is no order in the Universe; life events are random, I must be in control of all aspects of my life.

Whenever you have a limiting or negative thought, take the time to pinpoint the underlying core belief. Once you do, you can either simply drop the thought and remain in peaceful stillness, or you can consciously override the old belief with a new, more empowering belief. In the moment that you uncover the limiting belief, either say the new belief out loud, in your head, or write it down. This is a wonderfully empowering practice that will help you to recreate your reality from a place of conscious awareness. The following positive core beliefs would be suitable substitutes for the previous list of limiting beliefs:

1. I am good enough
2. I am worthy of other people's love and attention
3. I am capable and competent
4. I have control over my reactions and thoughts

5. I am meant to thrive in life
6. I am safe and protected
7. Happiness is always available as a choice I make in this moment
8. I am free to create my life however I choose
9. I am perfect and pure just as I am
10. I am free to recreate myself in every moment
11. I am free to have any experience I choose
12. How I feel matters
13. I take full responsibility for my feelings
14. There is order in the Universe; everything happens for a reason
15. I only ever have control over myself
16. I deserve to feel good
17. I have abundance in my life
18. I create the circumstances of my life
19. I am powerful

Letting Go of Concepts and Labels

Consciously creating loving thoughts about oneself is a powerful way to override limiting core beliefs. However, you can also dissolve limiting core beliefs by simply dropping thoughts altogether. The process of conceptualization takes the direct experience of life and compresses it into something the mind can understand. This process creates structure and order in your day-to-day life, yet also inhibits the fullness of your experience. The reason is that as soon as you attach a label to something, you create a mental "container" for it, thereby filtering your perceptions based on the parameters of the label. In fact, the very nature of language limits our experience of reality.

Imagine for a moment that there were no language...no words at all to describe the world around you. How would you experience life? How would you relate to the world around you? All words are merely symbols, representations of an energetic experience, but not the experience itself. Language, then, serves as a filter in the mind between you, and your direct experience of life. The world existed long before there were words to describe it, and the experience of reality can never be fully captured or expressed through words. To illustrate this point, try the following simple exercise:

Imagine that you are suddenly reborn in this moment without any knowledge of words or language. Right now in this moment look around the room you are sitting in. How do you experience it from this state of no words?....Look at an object close by. Notice that the first thing your mind does is try to identify this object by name—a book, a flower, a pencil, a vase. But does the word actually represent the full experience of this object? Take the time to really observe this object, noticing the colors, textures, and shapes. As you do, allow your mind to become quiet. What you may notice in this heightened state of awareness is a vibrancy and a freshness that you may not have noticed otherwise. You may notice that the object itself has an energy to it.

We have been conditioned to experience the world conceptually, labeling and categorizing everything, including ourselves. We have become more and more disconnected from the direct experience of life. When you see a flower you may have the thought, "pretty flower," and continue on your way, without actually seeing the beauty, light, color, and magic of what is before your eyes. This is how the constant chatter in the mind removes us from the experience of reality, and our connection to the Universal Life energy within and around us.

What will begin to happen as you practice quieting the mind and letting go of concepts and labels for life experiences, is that you will begin to feel the presence of energy within all objects; people, plants, animals, the earth, and your own body. You will not only see the flower, you will also feel the life energy within the flower. This feeling is a deepening of your connection to the Universe. Life takes on a new dimension, and an opening is created for a deeper experience of yourself and all forms of life. It takes practice and commitment to live in the present moment, free from mental interpretation. But the more you live in this awakened state, the more alive and empowered you will begin to feel.

Faith in the Process

Letting go of ego based thoughts, labels, concepts, and core beliefs requires a great deal of patience and faith. When the mind becomes accustomed to certain outcomes, it reinforces the belief systems that are already in place. The common adage, "I'll believe it when I see it," is generally the voice of the ego, which always reinforces its version of reality based on past results. A greater truth is this: "I will see it when I believe it." It takes faith and courage to believe in a new reality for yourself, one that is more expansive and liberating, but it is possible through practice.

One challenge to overcome is that the mind often believes that what it is focusing on is of the utmost importance, and that if you stop analyzing, thinking about, or obsessing over life situations (whether its your job, your relationships, your health, or your finances), then something bad will happen—you will have "dropped the ball." I have found this to be almost exactly opposite to what my direct experience has shown me to be true. As soon as I drop a compulsive thought pattern responsible for creating anxiety, and instead, come back to the present moment, I feel a sense of peace arise within, and life becomes a little bit lighter (which, initially, is felt as a very subtle shift). As I continue to stay in the state of presence, I usually become aware of a higher perspective on the situation. It is from this peaceful place of awareness that a solution generally arises on its own.

Though the mind is accustomed to always thinking about the future, this way of living is often not very efficient or practical (in addition to being anxiety provoking). If you were to briefly recall times throughout your life where you obsessed over future outcomes, you may notice how much of your time and energy was wasted preparing for events that never even happened. This drain on your energy distracts you from the guidance here and now, guidance that would otherwise allow you to efficiently address life's challenges in the moment thcy arise. It takes faith to let go of the mind's compulsive need to plan, prepare, and always be in control. But the more that you practice having faith, the more you open yourself up to receive guidance from the Higher Intelligence within.

I still practice this in my life everyday, and I have found that the more I learn to let go and trust, the more beauty and abundance flows into my life naturally. It may not come in the form that my mind believes it should, but I can always reflect back to see that it was the perfect experience for my growth and evolution, provided for me at just the right moment. It is quite amazing and wonderful to see how the Universe supports us in this way. And there is no use in ever beating yourself up for making a "mistake" in this process. How could you possibly make a mistake, when every experience is bringing you more awareness about yourself and the process of living from your heart?

One of the biggest challenges for many people is breaking free from the cultural norms that are a part of their conditioning, and which feel so familiar. Yet, it is many of our cultural norms that perpetuate much of the ego driven thought processes that cause so much suffering. It takes faith and courage to begin untangling yourself from unhealthy cultural influences, especially when the majority of people around you may seem content to remain relatively unconscious in how they are living. It can be helpful, then, to really begin dissecting the cultural values in which you are accustomed to, in order to see the motivating factors that have been shaping our collective experience for so long.

A Mind Dominated Culture

"It is no measure of good health to be well adjusted to a profoundly sick society" –*J. Krishnamurti*

When becoming aware of the ego it may seem startling to see just how much of our cultural experience is built around the ego. The economic systems of the world (for the most part) are focused around the individual having more, getting more, and working up the social and economic ladder. Beginning in early childhood most people have been conditioned to be in a state of neediness, always looking outside oneself for fulfillment in one form or another.

We are taught that in order to be happy we should create a life for ourselves which meet certain criteria; we should be successful, attain a certain level of social status, make a lot of money, have an abundance of material possessions, have many friends, find the perfect partner, and generally assert our will power out into the world in order to get our needs met. This message of individualism is woven into nearly every aspect of westernized cultures, perpetuating our collective feeling of separation; "It's me against the world, and I need to get my needs met in very specific ways in order to be happy and feel good about myself."

This conditioning comes from our family, and also the culture at large. The constant barrage of advertisements on television and online share a similar theme; you will be happier and have a better life if you buy specific products, subscribe to a specific lifestyle, and behave according to specific social norms. Having a nicer car, a bigger house, more money, and greater status can easily become the focus of attention when one remains unconscious to the influences of the collective ego.

The consumer-based culture in which we live also places a strong emphasis on being impulsive and engaging in self-gratifying behaviors. The inability of people to control their compulsions fuels much of the economy, and so advertisers and the media prey on this aspect of the collective ego in order to sell products and make money. The influence of the media over the last century has produced a population with very little self-control or self-discipline. Ads featuring sickly sweet and fattening foods are as ubiquitous in the media as images of half naked men and women. The underlying message is the same in both cases; "you want this and you want it now."

However, the ego can also strengthen itself in reaction against popular culture. There are numerous sub-cultures in which a person's identity is derived through rebelling against the norm. Taking on a spiritual lifestyle, for instance, and rejecting all things in the popular culture that are not "spiritual" could be a way of strengthening the ego. In this case the ego would become strengthened through a conceptual identity as being more spiritual or more evolved than the general public.

The seeking of knowledge, information, and specific skills can also serve to strengthen the ego. As long as a person remains unawake to their true nature, they will try to accumulate anything in order to strengthen their conceptual identity, and to provide themselves (as well as others) proof of their self-worth. You can see this phenomenon when observing the world or art, science, technology, or academia, for instance. It is quite common to see people seeking to enhance their self image through being an expert in their given field. Perhaps it is their passion and love for the subject that is driving them, or perhaps it is a deep-seated feeling of anxiety that causes them to look outside themselves for validation through their achievements. Likely, it is a combination of the two. Until a person becomes aware of the ego, it will subtly influence the motivations behind almost all actions, to varying degree.

Another element of ego that shows up in society is the culture of fear perpetuated by the media, government, and corporations. The more afraid you are of the "other" (whether it be another country, another race, another person, or another lifestyle), the more likely you are to give away your power. This takes the form of the fear mongering that occurs in the news and media, which can distort one's perception of reality to the point of creating intense paranoia and anxiety towards life.

Most news that gets reported is sensationalist, rather than an accurate depiction of the events occurring around the world. If you think about all of the amazing, positive, and uplifting experiences occurring everyday around the world (people helping other people, taking care of animals, and working towards rehabilitating the environment), notice how much of this kind of news ends up being reported. What you find is that very little of the news is positive. The predominantly negative news reporting is a mostly one-sided view of the world, and yet this is what we have come to expect from the media. These simple psychological techniques of using sensationalism and drama as a means of captivating one's attention, perpetuate a distorted mentality of fear and separation in the collective unconsciousness.

Imagine, instead, that the news consisted of a 50/50 balance of traumatic events and positive events. This simple shift might have a

102

profound effect on the collective consciousness. People might feel generally less paranoid, less afraid, and less anxious for the state of the world. Although, as I'm sure it is well known in the media and the world of advertising, truly happy and relaxed people are generally less likely to buy things they don't need, are less likely to put themselves in debt, and are less likely to work themselves to the bone to afford a lifestyle of excesses. Perpetuating anxiety, fear, and a mentality of separation actually lends itself to supporting the current economic paradigm.

Though the state of affairs in which we live has ultimately come about due to our shared collective unconsciousness, it is hardly a new phenomenon that those select individuals (and groups) that hold positions of power, have sought to subjugate the masses with the intention of keeping the general public ignorant and asleep. Consider doing your own research on this topic to see how the last century may have been an experiment by certain governments and corporations to see the effects of psychological manipulation on the masses. The British documentary series entitled, "Century of the Self," provides compelling evidence that the state of anxiety and ego in which many people live today is the result of strategic and intentional action taken by groups of people in power over the last century.

This information is not meant to create more anxiety, but rather, begin untangling the web of how we ended up living in such an egocentric and fear-based culture. When you look around and see so many people anxious, depressed, and disconnected, there are factors at play that have been subtly eroding our natural ability to feel connected to each other and the earth. Having this awareness can help a person break free from their addiction to the unhealthy and manipulative aspects of our culture, and provide greater motivation to awaken from the illusion of the ego.

It is also important to remember that no one is to blame for the state of things as they are now. We are each responsible for our own state of being, and paradoxically, it is through the suffering caused by the collective ego that we are each, in our own time, waking up to the greater reality beyond the ego. Allowing oneself to be manipulated or controlled (either consciously or unconsciously) can be a necessary step towards awakening and taking greater responsibility for oneself.

In that sense, the experience of being manipulated by another can even be viewed as a blessing in the process of awakening. This is true for our cultural experience, as well as in relationship with one another.

It is not as though there are evil forces in the world trying to keep the masses asleep. But rather, the only reason that anyone would be motivated to control and manipulate another person is if they do not feel much love in their own life, or feel their connection to the higher flow of energy from the Universe. It is the suffering of feeling afraid and alone that causes a person to seek control over others. Evil is no more than the result of a disconnection from love, from one's true essence.

Cultural Healing Through Love

It can be tempting, as one begins awakening to the magnitude of manipulation and corruption that has been perpetrated in the name of fear and greed, to turn against those in power as the "other," whom need to be overthrown. But keep in mind that everyone is seeking love and connection in their own way, even if that seeking takes the form of negativity or manipulation. And just like a child who has learned maladaptive strategies for getting attention by engaging in destructive behaviors, these wounds cannot be healed through force or punishment. It is only through love, acceptance, and compassion that negativity and fear can be healed.

Often the ego reacts with negativity towards that which is negative. What a paradox! The ego approaches ridding the world of ego by using force or negativity (guilt, blame, or shame). This approach will never work, in that whatever the ego resists or reacts against, only becomes strengthened among those having the reaction. When you react to negativity with negative energy, then you yourself are creating more negativity. No lasting solution or healing can occur when negativity is flowing from you.

If you desire to dissolve negativity and the collective ego, then learn to remain in control of your own thoughts and responses to life. View those who would use fear to control others with compassion and understanding, rather than judgment or condemnation. All of us know the experience of causing pain to others. We all know how it feels to close our hearts, and the suffering it causes. Holding this higher perspective about what motivates those misusing their power will allow you to see the painful events taking place in the world with greater acceptance and compassion. When you choose compassion and a loving perspective, this vibration is sent out into the world, creating a greater opening for healing to occur.

It takes commitment and awareness to stay focused on peace and love amidst some of the traumatic events that get played out on the world stage. Look at your own reactions to events playing out in the world to see if you hold any negativity towards them. Can you stay loving and compassionate towards the actions of others, even when they are destructive or negative? Can you see the higher perspective and wisdom in why painful events may sometimes be necessary for our collective growth and awakening? In practicing holding a loving perspective towards all of life, it can be helpful to understand that there are laws that govern how energy flows in the Universe.

We live in an attraction-based Universe, where negativity attracts more negativity, and alternatively, love attracts more love. This greater connection of energy is what the separatist ego mind can never understand. The fearful mind demands retribution and justice, claiming, "an eye for an eye." But as Gandhi noted in his infamous writings on peace, "an eye for an eye makes the whole world blind." Embodying love more fully in your life is truly the most powerful way to create positive change.

This idea of love healing all wounds is more than a hopeful sentiment. It speaks to the collective energy field in which all life is connected. Every thought that you think, and every emotion you create, ripples out through the collective energy field, creating a slight change in the vibration of the whole. Though you may not be able to see the collective energy field, and our current scientific instrumentation is not yet sophisticated enough to measure it, once you tune into it and feel it for yourself, you will know the reality of it. Initially, however, it takes faith and courage to step beyond the ego in order to begin feeling the interconnection of life energy. But by doing so, you offer yourself the opportunity to transform your own life, and very literally, the world.

In the process of freeing yourself from the culture of fear, it can be helpful to become more discerning with what you subject yourself to, and what you focus your attention on. Pay attention to what types of movies, books, or television programs you gravitate towards and why. Does the content of these sources of entertainment feel uplifting and inspiring, or is it more of a distraction, reinforcing experiences such as drama, violence, or suffering? Notice how when you watch television or go online, there are images constantly popping up on the screen vying for your attention, often with dramatic or sensational content. The techniques used to get your attention are abrupt noises, bright colors, flashes of light, rapidly changing imagery, and dramatic imagery. The ego loves drama and will gravitate towards it every time.

Notice, too, what physiological effect this type of mental and emotional stimulation has on your body. All of this stimulation is designed to increase your heart rate and create low levels of tension within you. When your breathing becomes rapid and your heart rate increases, your body releases cortisol. In this state you are much more likely to respond compulsively, as well as become more suggestible to outside influences.

Any moment you find yourself slipping into negativity while engaged in the world, return to your breath, and detach from whatever activity your were engaged in for a few moments. Find your center and allow peace to return naturally. In this way you will be taking back conscious control over your state of being; a simple act that has profound implications in your spiritual growth. Be sure to take frequent breaks from the television or computer, and to stay connected to your breath while you engage in these activities. Spend as much time outdoors in the sunshine, breathing the fresh air, and engaging in positive and life affirming activities whenever possible. Your commitment and intention to release yourself from cultural manipulation will improve your sense of autonomy, well-being, and overall confidence in yourself as the creator of your own reality.

The Curse of Comfort

"comfort...that stealthy thing that enters the house a guest, and then becomes a host, and then a master." -Kahlil Gibran, The Prophet.

One of the biggest myths of the collective ego, a myth that is greatly perpetuated in popular culture, is the idea that an abundance of comfort and security will result in happiness and a meaningful life. Beginning as early as childhood we are fed the belief that if we work hard enough we can eradicate all discomfort, avoid all pain, and finally feel safe, happy, and content. While the ego would prefer to erase all the unknowns of life, and remove all potentially uncomfortable or painful experiences, this would actually be a recipe for suffering.

Imagine if your ego had every one of it's desires met. Imagine you could actually control every aspect of your life, being able to avoid all discomfort or pain, and instead, have everything that you wanted. If it were up to the ego, you would likely be very wealthy, never having to work again, with every one of your whims met instantaneously. While this might initially sound like heaven, in reality, this type of life would very quickly lead to some kind of hellish experience. You can see very clear examples of this in many wealthy people who have amassed large fortunes, yet still need more, and remain rather miserable despite having everything they ever wanted.

An episode of the classic television show, "The Twilight Zone," exemplifies this paradox regarding the desires of the ego. In the episode a thief is killed during an attempted robbery. In the afterlife he finds himself in what appears to be heaven. This version of "heaven" is a casino where every bet the thief places, he wins. There are beautiful women at his side, and an endless buffet of decadent food to eat.

For the first week the thief is elated, indulging himself in every gluttonous desire. As he continues to win every bet he places, and have every one of his whims met, he becomes bored and uninspired. Very quickly he finds himself completely miserable, frustrated by the lack of excitement or meaning in his new environment. Without the element of surprise, and the challenges that come with the many unknowns of life, the joy quickly disappeared from the thief's experience. What he had always believed would make him happy was actually a horrible fate. The twist at the end of the episode occurs when the thief realizes that what he thought was heaven, was actually hell.

This is a perfect example of the paradox of the ego, which is always searching for what it believes will get you closer to paradise, while slowly paving the road towards a life of stagnation, emptiness and suffering. The ego mind believes that all of those temporary experiences of comfort or pleasure will ultimately bring you happiness, while in reality, they create a form of padding around you, dulling your inner fire and passion for life.

When you fulfill the desires of the ego for greater comfort, you are putting up a wall between yourself and the direct experiences of life. This will never satisfy the heart and Soul, which desire to know the full range of human experience; deep joy, love, bliss and ecstasy, as well as deep pain, sadness, and grief. The heart knows that you cannot have joy without pain, or ecstasy without sorrow; they are, in fact, two sides of the same coin.

And the paradox is that once you have become thoroughly insulated from having to experience any discomfort or pain, you become miserable. You become anesthetized to life. You long to feel something, anything, just to know you are alive. And so the ego becomes even more self-satisfying as a way to feel something (which takes the form of compulsively seeking pleasure gratification, greater comfort, or even self-destructive behaviors). This is the state of our collective unconsciousness now; continually seeking greater comfort as a way to insulate ourselves from life, while simultaneously compulsively seeking pleasure gratification (in all its various forms) as a means to artificially feel alive.

So become alert throughout your day as to where you may be avoiding discomfort, uncertainty, or the unknowns of life, and allow yourself, instead, to be present with it. Yes, a certain amount of comfort and consistency is necessary in order to be effective in the world; a comfortable home space, comfortable clothes to wear, a reliable mode of transportation, and a pleasant place to work. But watch how the ego can be very slippery in its desires, wanting to "upgrade" in subtle ways; "life would be a little better only if..." Suddenly you need a bigger place to live, more features in your car, or you find yourself wanting the newest gadget because it will make life a bit easier. Stay alert and present to be sure that your "needs" truly are what you need in order to be healthy and happy.

Begin to allow more space in your life for discomfort. Make a point of letting yourself feel pain and discomfort when it arises. No need to be masochistic about it, but rather, find the balance between comfort and discomfort, pleasures and challenges. The next time you get a headache, for instance, instead of immediately going to the medicine cabinet for the painkillers, simply let yourself feel the pain. Breathe into the pain and allow it to soften.

Can you sit with the discomfort of the unknown, without needing to be in complete control of your experience? How much unknown are you comfortable with? Let yourself really unravel the conditioning regarding control and comfort, giving yourself the opportunity to have a richer and more meaningful life by consciously engaging uncomfortable experiences. Become like a flower, absorbing the light of the sun when it is shining, but also like a warrior, facing challenges, pain, and discomfort head on when they arise, without needing to anesthetize yourself with some form of escapism or padding.

Everything is Grace

No matter how spiritually awakened a person becomes, life will continue to present situations that are challenging and potentially uncomfortable. This is the nature of life, a dichotomy of pleasure and pain—two sides of the same coin. However, despite the drama or chaos that a person may be experiencing internally in the midst of a challenge—"Why does this always happen to me? I wish this wasn't happening to me!"—ultimately, every experience is grace. Every event that has happened to you, the "good, the "bad," and everything in between, is serving your growth and awakening.

Every challenge provides opportunity for growth, for evolution, and to learn more about oneself and the nature of reality. If there were no challenges, life would not only be very boring, but our experience would not progress. We would remain stagnant, without inspiration to move or change. The ego would prefer to erase all painful experiences from life, not understanding that to do so would rob a Soul of the catalysts essential for transformation. Holding this new awareness, then, how could you ever wish for the events of your life (or in the lives of others) to have played out any differently?

Looking back on my own life, I see how losing my father at an early age, developing a disease, and going into deep states of anxiety and depression all served as a catalyst for transformation and awakening. It is through our suffering that we develop such a strong motivation to know ourselves beyond the limitation of the mind. Suffering causes us to look more closely at ourselves, to understand how the mind works, and to begin creating our thoughts, emotions, and actions more consciously.

For many years of my life I did not know what my purpose or passion was for living. I was simply plugging away like many people do, unaware of the greater reality within and around me. But as my suffering increased through living a shallow and disconnected life, I found myself seeking for answers and meaning with greater focus and determination. The suffering is what propelled me to dig deeper, and resulted in a profound shift in my inner reality. It truly couldn't have happened any other way.

Suffering arises when the mind reacts against the present moment, believing that "this shouldn't be happening." But if it shouldn't be happening, then it truly wouldn't be happening. Just the fact that it is happening, lets you know that the experience is serving a purpose. You may not be able to see what that purpose is now, but as you move through the experience, you will likely gain a greater perspective on why that event occurred in your life. The more you embrace challenges, and the full spectrum of human experience, the more you will begin to see that everything truly is grace.

Beyond the Ego

There is an energy within all of life that exists beyond the mind's ability to fully comprehend. This energy has been called Prana, Chi, Universal Life Energy, Source, Great Spirit, God, Truth, and Love, to name a few. The name for this energy is not as important as learning how to experience it directly, as well as to understand how the function of the mind inherently limits one's ability to feel their connection to this energy.

At the most fundamental level, everything in creation is made up of energy. Your physical body, your thoughts, and your emotions are all temporary expressions of this greater source of energy as it moves into form. Quantum Physics has been uncovering the nature of this energy for the past few decades, slowly bridging the gap between science and spirituality.

But you don't need to understand the science in order to connect with subtle spiritual energy. What is necessary, however, is to take your attention away from the thoughts in your mind, and allow yourself to actually feel the energetic field within and around your body in this moment. The thinking mind, in a sense, is like the gatekeeper as to how much of this energy you are aware of. The louder and more compulsive your thoughts are, the more this subtle energy becomes covered over, preventing you from feeling what has always been within you.

While the intellect is absolutely useful for navigating the physical world, and the advances made by science over the last century have provided amazing benefits to humankind, the faculties of the mind are mostly limited to working with the physical world. But what we perceive in the physical world through our five senses is only the tip of the iceberg of the greater reality occurring beneath the surface. As one awakens more, this greater reality becomes known through direct experience. And the feeling of this connection is that of love, joy, and well-being. No thought or concept can adequately describe the experience, it has to be felt directly in order to know what it is.

The Energy Within

Try the following exercise to practice heightening your awareness of the energy field within:

1. Bring your focus and attention into your body and to your breath. Begin taking deep, slow breaths. And notice as you breathe in a very slow and methodical way, that your mind slows down, your emotions become still, and you begin to feel more peaceful with each passing moment. When you keep your attention in the body longer, you can begin to feel very subtle tingling sensations, or a slight vibration within—this is the essence of Life Energy within you. In order to feel it, however, your mind must be relatively quiet. Slowing down the breath helps develop the sensitivity to this energy.

2. Now bring your attention to the energy within your hands, keeping your attention on this energy no matter how subtle it may feel at first. When thoughts arise, take a deep breath and bring your attention back to your hands. Continue to keep your attention here for as long as you are able. When the mind wanders bring your focus back to the breath, and then back to the energy within. Now see if you can feel this energy in your wrists and forearms...how about your upper arms? Now move your attention down into your feet, can you feel the energy there? It will take some practice to keep your attention on the energy in your body, but the more you do it, the more your awareness of this energy will grow.

Notice as your thoughts begin to become active again, what causes you to lose awareness of this energy? It is when your attention is consumed with concepts, thoughts, and the mind-made reality, that you miss the actual experience of reality occurring within you in each moment. The true power that we each possess rests in our ability to be in control of where we focus our attention. Wherever you focus your attention—whether it be on your thoughts, the energy of your emotions, the subtle energy in the body, or on the world around you— will determine which experiences in your life become more energized and actualized. This reflects what has commonly been described as

112

the "law of attraction," a principle that describes how the subtler energies of our thoughts and emotions manifest into the world of form.

The Law of Attraction

"What we are today comes from our thoughts of yesterday, and our present thoughts build our life of tomorrow: our life is the creation of our mind." -Gautama Buddha

The law of attraction refers to the phenomenon of resonant fields of energy, whereas the vibrations of mental and emotional energy that you empower with your attention, attracts people and circumstances into your life of a similar vibration. The idea is that every thought and emotion actually exists as a frequency of energy emanating out from within, beginning in the mind, moving into the emotional field, and out into the world. As this energy moves out into the collective energy field it resonates with similar frequencies of energy being expressed by other forms of life, and by the Universe itself. This resonance acts much like a magnet, attracting similar vibrations together for the purpose of co-creation, growth, and learning.

A good analogy of this would be that of a radio dial. At any given moment there are hundreds of different radio stations being broadcast through the airways. If you want to experience a specific station, you would need to turn your dial to match that frequency. Mental and emotional energy operates in a similar way. If you want to have certain experiences, you can learn to change the dial of your thoughts and emotions in order to match the frequency of the experience that you desire to have in your life.

Having control over your mind and emotions, then, allows you to be in control of the signal you are sending out, and consequently, the life experiences that you receive back from the world around you. Through meditation and mindful awareness practices you can cultivate your focus and intention. This creates a solid foundation to consciously change the vibration you are expressing, and consequently, your experience of reality.

The popular New Age phrase sums up this phenomenon quite appropriately; "where attention goes, energy flows." This simple yet profound statement says it all; whatever you focus your attention on receives more of your creative energy, which empowers more of that experience in your life. If you focus on all the things wrong in your life, these experiences receive more of your energy, and you will find they become more prevalent in your experience. Conversely, when you feel gratitude and appreciation for aspects of your life, these experiences also become more energized, attracting more positivity into your life.

It can be helpful to understand that the Universe cannot tell the difference between what you say you prefer, versus what you actually focus your attention on. For instance, if you say "I hate my job, it's horrible, I want a different job," the Universe receives the message that you must love your horrible job, otherwise, why would you be focusing on it so much. And consequently, you would likely find very few new career opportunities opening up for you, as your energy will continue to be flowing into what you say you do not prefer.

The key to utilizing the law of attraction is to become adept at where you place your attention. If you want a new job then focus on the kinds of uplifting work you would prefer to be doing, versus how much you dislike your current job. If you want to heal your body then focus on everything right and healthy within your body, versus what is wrong with it. This process is in stark contrast to what most of us have been taught about the world; that in order to find a solution to a problem you need to focus on the problem. While this is true in some regards, the fundamental solution to any problem is always an energetic one. Because ultimately, even if you solve the problem, but do so with resistance, anxiety, or negative energy, you will undoubtedly encounter more of the same problems down the road.

It is a paradox that baffles the mind, and requires focus and discipline to observe those things in your life which you do not prefer (without generating fear or resistance towards them), while simultaneously moving your attention onto the positive things which you do prefer. Often times people are unable to do this due to their own emotional reactions. They cannot help but become angry, agitated, or upset by the circumstances. The more you realize, however, that everything you react against is truly a reflection of yourself in some way, the more efficiently you can learn from these situations, allowing yourself the opportunity to transcend beyond them.

Learn From the Reflection

One of the most effective ways to utilize law of attraction is as a tool to better understand your own karmic blockages and energetic expressions. Simply observe the people and experiences that come into your life, always with the understanding that what you are experiencing is a direct reflection of that which you are expressing. If you have resistance to others, or are not inspired by the people around you, then take a good look at why. Observe how these people view the world, what core beliefs they have about life, and what kinds of thoughts and emotions they express, and then take a good look at yourself. You may notice some unsettling similarities.

And when you do, it is a time for celebration! This person or situation has just helped you to see yourself more clearly. Hold gratitude in your heart for them and the reflection they provided you, and then begin consciously changing yourself to be more in alignment with the reality that you do prefer. Work towards dissolving the ego, and focus instead on positive, life-affirming aspects of yourself and your situation. Meditation, mindful awareness practices, positive affirmations, prayer, and visioning are all useful tools in this process.

Though our surface layer thoughts are absolutely related to what vibrations we send out, and consequently what we attract back into our lives, of deeper significance are the underlying core beliefs and ingrained mental and emotional patterns within. While many people try to implement positive affirmations, mantras, or prayer as a way to utilize the law of attraction to their benefit, to truly reap the rewards from this conscious way of living is to go through the process of letting go of the ego on a deep level.

Commit to letting go of fearful and restrictive core beliefs that are limiting your happiness, joy, and peace, and you will find that the law of attraction naturally works in your favor. Instead of simply trying to overwrite the old programming with positive thoughts, be sure to first dissolve the old programming. If you ignore the deeper blockages within, your baseline vibration will not shift very significantly, and what you attract into your life will continue to be a reflection of the old ego patterns.

The ego loves the idea of the law of attraction; "yes, I can finally get what I want!" Good luck ego, it doesn't quite work that way. For what is the energy truly underlying the ego's desires? It is fear. Fear motivates the ego to want what it wants. Yet, what each Soul truly desires is love. Forget about all those shiny toys that provide fleeting experiences of pleasure or anxiety relief, and instead, focus on becoming a beacon of love, sending out the message to the Universe, "I choose love! I choose love with every thought, feeling, and action. May all sentient beings feel love, joy, and peace!" Focus your life around allowing more love into your own life, and the lives of others, and see how the law of attraction naturally brings into your life that which your Soul truly desires.

The Choice for Love

"Even after all this time the sun never says to the earth, 'you owe me.' Look what happens with a love like that, it lights the whole sky."
-Hafiz

Each one of us has come here to uncover greater depths to love. Even if your conscious mind has yet to acknowledge this Soul level need, if you were to search the deepest parts of yourself, you would undoubtedly uncover this desire to know unconditional love with every fiber of your being. We did not come here merely to survive, to fill a void, or to tinker around. We came here to bring a love so powerful into this world that it would illuminate all darkness with light. We came here on a divine mission to dissolve fear and limitation back into the eternal love of who we are in our essence.

In every moment you are offered this profound choice; love, or fear. When you stay open, relaxed, and in a state of acceptance, you are choosing love. When you resist life, close down, or become reactive, you are choosing fear. The choice for love or fear may be very subtle from moment to moment, and can feel so automatic that it may not even seem like a choice, but in reality, it always is. And you know the difference immediately between love and fear based on the sensations and feelings in your body. Love feels open, expansive, and freeing, while fear feels restrictive, limiting, and isolating. It is never the circumstances of life that dictate whether you experience love or fear, but rather, a moment by moment decision made from within—a decision that profoundly shapes your experience of reality.

When you choose love, you are choosing to look beyond the fearful conditioning within yourself and others. Choosing love means remembering that each one of us is an expression of divine energy longing to be seen more fully. Choosing love means unlocking doors, taking down walls, and being open to all that life has to offer in each moment. Choosing love sometimes means letting go of that which is logical and practical, letting yourself do the unexpected, the thing that perhaps you were taught was unacceptable by societies standards—such as feeling love when it goes against all reason.

How can you hold love in your heart for a murderer? How can you hold love in your heart for those who are greedy and selfish? Not by thinking about it, but simply by allowing love to flow from you. Love is our natural expression. Surrender into love, allow love to flow into every breath, every thought, and into each movement. Become a channel for love by holding this intention in each moment. Love is who we are, and exploring the depths of love within the human experience is why we have come here.

One of my favorite spiritual teachers who lived a life embodying love is a woman by the name of Peace Pilgrim. This lesser known saint of modern day times was an American woman, who in the 1970's decided to devote herself to living in the highest spiritual light, striving to always choose love in every situation. She decided to give away all of her possessions and travel the country on foot, spreading the message of peace. She made the pact with herself not to take shelter or food unless it was offered to her, and to keep walking until world peace had been achieved. She carried only a few simple possessions, and wore a blue tunic that read "Peace Pilgrim" on one side, and "25,000 miles on foot for peace" on the other. By the end of her pilgrimage she estimated that she had traversed the country several times on foot. She spent her life teaching the ways of living in peace and harmony to thousands of people across the country.

In a book of stories compiled by her numerous followers, Peace recounts her incredible experiences while traveling. Many of these stories left a strong impression in my heart, and serve as a constant reminder of just how powerful the choice for love can be. Peace describes a variety of situations of being confronted during her travels by violent or aggressive people. And in each situation she was able to hold a loving vibration towards the troubled Souls who would have otherwise inflicted harm on her or another, thereby transforming the situation.

In one instance, Peace stands between a helpless girl and a large man who intended to harm the girl. Peace holds her ground, while showering the man with compassion and love. The man, disarmed by Peace's loving energy, backs off and drops his aggressive behavior, to which Peace later wrote about in the book dedicated to her good deeds:

"Now what was the alternative? Suppose I had been so foolish as to forget the law of love by hitting back and relying on the jungle law of tooth and claw? Undoubtedly I would have been beaten—perhaps even to death, and possibly the little girl as well. Never underestimate the power of God's love—it transforms! It reaches the spark of good in the other and the other person is disarmed."

Love is the most natural and effortless way to be, and has the power to heal all wounds. Let go of judging and analyzing life, and instead, return your attention to your heart and to this moment. Feel the love within, and allow this love to flow from you out into the world. Allow yourself to soften, to lighten up, and to remember that this human drama is not what we think it is. Life is not as serious as the mind makes it out to be. Even those Souls who have inflicted incredible suffering on others are serving a purpose in the flowering of our collective consciousness. Intense fear and resistance on the part of a few (and the consequent pain inflicted out in the world through their behavior) can spark a journey of awakening among the masses, igniting self inquiry, compassion, and heart opening moments of shared unity and love.

There is a greater undercurrent of growth, learning, and expansion occurring for every Soul across the planet, a process that cannot be fully comprehended by the mind. And we are all playing our part in this schoolroom; the rich, the poor, the joyful, the vengeful, those who would do harm, and those who would bring peace. When you choose love, you honor the wisdom of each Soul in creating their reality for their particular purposes of growth and learning. Choose love, and have faith that even though you cannot understand the rhyme or reason for the events of the world, everything truly is happening for a reason.

An Exercise in Openness

Try this simple exercise to see how powerful a small decision to love can be in your life. Choose one day to commit to acknowledging in some way every person that you encounter throughout your day. For every time you acknowledge another person in some way, it is actually a gift of love. And when you greet the person, do it with as much presence as you are able, taking the time to say hello, make eye contact, smile, and truly acknowledge the other person.

Greet everyone you encounter in a loving and compassionate way; the person standing next to you in line at the supermarket, the checker at the supermarket (and the bagger too), as well as the people you pass on the street. Wave, say hello, and smile to all of life around you, including children and animals. You can even say hello to the flowers and trees. Do not be concerned what others may think of you,

119

but instead, pay attention to how good you feel as you open up to life around you. This simple exercise may sound trivial, but if you commit to trying it for one full day, you will understand the power of this practice. Very likely, by the end of the day it will have been one of the best days in recent memory.

By making the commitment to stay open and loving towards others, you can reverse the many subtle habits of fear. While most people are consumed with trying to get their needs met by receiving attention and validation from others, instead, be the one who freely gives attention, and who lovingly acknowledges others. We are all longing to be seen and honored. When you decide to be the one to see and honor others, without expecting anything in return, you are offering the greatest gift possible; that of unconditional love. The secret is that through the act of giving, you receive so much. There is no better feeling than to give love to another, to bring a moment of warmth to an interaction where there was no warmth before.

Yet many people experience a fear of love, a resistance to sharing love openly with others. Due to past experiences of rejection, pain, and hurt, we often put up walls and barriers around the heart, shutting ourselves off from love. In the process we learn patterns of giving and receiving love conditionally. To begin allowing unconditional love back into our lives, is to begin unraveling the myth of what love is, and to discover the true Source of this divine energy within.

Decoding Codependency

"Your task is not to seek for love, but merely to seek and find all the barriers within yourself that you have built against it." -Rumi

When most people think of codependency, they think of the classic example of the drug addict, and the person who bends over backwards to enable the addict to maintain their addiction. Though the codependent behaviors I am speaking of in this section are much more subtle than this classic example, the phenomenon is the same. In reality, most everyone on the planet is dealing with the same fundamental addiction, and yet many people aren't aware of it. Most everyone is addicted to looking outside of themselves for love. It is the addiction of seeking relief from the separation anxiety we feel from our own hearts; the anxiety of feeling cast out of Oneness, disconnected from our greater connection with the Universe, God, and unconditional love. And just like any addict, most everyone is searching for that feeling of connection once again.

Codependency, then, is a result of this underlying anxiety that most people are unconsciously motivated by. In order to relieve this anxiety it is common for people to either give their power away to others, try to control, change, or influence others, appease others, or attempt to gain the validation of others. Any attempt to get your needs met from others, without honestly and transparently communicating those needs, can be referred to as "codependency"—you are dependent on another person for your well-being, happiness, or sense of security in the world in an unclear way.

These patterns are usually so deeply ingrained, as well as normalized within our culture, that most people are not even aware that it is happening. It should also be noted that there is nothing inherently wrong with these types of behaviors or relationships. Codependent patterns only become a "problem" if a person begins to suffer because of it. Codependency can allow a person to derive a sense of identity, purpose, safety, and control in their lives, but always in relation to, and dependent upon, another person. The more self awareness one gains, however, the more these types of connections begin to feel shallow, limiting, and restrictive, rather than comforting.

Codependency takes the form of energetic "contracts" forming between two people, whereas the creative life energy of each individual is forfeited to the other, in the hopes of securing love and acceptance—even if it is only conditional love. "If you help me get my needs met, than I will do the same for you. I will put aside my needs and heart's desires in order to stay close to you. I will be sure not to shine too bright, lest it make you uncomfortable. I will do whatever I can to alleviate the anxiety you feel in your life." But always with the caveat that the other person do the same for you. You begin to lean on another in subtle ways, and allow others to lean on you. Though this may feel comforting initially, ultimately it does not allow for much growth or evolution in a relationship, nor individually. And at some point this restrictive dynamic will likely contribute to conflict down the road.

While the ego seeks this form of connection as a way of appeasing anxiety, the heart knows there is another way. Your heart knows there is nothing more empowering, more liberating, or more beautiful than standing on your own two feet, your roots planted firmly in the ground, and living your life with purpose, clarity, and focus. To know who you are in your essence, and to share your loving energy with others without needing anything in return, is one of the greatest gifts that you can offer yourself and the world. The nineteenth century poet and philosopher, Kahlil Gibran, expresses this sentiment most eloquently in his masterpiece, "The Prophet," where he writes:

Love one another, but make not a bond of love:
Let it rather be a moving sea between the shores of your souls.
Fill each other's cup but drink not from one cup.
Give one another of your bread but eat not from the same loaf.
Sing and dance together and be joyous,
But let each one of you be alone,
Even as the strings of a lute are alone
Though they quiver with the same music.
Give your hearts, but not into each other's keeping.
For only the hand of Life can contain your hearts.
And stand together yet not too near together:
For the pillars of the temple stand apart,
And the oak tree and the cypress grow not in each other's shadow.

To allow for such depths of love to flow in relationship is to honor the space between one another, to remain centered and focused on the purpose of your life, rather than becoming over-enmeshed in someone else's life (what is commonly mistaken for intimacy). True intimacy, however, is born from deep energetic autonomy, knowing who you are, and how to tend to your own mental, emotional, and physical well-being. This creates a solid foundation of trust, whereas you are not seeking to take from another in any way, nor are you interested in receiving those "gifts" born of the insecurity from another. To move beyond codependency is to begin asking yourself some fundamental questions; "what is my purpose in life? What are my unique gifts to share with this world, and how can I truly honor my own needs more fully?"

This can be one of the most exhilarating, and simultaneously frightening questions to ask oneself. Many people have been suppressing their heart's desires (as well as their day-to-day mental, emotional and even physical needs) for so long, that just opening up to the possibility of truly being free and happy may evoke sadness, pain, or fear. The thing that we each desire most—love, freedom, and purpose—is the very same thing that we are afraid of. But why would we be so afraid of love, afraid of our own creative power? The answer to this question resides in a lifetime of conditioning that has resulted in a profound misunderstanding regarding the very nature of love.

The Roots of Codependency

We all come into this world emanating unconditional love, joy, and peace. You can feel this in the energy of children, who express a natural vibrancy and joy just for the sheer experience of being alive. In the early stages of childhood, children give their love unconditionally, remaining open and in a state of innocence and presence. As a child grows, however, he or she begins to have the experience of feeling abandoned by their parents, of rejection from family and friends, and a belief begins to form in the young psyche that feeling unconditional love is neither acceptable nor safe. We form the belief that who we are in our essence is not okay. The implications of this are profound. We actually begin associating the idea of unconditional love and freedom with feelings of hurt, vulnerability, and even fear. In this way we learn to fear love, we learn to fear the very essence of who we are.

In order to protect ourselves from this pain, the ego begins to firmly take root in the developing psyche during childhood. We begin putting up defenses, guarding against others, and in the process, we begin expressing love conditionally. We learn to only give when we will get something in return. We begin limiting how much love we express, and in doing so, limit how much love we feel in our own lives.

In this deficit of love we begin to become self-centered, seeking to get our own needs met from others. And in times when we are unable to get our needs met from others, we often shut down, becoming angry, bitter, or frustrated. This creates conflict with the people in our lives, with blame often resulting; "if only you were behaving differently in some way, then I wouldn't have to be upset right now...I need you to change in some way so that I can be happy." In the moment, closing down serves as a form of self preservation. Though this defense mechanism allows one to survive, every time the decision is made to shut down, it enshrouds the heart in one more layer of forgetfulness—forgetfulness of the truth of who we are as loving beings. And there is no suffering greater than denying ourselves and others the love which is our natural expression.

The Cords of Codependency

An example of a common cord of codependency is the process of being supportive for friends. When a friend comes to you feeling upset, anxious, or depressed, the common reaction is to take care of your friend. But what does it mean to "take care" of your friend? Often times it means listening to them talk about what is wrong in their life that is causing them to feel bad. And yet because most people do not actually know how to tend to their own emotional needs, this commonly results in a person simply venting. The person talks about how someone else is the cause of their problem, how upset they are, or how hard and overwhelming life is. More times than not, when a person comes looking for support, they are looking to release the negative energy they feel within themselves as a form of anxiety relief.

You may also sense that your friend is subtly looking for your sympathy, or some form of acknowledgment of their hardships. Notice, then, how you begin to feel within as your friend vents their negative or anxious energy, seeking your support in some way. You may find yourself feeling obligated to offer a supportive comment; "oh, that's not fair, that sounds rough." But what you may also notice is that as you extend your energy in this way, you begin to feel drained, uneasy, or not fully honored through the interaction.

Ultimately, this exchange neither nourished you, nor truly brought about healing for the other person. Yes, it allowed your friend to feel some relief from their negativity, but no real growth or change occurred. After the exchange you may find yourself feeling slightly used, less than optimistic about life, or even mildly anxious. Most people accommodate this occurrence with their friends because, "that is what a good friend does." Over time, however, this type of dynamic will likely cause resentment, frustration, or anger to build.

This is codependency in action. You compromised your own emotional state for another. Did it actually feel good to receive the negative energy from your friend? Not likely, and yet you put up with it because that is the social norm, and what is expected of a "good friend." This is the same phenomenon that occurs between an addict and an enabler. You enabled your friend to continue creating a negative experience for themselves by engaging in this type of codependent behavior. This does not truly empower your friend to make positive changes in their life, nor does it empower you in any way.

So why did you compromise your energetic state, giving your power away in this interaction? Likely it is because you wanted something from the other person; you wanted to ensure that this person would stay in your life. At the heart of codependent behavior is that fundamental belief that you are not deserving of love, and that if you were to truly embody your power, honoring your feelings and needs, then the people in your life would leave you. It is the belief that who you are in your essence is unacceptable. It is an irrational fear, but a powerful one nonetheless.

From this deep seated fear we learn to compromise our own needs in place of meeting the needs of others. We mute the voice of our own heart, our passion, and joyful inspiration, lest it jeopardize the homeostasis of our relationships. We don't want to make others uncomfortable, appear rude or selfish, and actually find ourselves alone out in the world. But ultimately, this form of connection creates very little room to expand, and at some point the relationship must either be dissolved or transformed if both people are to continue growing.

A cord of codependency will generally feel like a drain on your energy, and usually take the form of negativity such as complaining, trying to exert control over others, or expressing thoughts of doubt, worry, or frustration. Conversely, you may also notice another person going out of their way to try and please you, or to give their energy to you in some way. Likely you will feel a neediness arising either in yourself or another person, which is in response to feeling helpless about the situation. From this place of anxiety, the ego mind looks to the external world for relief. It is in these moments that you must remain very alert in order to connect to the Source of your own love from within.

Feeling the Love Within

Once you recognize a codependent behavior in yourself (or in another) simply pause in that moment and bring your attention to your spiritual heart. The spiritual heart is located slightly to the right of your physical heart (located in the center of your chest), and is your direct connection to the Universal energy of unconditional love. By refocusing your attention on this energy center within, you are connecting directly to the source of true power, love, and feelings of well-being.

There is literally a wellspring of unconditional love pouring out from your heart center in every moment, and by taking your attention to your heart you allow love to flow more fully into your life in each moment. The love flowing from your heart must be felt directly, and so it is essential to actually take your attention to the heart center. This is an energetic phenomenon, and something the mind may not understand so easily. Try it for yourself and experience the power of the practice firsthand.

Feeling your heart is the first step to healing codependency (the second step involves learning to honor your own needs more fully, which will be addressed in the following chapter). By redirecting your attention to your heart you begin dissolving lifelong patterns of looking outside yourself for love. For a more detailed description of this process, reference the section entitled, "Meditation on the Spiritual Heart" (pg. 161).

Keeping your attention on your heart, however, can sometimes feel quite challenging, and you may find yourself distracted by other people, the world around you, or feel a strong pull to revert to old patterns. You may notice a compulsion to say something, to take some action to appease others, to get the attention from another, or simply to affect the other person in some way. Do your best to keep your attention focused on your heart. It takes practice, and every moment you notice a codependent behavior arising is an opportunity to practice. In this way, be grateful for those in your life exhibiting strong codependent tendencies, as it affords you the opportunity to practice greater focus and self-mastery.

As you feel your heart you also may notice a sadness or sense of loneliness arising within you. But whatever comes up for you, it is time to sit with it, to feel it, and to no longer run from it by looking outside yourself for relief. Honor your feelings as you sit with what comes up from within. No need to blame anyone, just simply be aware. In order to connect more fully with your inner source of love, it is often necessary to first clear away any pain or sadness that has been stored around the heart for so long. Let yourself have time and space to do this process, crying or grieving when you need to.

Fear in Love's Clothing

One potential challenge of breaking codependent patterns is the subtly in which fear can be expressed. Often what appears on the surface to be an expression of love, is actually an expression of anxiety or fear. Think of the typical mother-child interaction, for instance, where the mother is pestering the child with questions about his or her life. "How is your job, how is your relationship, how is your health, are you eating enough?" Though these questions may seem loving in nature (and surely the mother would claim to have completely loving intentions), the underlying energy is often that of fear. The mother is anxious for the child's well-being, and has learned to appease her own anxiety by effecting change in the child's life, rather than learning to connect to her own source of love within. In a sense, the mother is using her relationship with the child in order to get her own needs met.

Now think of the child's reaction in this scenario. The child, feeling the mother's concern, begins to feel worried about his or her own life, as well as anxious about mother's well-being. Not wanting to be the source of any anxiety or worry, the child may offer some appeasing words, "don't worry mom, I'm fine. My job is great, my relationship is great!" Feeling uncomfortable with the idea of mother being anxious, the child has learned just what to say in order to appease mother's anxiety. And in a sense, the child has used the interaction with the mother to appease his or her own anxiety.

This is fear in love's clothing; behaviors that appear loving on the surface, yet are actually rooted in fear. And of course the mother and child truly do have a great deal of love for one another, but in these instances, love is not what is being expressed. And why would anyone choose to express anything other than love with those whom they care about? The answer, or course, is that these are not conscious decisions, but rather unconscious and automatic behaviors arising from the ego. Bringing awareness to these codependent patterns is the first step to healing them.

Another example of this phenomenon might occur at a social gathering where there is a certain level of tension in the air. You may notice that your friend, in particular, seems a bit anxious, and is sticking by your side rather closely. You notice your friend wanting to dominate your attention, talking to you about experiences the two of you have shared, and making an effort to connect with you. On the surface this may look like an expression of love towards you, when in actuality, your friend is mostly focused on appeasing his or her own anxiety by eliciting your attention and energy.

Notice, too, what your reaction might be in this situation. Feeling uncomfortable with your friend's anxiety, you may try to offer a kind word, some support or comfort, and give them your attention as a way to help them try to relax. Though this might seem like a loving act, in reality, you are most likely attempting to soothe your own anxiety about the situation by effecting your friend in some way. If you can find a way to help your friend relax, then you too can relax. This is fear dressed in love's clothing, and another example of codependency.

There are many common cords of codependency that appear to be loving or friendly gestures, when in reality, are often rooted in anxiety or fear. Many of these behaviors are so normalized in our culture that one has to be vigilant in order to disengage from them. Some common cords often occur through the following behaviors:

-Seeking to become over-enmeshed in another person's affairs.
-Offering unsolicited opinions or advice.
-Seeking advice or support as a way to elicit sympathy or form a bond with someone.
-Performing in some way as a means to gain other people's attention.
-Using humor as a way to get validation from others.
-Trying to comfort someone in order to appease your own anxiety.
-Gossiping as a way to bond with others.
-Trying to be polite or friendly to please others, or appease your own anxiety.

This is not to say that one should never help another person, never offer support, or take loving action for another person. What it does mean is that your priority becomes connecting to your own source of love within first, before trying to elicit change in the world around you. Once you find your center, then helping others comes naturally; you offer a kind word, a loving gesture, or perhaps, do nothing at all. Sometimes doing nothing is the most loving thing you can do. Holding the awareness that your friend or family member is an expression of pure love in their very essence, without choosing to believe in their self imposed limitations and fears, is a powerful gift to give to another. Doing so allows another person to face their fears head-on without you providing a crutch for them to lean on.

When transforming codependent behaviors do not be surprised to find others becoming angry, annoyed, or upset with you. This is a common ego response to any form of change, especially when it comes to relationship dynamics. This can be particularly true for close friends and family who have grown accustomed to you behaving and interacting with them in familiar ways. It is common for people to become uncomfortable as you no longer relate in a familiar way, and instead pause to feel your heart and inner energy field. There may be a silence that makes others uncomfortable, causing them to leave your company, or say something to try and get your attention. This is fine, just allow others to do what they do, while you continue to find your center and feel the energy within. As you go through this process, really commit to it, honoring yourself and your desire for energetic autonomy.

The Mother of All Codependency

As I engaged in this process in my own life, many friends and family members became upset with me. My mother, for instance, found it very challenging as I began consciously transforming my relationship with her. Whereas before I would share many personal details with her to elicit her support, do my best to appease her anxiety, and engage in many other codependent patterns, I instead began to spend the majority of my time around her in silence, feeling my heart, and paying attention to my breath. Sometimes I would even close my eyes in order to focus more fully on my own energy field. When I did speak I was very conscious as to what I shared with her, being sure that I was speaking from my heart, and offering only love.

My mother became very uncomfortable with my change in behavior, and at times became quite upset, saying things such as, "why are you doing this to me?" and "I don't even know who you are anymore." The codependent compulsion in me wanted to explain to her that I was just dissolving codependent patterns, and that she had nothing to worry about. However, I quickly realized that it wasn't even in alignment for me to explain my process at that point, because my desire to do so was still motivated by my own anxiety and desire to appease her. So I chose to remain in silence instead.

But an amazing thing happened during this process. My mother began to go through her own awakening. Because I was no longer engaging in fear-based interactions with her, it allowed her to begin to see more clearly her own energy and behaviors. After my mother's initial fearful emotional reactions faded, she began to inquire about what I was going through from a place of sincerity. When I explained my process, I could see an arising awareness within her. It was painful and uncomfortable for her to see these things, but she ultimately realized it was a blessing.

Over the following months and years I witnessed a significant change in my mother's behavior towards me, to the point where we now share such a loving, healthy, and wonderful connection—one with very clear boundaries. As uncomfortable as it was for my mother to go through it, she now openly offers gratitude and appreciation for my courage to consciously change our relationship dynamic, which she also acknowledges has had a significant positive impact on other areas of her life, including the quality of her relationships. At the time I had no idea that by honoring myself it would serve as a catalyst for someone else to do the same.

But you cannot engage in this process with the secret hope that other people go through it with you. Just stick to your process, honoring yourself, and let others find their own way. You cannot truly help another person until you are rooted in your own self-love, nor until the other person is truly open to receiving. If they have questions about your process, then they will likely ask you. And you will likely answer—from the wisdom within your heart, without needing anything in return.

When you take the time to connect to yourself first, you can then share love with others freely, because you are no longer dependent on anyone else for it. Be really honest with yourself, however, regarding your motives for interacting with others, and be very committed to breaking codependent patterns by coming back to yourself first. You cannot do this process as a way to subtly change another; "if I can only find my own love first, then I can help heal this other person." You truly have to let go of your attachment to try and change another.

The key is to remember to only extend your hand to another when you feel centered, peaceful, and loving. And conversely, only take the hand of another when you can sense that they are truly rooted in their own self love. Getting centered often involves, not only feeling your heart, but also deeply understanding what your needs are in the moment, so that you can begin taking care of yourself on a deeper level. As you learn to meet your own needs in life more fully, it will bring you a sense of empowerment and security, allowing you to more readily connect to the love within.

Reclaiming Your Personal Space

Once you have noticed codependency in action and have focused your attention on your heart, begin reorienting yourself towards addressing your own needs. Initially, you will likely need some time to yourself in order to clear your mind and energy field following a codependent interaction. It is essential to regain your personal space at the first signs of any arising negativity within you, so as not to pull someone else into unconscious patterns of negativity, codependency, or conflict. Expressing your needs for personal space with a statement such as, "excuse me, I'm going to take some time for myself," can be a simple and straightforward way to communicate this to another person. You don't necessarily need to leave the situation, but it is necessary to withdrawal your attention away from social interactions to refocus your attention inward.

Once you have withdrawn yourself from the situation, begin clearing your energy in whatever way you need to. Keep your attention on your heart while you relax your body, taking deep slow breaths. Many times simply breathing and relaxing will be enough to dissolve any negativity. Other times you may find it helpful to drink some water, take a walk, spend some time in nature, or meditate for a while in order to find your peace. For intense negativity you may find that a hot shower helps, while smudging yourself (or your environment) with sage, cedar, or lavender can also help clear any negative energy. Using either water or smoke for purification are ancient techniques for clearing energy, both of which are extremely effective. Once you get clear within, begin reflecting on the preceding situation in which the negativity arose, bringing awareness to any needs you may have had, yet which were not being addressed.

Honoring Your Own Needs

The second step in dissolving codependent patterns is learning how to honor your own needs (to the best of your ability) on every level; spiritual, mental, emotional, and physical. One of the most effective places to begin is with the spiritual, by seeking to get greater clarity as to your Soul's purpose for this lifetime. It is important to address this foundational aspect of your experience, otherwise no matter how well you try to meet your needs in other areas, you will likely always feel that something is missing from your life. However, you can also work towards meeting needs in other areas of your life before you have fully clarified your Soul's purpose (and as I will explain, the two often go hand in hand).

Take the time to tune into the themes that your Soul has come here to experience, and then begin honoring your heart's desires more fully in the way that you prioritize and live your life. This can take much investigation, meditation, prayer, and patience. For more in-depth guidance on this process, refer to the chapter entitled, "Uncovering Your Soul's Purpose" (pg. 157). By simply holding the intention to receive guidance about your Soul's path, you will begin tuning in more fully to the intuition from within. Getting clarity regarding your Soul's purpose is generally an ongoing process, which, unlike mental, emotional, and physical needs, may not be met in such a straightforward way.

My feeling is that often the Soul's purpose is not necessarily a singular purpose (to become a healer, an artist, a doctor, or business owner, for example), but rather, it is a way of living with balance in all areas of your life. The more you create balance between your day-to-day mental, emotional and physical experience, the more solid and whole you feel within, naturally increasing the love you feel for yourself. As you increase self-love through living a balanced life, it establishes a solid foundation from which to cultivate your unique gifts. And it is through sharing our unique gifts with others that we bring more of our authentic and loving energy into the world around us. This could be considered the purpose of the Soul.

So in a sense, understanding how to best attend to your mental, emotional, and physical needs is a step on the path towards actualizing your unique gifts, and ultimately, your Soul's purpose. It's almost as though you need to first prove to yourself that you can take care yourself, before you feel ready to begin helping others, and actualizing your greater Soul purpose. Committing to living in greater balance sends the message to the Universe that you are ready for the next step, ready to embody more of your Soul's purpose of sharing your love and unique gifts with the world. And any time negativity or codependent behaviors arise within you, it can be a potential indication that you are ignoring your needs in the various area of your life.

In such moments, take the opportunity to review the situation in which negativity or codependency arose, and ask yourself whether or not you were fully honoring your own highest good during the experience. Were you engaged in behaviors that were truly uplifting, positive, and productive? Or were you perhaps being subtly destructive or irresponsible with your energy, attempting to ignore or escape some aspects of your life from a place of anxiety? Perhaps there are other projects, goals, or tasks that you could have focused on which would have been more nourishing on a Soul level. Take the time to reflect on the various areas of your life which may need more of your energy, attention and care.

Mental, Emotional, and Physical Needs

Begin by examining the needs of your mind, in order to see if you are providing yourself with enough mental stimulation in your day-to-day activities. Without adequate mental stimulation energy often becomes either stagnant or manic, resulting in apathy, anxiety, depression, or an overactive mind. I have found that generally a few hours of mind-focused activity each day is necessary to have balance in this area of my life. Focusing on tasks that require mental processing, logic, or the analytical function of the mind (such as writing, building, designing, planning a project, learning a new skill, or work that involves problem-solving) can be essential for giving the mind a good work-out. This will also help increase inner silence in times when you are not actively using your mind.

The mind is a tool and has a purpose, and when you give it what it requires in order to feel useful, then it is less likely to act up with excessive chatter during the rest of the time. Conversely, engaging your mind excessively can easily lead to an overactive mind, and so it is essential to find the balance between using your mind, versus learning when to consciously turn off thinking. This takes time and practice to master. Many people's jobs require them to be in their heads for the majority of the day. Because of this, it may require particular diligence in order to find balance in how you use your mind.

Next, take the time to reflect upon your emotional needs. When we forget to honor our emotional needs it can easily lead to feeling hopeless, lost, or confused about our purpose in life. I have found that a few hours each day engaging in work with others in positive and uplifting ways feels deeply nourishing, and is also a natural expression of my Soul's purpose. If the work you do doesn't include uplifting human interaction, then consider volunteering some of your time to help those in need. Volunteering can be wonderfully heart opening, and can enrich the emotional experience within your life tremendously.

Tune into your heart to see just how best to meet your emotional needs in this regard. Are you drawn more towards deep connections with others, or do you prefer lighter, surface layer interactions? Do you like spending time connecting one-on-one, or do you feel more fulfilled through being in groups? Notice the kinds of interactions that nourish you most, and begin inviting more of these experiences into your life. Emotional connectivity can just as easily occur through spending time with other forms of life, such as with animals, and to a lesser degree, through time spent in nature. Finding the most effective way to meet your needs in this area will be unique for every person, and require personal investigation.

In addition to spending quality time with others, creative expression is a wonderful way to satisfy emotional needs. Just the act of being creative gets your emotional juices flowing. Writing, painting, making music, or working on any creative project helps stir the embers of life energy within you. Through being creative you uncover deeper layers within, have new insights about yourself, feel inspired, and discover more about your unique passions and gifts—all of which is deeply emotionally nourishing.

Learning to take care of your physical needs is just as essential as meeting spiritual, mental and emotional needs. When we don't truly understand how to tend to our own physical needs, it can leave us feeling drained, and consequently, dependent on others for energy and inspiration. Though it may sound trivial, making sure that you are adequately hydrated, are well fed and well rested throughout the day are all very important for maintaining vibrant energy. Be aware of the kinds of foods that you regularly consume, to see if your diet may be contributing to feeling negative or energetically drained. Diets high in sugar, caffeine, or other stimulants, for instance, can cause chemical imbalances in the body, brain, and energy system, often leading to energetic depletion. And again, when the body is compromised in some way, it can open the door for negativity and codependent tendencies.

Other commonly overlooked physical requirements might include getting adequate exercise, as well as getting plenty of fresh air and sunshine. Much of this exploration involves nuance and subtlety, which can take some time to flesh out. For a more in-depth discussion on how to best nourish yourself in all areas of your life, reference the chapter entitled, "Conscious Nourishment" (pg. 189). As you begin observing your patterns of self care, keep a journal of your notes and observations to track your progress.

If you are suffering from physical disease or illness, learning to meet your own needs in each area of your life can be powerful medicine. I mean this in a very literal sense. My experience of illness is that it is often a reflection of areas in our life where we are not fully taking responsibility for ourselves. This lack of self care reflects a greater lack of self love. By learning more about ourselves, with the intention of meeting our own needs, we increase the love within, helping to dissolve energetic blockages that may be at the heart of physical dis-ease. The last section of this book entitled, "The Holistic Healing Process" (pg. 235), serves the purpose of guiding a person through the healing journey by uncovering many of the potential energetic blockages that commonly result in illness.

Expressing Your Needs to Others

There are, of course, many instances when you are dependent upon others to get your needs met, and must express your needs clearly to another in order to take care of yourself, or create healthy boundaries. In addition, sometimes circumstances don't allow for you to remove yourself from a situation, or to go inward for your process. In these instances it can be helpful to have practical tools for communication that enable you to effectively express your feelings and needs in moments when it is necessary to do so.

It should also be noted that the goal is not necessarily to try and meet your needs in every situation, but rather to learn to take care of yourself to the best of your ability. By doing so, you empower yourself to no longer lean on others for support. Receiving support from others is a blessing when it comes, and there is an art to receiving, but for this section we are focusing on the nuts and bolts of taking care of oneself.

I have outlined a simple and straightforward process for expressing your needs to others, which can be found in the chapter entitled, "Heart Centered Communication" (pg. 226). This technique is a modified version of the technique created by the late Marshall Rosenberg called, "Conscious Communication" (formerly known as "Non-Violent Communication"). Rosenberg's technique is powerful in it's own right, although I have found that some aspects of his process open the door for codependent patterns to emerge, which is why I have modified and simplified it. The process I outline is an effective and simple form of expressing oneself that holds the power to dissolve codependent patterns, as well as create greater clarity regarding your feelings and needs.

The Divine Purpose of Relationship

It can be helpful to understand, however, that another person can never offer you anything that you do not already have within. The degree to which you love yourself is directly proportionate to the love you are able to receive and share with others. So when a new relationship enters your life, remember, this person is merely a divine reflection of you. Instead of seeking love from them, learn from their reflection, seeking to understand those areas in yourself where you continue to deny yourself love.

When relationship is viewed from this perspective, you will no longer need to try and hold onto another, because you will see that people truly come into your life for a purpose, showing you so much about yourself. When the learning is complete, the relationship will dissolve. And you wouldn't want it any other way. Why cling to a relationship that no longer serves the growth of you or the other person? To do so would only cause suffering.

Though relationship is a divine reflection, you cannot rely on the other person to reflect your light. We are all human, engaged in our own process of working through the veil of illusion, often swinging like a pendulum between love and fear, between self-mastery and inner struggle. Work to actively uncover your own inner light through spiritual practice, without expecting anyone else to do the same. By honoring your feelings, needs, and Soul's purpose, you keep your own roots firmly planted in the ground. And as you do, you will naturally feel your own light, as well as see the light in others, without needing them to reflect it back to you. When the loving reflection does come, it is experienced as the joy of receiving a wonderful gift, rather than as a relief born of expectation.

What you may begin to become aware of as you engage in relationship in this conscious way, are patterns throughout your life of being drawn to other people who balance you out, or "complete" you in some way. You may notice that being around these people feels satisfying, as if they are filling in the gaps of your own energetic expression. This reflects a profound phenomenon relating to the two primordial energies in the Universe being expressed within all of Creation; the divine masculine and the divine feminine. Each person is seeking the balance of these two energies within, and relationship serves the purpose of helping each one of us understand and integrate these two aspects of the Self more fully. When a person lacks awareness of their masculine and feminine energies within, they often rely on others to provide this sense of balance through relationship, which commonly results in codependent patterns forming.

These two energies are referred to in Taoism as yin and yang energy. As you consciously begin honoring your own needs, you may notice areas in your life where you either feel overly attached to the masculine expression, or the feminine expression. Any attachment you feel in this regard is often a reflection of patterns of imbalance between the yin and yang energies within. The more you bring awareness to the yin and yang expressions within your life, the more empowered you will become to embody balance, peace, and love, no longer relying on others for this feeling of wholeness within.

Yin and Yang Energy

Yin and yang are the names given to the initial division of energy coming from the one source of Universal Energy. These two flows of energy have been described as the in flow and the out flow, as well as the divine masculine and divine feminine (I'll use these terms interchangeably throughout this section to reinforce non-attachment to any one set of terms). If you think about the masculine and feminine being two halves of the whole, learning to embody both can allow a person to truly feel their wholeness. Finding the balance point between your yin and yang energy, and cultivating a life around this balance, creates a doorway to return to the state of oneness and unity consciousness.

In this sense, yin and yang theory is another model for the awakening process, one that bypasses the idea of the ego. Instead of doing battle with your ego, enlightenment is viewed as the process of gaining mastery over these two fundamental energy forces within. Viewing spiritual liberation through the lens of yin and yang helps depersonalize the process, allowing the mind to see that you are working with primordial energies that extend far beyond the personal self, or the the individual ego.

The idea of two flows of energy coming from the One Source of energy are described in many spiritual traditions. But this idea, like all thoughts and concepts about what life is, may ultimately be discarded as the two states become integrated back into balance. As one moves back into wholeness, even the distinction between two flows of energy becomes unnecessary. And though yin and yang theory may seem a bit heady or intellectual, holding a loose conceptual understanding of the phenomenon can be a powerful doorway to deepen your direct experience of Oneness.

You can directly observe and feel the yin and yang energy within you, and in the external world around you in every moment. Every aspect of creation has either a yin or yang expression. The breath, for example, has two components; the inward flow and the outward flow. The seasons of the year, the times of the day, and the cycles of life all follow a similar pattern of rise and fall, in and out, birth and death. The sun, for example, can be considered yang, giving its energy outward. The moon, on the other hand, may be considered more yin, receiving the light of the sun and reflecting it back out again.

The yin and yang are not meant to be concrete labels, but rather a description of an energetic state existing in a moment of time. And within each state there always exists the potential for the opposite state to exist as well. The sun, for example, would be considered yang in relationship to the moon, but could also be considered either yin or yang, depending on whether it is rising or setting. A sapling tree exists in a yin state (for the time being), while the mature tree exists in the yang state. Other examples of yin and yang are: cold and hot, light and dark, the pulsing of blood in and out of the heart, birth and death, creation and destruction, and growth and decay. Each state is defined by its relationship to its opposite. There can be no light without dark, no heat without cold, and no birth without death.

It can help to become familiar with the general characteristics of each state so that you can begin to notice the subtler expressions of these two energies within yourself, and within the world around you. The energetic characteristics of yin energy are femininity, receptivity, fluidity, creativity, intuition, allowance, gentleness, softness, inspiration, transformation, introversion, and nurturing qualities. Physical characteristics of yin are cool, dark, soft textures, rounded shapes, sinuous lines, cool colors, water, earth, and air. Yin is associated with the heart, wisdom, and feeling tones.

Compare this with the quality of yang energy, and you can see that they are distinctly different from one another. The energetic characteristics of yang energy are masculinity, structure, logic, control, power, decisiveness, extroversion, assertiveness, and the act of creation. Physical characteristic of yang energy are hot, light, hard textures, geometric shapes, warm colors, fire, rock, and metal. Yang energy is associated with thinking, knowledge, and the capacities of the mind.

The inner conflict that many people feel within their lives often reflects the repression of either their masculine or feminine energy. Many people are still closely identified with the energy associated with their gender, causing an unconscious repression of the seemingly opposing energy. On the other hand, there are many people who have reacted against traditional gender roles, identifying more strongly with the opposite energy. The paradox is that both energies can exist simultaneously in balance, even while outwardly appearing to oppose one another.

You can observe the conflict between the masculine and feminine energy by observing relationship dynamics between many men and women. This is a phenomenon commonly referred to as "the battle of the sexes," whereas each person is trying to prove that either the masculine or the feminine way of being is superior. In this situation each person is overly identified with either their own yin or yang expression, failing to recognize that what they are really seeking is a balance of the two energies within themselves. This externalization of the internal conflict can cause defensiveness and polarization towards one's partner. Instead of observing, appreciating, and integrating the energetic expressions of their partner, many people tend to resist this learning due to their own lack of awareness, and the compulsion of the mind to mistakenly identify with their predisposed expression (either masculine or feminine), and then defend it as though their sense of self were being threatened.

The flip side is that we also come to depend on the masculine and feminine expressions in our romantic partner, friends, and family members, because it allows for a natural balancing out of our own energy. It is quite common to see a strong connection form between a person demonstrating strong masculine qualities, and a person expressing more feminine qualities. These connections generally feel satisfying because it allows each person to learn and integrate the opposing energy more fully into their lives through their interactions with the other person. It is a beautiful dance, and when experienced consciously, can allow for growth and powerful inner transformations to occur.

In truth, both flows of energy are equal, and can only exist in relation to the other. There can be no masculine without the feminine to define it, and vice versa. This is a simple concept, yet profound in its implications in a person's day-to-day life. These two energies are flowing within you all the time, seeking to exist and be expressed in a balanced way. You can observe this in yourself in how you move your body, how you use your mind, how you structure your day, how you socialize, how you prioritize your life, and how you interact with the world around you.

The balance of yin and yang energy is as subtle as how much tension you are holding in your body at any given time. Holding a certain amount of tension in your body while you are performing tasks is necessary to stay focused, alert, and simply to keep your body upright and all the muscles functioning properly. This yang expression of tension, however, must be simultaneously balanced with conscious relaxation (the yin energy). If not, over time you will likely find yourself becoming agitated, irritated, or exhausted.

Are you able to hold just enough tension in your body to complete a task, simultaneously relaxing your body with each exhalation? Can you move fluidly between tension and relaxation moment by moment? Is your energy flowing through you like the tide of the ocean; smooth, fluid, and with an even in-and-out movement? Or does it feel more like a river that is flowing one moment, and then stopped up the next moment?

As you breathe, each moment of inhalation is bringing in and cultivating more energy in your body (the yang expression), and each exhalation is releasing and dispersing energy through the body (the yin expression). Notice for a moment how you are breathing. Are you allowing the yin and yang to remain in balance during each breath, or are you continuing to hold tension even while you exhale? Are you taking shallow inhalations and forceful exhalations, consequently releasing more energy than you are cultivating? If you often yawn or release big sighs, these can both be indications of imbalance. The flow of breath is a wonderful place to begin your practice of balancing your energy, for it affects every other aspect of your life. Balanced breathing creates a relaxed mind, steady and even emotions, and reflects the deeper balance of yin and yang energy within.

At the core of yin and yang theory is the union of the heart (the feminine principle) and the mind (the masculine principle). When these two energies are aligned, where the mind is consciously being used in loving service to the heart, an inner environment of peace and harmony is created. Finding this balance point between heart and mind will be different for everyone, depending on the kind of experiences that a Soul has come here to have.

The first step in finding this balance, however, is to really familiarize yourself with the experiential difference between yin and yang energy. You can do this simply by holding an awareness of the masculine and feminine qualities as you go about your day, observing the dynamic interplay between these two energies in life all around you. For a more detailed description for balancing these energies within, refer to the chapter, "Balancing Yin and Yang Energy" (pg. 205). The more aware you become of these two aspects of creation, the more you will begin to notice them within yourself, seeing areas of your life where you may be imbalanced. Gaining greater energetic sensitivity in this way is the foundation on the path of self-mastery, allowing you to create your life with greater conscious awareness.

Part III
The Path of Self-Mastery
~*~

"No one can save us but ourselves. No one can and no one may. We ourselves must walk the path." Gautama Buddha

As the old ego structures crumble away, a deep joy and excitement begin to arise for creating a truly heart-centered life, one where you naturally gravitate towards positive and uplifting activities. The focus of life often shifts from the personal to the Universal, with a desire springing forth to offer your energy for the highest good of all life, rather than from selfish desires. Life becomes imbued with a new dimension of magic, beauty, and grace—a quality of experience that is beyond the mind's ability to fully comprehend, and must be experienced first-hand to truly know it.

The path of awakening is not always an easy one, however, and you will undoubtedly be faced with new challenges and obstacles along your journey of deepening self-awareness. If you remain open to such challenges, learning to exercise greater conscious choice in your reactions, then you are walking the path of self-mastery; becoming masterful over how you use your thoughts, emotions, and actions in the world. This process often involves cycles of growth, combined with periods of integration and processing. It requires discipline, focus, and a deep commitment to Self in order to progress on the spiritual path, but to do so will transform your life in incredible ways.

The techniques in this chapter can allow you to begin

consciously creating your life in the way your heart truly desires, building a strong foundation for spiritual growth and inner peace. These techniques also aid in the process of integration, allowing for a smoother journey. You can simultaneously do these practices while continuing to dissolve the ego through the practices outlined in the last section. In fact, the two go hand in hand. As you continue dropping the ego, your heart naturally begins to come alive, showing you through your intuition and feelings how to live your life in greater alignment with your Soul's purpose.

Daily Spiritual Practices

It can be very powerful to create a daily routine of spiritual practice in your life. By doing so, you create a strong commitment to yourself, and a solid foundation for spiritual growth. A daily spiritual routine will ground you, help you stay connected to your center, and increase your clarity and inner peace. Find practices that you truly resonate with, using your intuition to modify and change your routine as you progress along your journey. Though initially it may feel restrictive to commit an hour or two of your time each day to spiritual practices, over time you will likely find that it creates an inner freedom, peace, and expansiveness that is well worth the time and effort.

Meditation

"To the mind that is still, the whole universe surrenders" -Lao Tzu

The basic purpose of meditation is two-fold: to cultivate focused discipline over your mind, and secondly, to take your attention deeply into the present moment. The more focused the mind becomes, the easier it will be to remain in the present moment. And as you merge more fully with the present moment, you uncover within yourself the direct experience of God consciousness, and deep feelings of love, peace, and well-being.

You can practice the first step of meditation (cultivating mental focus) all day long. Give whatever you are doing your full attention. Be fully present in every activity. When the mind wanders or becomes overly active, use your breath to come back to the present moment and relax. When you are not actively engaged in a task, rest in the present moment. During sitting meditation this is also the practice. When any thought arises, bring your attention back to being present. As you attain greater mastery and focus over your mind, your meditations will take on a new dimension as you journey deeper into the stillness of the eternal now.

Sitting meditation is best practiced 20-90 minutes at a time in the early hours of the morning (between 5am and 8am), and in the evening hours of the day (between sunset and the time you go to bed). If you have ever tried meditating at 5am, you know how amazing the experience can be. At this early hour of the day the energy of the earth is very still, creating a palpable stillness in the air. We are each synchronized to the earth's energy, and we can use the earth's peaceful energy at this early hour to aid our practice in finding stillness within. Of course, whenever you can make time to meditate is the perfect time.

When meditating, keep it simple. Sit in a cushion or chair, and wear comfortable clothing in an environment where you can relax. Set a timer, committing to meditate for the entire period of time that you choose. Begin by bringing your attention to your breath and relaxing your body. Keep your spine relatively straight without making yourself uncomfortable. As you breathe, continue checking in with the various parts of your body, relaxing your muscles as you do. Hold just enough tension to keep your body upright. Keep your attention on the breath, allowing it to naturally slow down as you relax.

When a thought arises, return to the breath. Do not be concerned at all with the content of your thoughts. Instead, focus on being present with your breath. Even if you have to bring your attention back to your breath a thousand times, it is a very successful meditation. In fact, there can be no unsuccessful meditation. Just having the intention and commitment to cultivate inner peace makes your meditation practice a success. Your intention is so powerful that if you stick with it, there can be no outcome other than inner peace. It is only a matter of time.

What you will notice through meditation is that your breath is a doorway, allowing you to travel more deeply into the center of yourself and the present moment. Follow your breath, allowing it to slow down and become quieter and more shallow. This does not require effort, so much as conscious relaxation and alertness. As the breath becomes quieter and more subtle, everything within you becomes more still. Your body may begin to feel heavy like stone, you may feel yourself expanding beyond your body, or you may feel as though there is infinite space within your body. Stay with your breath and whatever sensations arise from within you. There is no need to feel discouraged or frustrated, for the path of self-realization is a noble pursuit that takes commitment and time.

There are a few variations on meditation that I present in this book, such as the meditating on the spiritual heart. More important than where you place your attention, is your ability to focus your attention. Whether it's your breath, your heart, or one of your chakra points, focus on mastering your ability to concentrate the mind.

When it comes to meditation, consistency is key. This cannot be understated. Watch your mind as you begin a regular practice of meditation and it will likely say, "this isn't working," or, "I'm not doing this right." Really? Who's telling you that? Why, it's that wily mind that is making up those stories. Stick with it and you will absolutely see results. Tap into your childlike innocence, curiosity, and sense of adventure, and most of all, enjoy the journey.

Meditation is a practice that has been used for thousands of years and is proven effective for increasing mental, emotional, and even physical well-being. Meditation clears away the veil of illusion that has been clouding our ability to see what this human experience is, and who we truly are. The process of meditation breaks the addiction to thinking, it is a cumulative practice, and it takes time. It takes dedication and commitment. If you want to know a deeper dimension to life, to know yourself beyond the filters and limitations of the mind, then meditate.

Yoga

Yoga is a wonderful practice for getting out of the head and into the body, helping you to cultivate greater mental focus and discipline. Yoga helps keep your body limber and healthy, as well as allow you to become more comfortable with discomfort. In addition, it is common for emotional traumas from the past to become stored in the tissue and muscles of the body. Yoga, then, can be very helpful in releasing these old energies, keeping your body free from energetic blockages and physical illness. Most of all, yoga helps to prepare the body for meditation, and is best practiced before sitting meditation. Slow methodical movements, coupled with relaxed deep breathing, creates an inner environment of peace and calm, both of which are conducive for meditation.

You don't have to be an expert at yoga to do the basic postures necessary to cultivate greater discipline, focus, and self awareness. Though many yoga teachers would likely disagree with this statement, I truly believe that using your intuition to find your own yoga flow will be most beneficial for spiritual growth. This is in contrast to becoming overly focused on one particular style or teaching.

This might not be the case, however, for those using yoga as a physical workout, in which case precise instruction may be most beneficial for strengthening the body. But for the spiritual benefits of the practice, I suggest finding your own flow, which will allow you to listen and feel the unique needs of your body. The wisdom within your body is accessible to you when you take the time to go within and find it for yourself. Before there was "yoga," there were people who just stretched their bodies because, intuitively, they knew there was wisdom there, accessible to those with the patience and commitment to uncovering it.

Listen to your body, feel into where it needs to be stretched, and make slow and methodical movements to achieve the stretch. Be focused, moving and breathing slowly and steadily, taking your time to hold each stretch for a few breaths. Find a routine that works for you, and be open to adjusting it as you progress in your practice.

Doing yoga everyday, particularly in conjunction with a meditation practice, anchors your energy to the earth, and gives you stability as you go about your day. Starting each day with a commitment to Self sends a powerful message to the Universe that your own state of peace, happiness, and health is your priority and focus in life.

Mindful Awareness

Being mindful throughout your day means staying aware of the thoughts, emotions, and actions that you are creating in your life moment by moment. When a negative thought arises, come back to the breath and let it go. When a negative emotion arises, come back to your breath and relax your body. Staying in this continual state of presence will change your life. Being mindful will allow you to see the higher perspective, dissolving your attachment to many aspects of life that no longer serve your growth and happiness.

What could be more important than living in peace? Most people are so consumed with the outer world, searching and seeking for something that they believe will make them happy (or at least remove their anxiety), that they fail to recognize the peace that exists in the present moment. Within peace you find happiness, within happiness you find love, and within love you find God. Finding inner peace is the first step. And peace is available to you in every moment as soon as you drop the need to get somewhere else, or become something greater, and instead, choose to come back to the present moment, to what is right here and now.

Retracing

One useful mindful awareness technique for cultivating presence, as well as learning to have greater mental mastery, is a practice called retracing. This technique is especially useful for dissolving patterns of reoccurring thoughts of a negative nature that may play like a broken record in your mind. Experiment with this technique to see under what circumstances it is most helpful for you.

As soon as you notice a negative thought arising, begin tracing it back, scanning each previous thought until the original "seed" thought is reached. As you retrace each thought, notice how your mind made certain mental connections that led you to your current thought and negative state of mind. This process can take a few seconds, or longer, depending on the intensity of the train of thought you were caught up in.

An example might be a stream of reoccurring negative thoughts about a past romantic partner. You might catch yourself having thoughts that this person treated you poorly, making negative judgments of their character. As soon as you notice this thought in action, you would then recall the thought that directly preceded the judgment of your ex partner. You may have been thinking about the relationship and where it went wrong.

Continue retracing your thoughts and you may see that you were thinking about the direction and goals of your life, and how you felt derailed by the relationship. Before that you may have been thinking about your current work situation and how you are not happy there. Before that you may have simply been walking down the street and observed a happy person. In reaction to the happy person, you might have had the thought, "I'm not as happy as that person, my life is not so great."

It is really amazing to witness in yourself how one unconsciously created negative thought can lead to a downward spiral of negativity. By retracing your thoughts you shed light on how your mind makes certain mental connections. This technique can help you take back conscious control over your thought process. It is akin to taking a broom and dustpan to your mind, cleaning up all junky thoughts that have been draining your energy and distracting you. Over time an amazing thing happens; you catch yourself at the original thought before it escalates any further. It is a really glorious moment to see the seed thought, smile, and decide not to water that one, because you know exactly how it will grow.

Mindful Reflection

When applied to your own spiritual evolution, the mind can be a very powerful tool. While dropping compulsive thinking frees you from suffering, you can also actively engage your mind in the awakening process. Similarly to the previous technique of retracing, you can use your mind to deconstruct and unravel the dysfunction within your own mind through the process of mindful reflection.

To do this, give yourself time each day to reflect on your process. Give yourself 20-30 minutes once a day to review the experiences of the day, and how you responded to them. Use your mind to study itself as though you are a scientist in the laboratory gaining greater data on how your own mind works. Do not be so concerned with the contents of your thoughts and emotions, but rather, observe the patterns within your mental processes. How were you choosing to perceive life in the moments when certain mental and emotional reactions were triggered? Bring awareness to the core beliefs, patterns, and themes that arise again and again in your daily inner experience, without creating any judgment or resistance towards them. As you do, explore alternative perspectives that you could have held in those situations which would have shifted your experience. Notice how your reaction to any given situation is only one of an infinite number of reactions that you could have held.

The ego operates very much like a computer, running the program that you were taught early on in your life. Instead of worrying about the contents of the program, look at how the actual software program itself operates. You do not need to do anything about what you discover. Merely bringing awareness to these phenomenon will increase your conscious control over your thoughts, emotions, and actions. As you do this process you may notice your mind begins to wander, getting pulled into the content of the experiences. If this happens it is important to get refocused on the bigger picture, and to remain clear about the task at hand.

They key to using this practice in a conscious way is to not spend idle time thinking about the past. Once the 20-30 minutes of mindful reflection is complete, put your thoughts down once again. Let go and return to the present moment. When the mind wants to return to past experiences, or gets pulled into drama from past situations, be vigilante to return your focus to the present moment. It can be very easy to slip back into unconscious states if you do not stay aware of how you are using your mind. It can be helpful to keep a journal, keeping notes and observations about your process.

Breathing Techniques

One of the greatest tools for transformation is your breath. Beyond simply focusing on the breath as a means of coming back to the present moment, you can practice changing your breathing patterns to effect change in your mind, emotions, and body. The benefits of conscious breathing practices are just as impressive as the benefits of meditation; increased immune system functioning, improved circulation and heart health, increased nervous system functioning, and improved cognitive functioning.

I would also suggest experimenting with different breathing patterns intuitively to see how the breath can change your state of being. When we take the time to experiment different techniques for ourselves, rather than simply following a technique step-by-step from another person or a book, we can have a much more powerful and direct learning experience. Your intuition knows the path back to wholeness, and will guide you appropriately when you hold the sincere intention to uncover more of your true nature.

Deep, Slow Breathing

When you consciously slow down your breath while still breathing deeply, you can quiet your mind, calm your emotions, while continuing to remain alert and present. Compare slow and deep breathing with the slow and shallow breathing that often accompanies meditation. Shallow meditative breathing can bring your mind and emotions to an even deeper level of stillness, but is also more likely to cause sleepiness, reducing your energy and alertness.

By taking deep and slow breaths, however, you can remain energized while also slowing and stilling the mind. This is useful as a practice for harmonizing your energy when you feel unbalanced in any way, and for when you are active out in the world. Breathing this way allows you to return to peace and calm without losing your energy and vitality. I have found it very useful for resetting my mind and emotions, and for getting grounded while engaged in daily activities.

The idea is to breathe deeply and slowly at a comfortable pace, allowing your lower lungs to fill with air first. As you inhale, allow your belly to extend outward as your lower lungs fill with air. Once the lower lungs have been filled (about halfway through the inhalation), focus on allowing the mid and upper lungs to fill with air until your lungs have reached a comfortable capacity. As you exhale, allow the air to leave your lungs in the reverse order, beginning with the chest, and ending in the belly. Stay present with the exhalation until all the air has exited your lungs and your belly has retracted back towards your core. This breath can be compared to the tide of the ocean, and feels much like a wave of air coming in and out of your body in a rhythmic manner. Remember, this breath should not be forced, nor should it feel uncomfortable in any way. It may feel a bit awkward or unnatural at first, but over time it will become like second nature. Try it now…

If re-learning to breathe seems like a strange concept, remember that breathing slowly and deeply from the abdomen is actually the most natural way of breathing. It is only that most people have unconsciously adopted shallow chest breathing, which is why it may initially feel more "natural" to breathe shallow. Deep and slow breathing from the abdomen allows the full capacity of your lungs to be reached as you breathe.

This style of breathing also activates your parasympathetic nervous system, effectively calming your nerves and releasing neurotransmitters in the brain. Over time, conscious breathing will retrain the nervous system to be in a state of relaxation and peace, rather than anxiety and tension. I suggest practicing this throughout your day whenever you can remember, and particularly a few minutes before each meal.

Breath of Light

The breath of light is a wonderful way to utilize the energy in the air (prana) to harmonize and expand your own energy field. By breathing deeply in this way you bring more energy into your system, allowing you to feel greater physical energy, greater mental clarity, and increase your feelings of peace, well-being and vitality.

Take deep breaths in through your nose, exhaling out through your mouth. As you breathe allow your body to relax, feeling your breath flow like the tide of the ocean, in and out in a circular motion. Breathe deeply and in a slightly energized manner. Allow each breath to be full, but not forced in any way. As you breathe keep your attention on your heart, as though you were breathing energy in and out with your heart. Feel the energy cultivate and build in your heart on the in breath, and then feel the energy spread through every cell of your body on the exhalation. Feel the energy expand out beyond the physical boundary of your body to fill your energy field. Continue to feel your energy expanding and flowing all around you. Allow your body to become soft, permeable and fluid.

This will take practice to actually feel the prana expanding, so keep your attention down in your body on the actual sensations of energy as you breathe. After a while you will begin to sense yourself expanding through your breath and out beyond your body. Practice this breath throughout the day in order to stay centered, grounded, energized, and present. The key is to take deep, slow, natural breaths, while relaxing and keeping your attention on the prana as it expands out from your center.

Breath of Fire (Agni Pran)

Breath of fire is a yogic breathing technique for cultivating your energy, and increasing mental alertness and physical energy. This is a wonderful breath to practice before or after your morning routine of yoga or stretching. Breath of fire invigorates, energizes, and stimulates the cells, tissue, and organs in your body, aiding in the natural processes of detoxification. The breathing technique is particularly good for increasing physical energy, mental clarity, focus, and emotional balance. The breathing pattern consists of quick rhythmic breaths through the nostrils, taking approximately 2-3 breaths per second.

To begin, sit in a comfortable position with your spine straight, your shoulders relaxed and dropped, and your body relaxed. On the exhalation quickly contract your abdominal muscles in towards your spine, drawing your navel in and up towards your diaphragm. This contraction should rapidly push the air out of your lungs as you quickly exhale through your nose. On the inhalation, simply relax your muscles, allowing the air to naturally be drawn in through your nose and down into your lungs. Your inhalations and exhalations should be even and quick (2-3 breaths per second). Practice breath of fire for 1-3 minutes at a time, being sure to take even inhalations and exhalations through the nose. Practice this breath throughout the day, particularly when you feel depleted in energy, sluggish, or unable to focus or concentrate.

Breath of fire should not be practiced during pregnancy or during menstruation. Breath of fire can cause some tingling or light-headedness to occur (on account of the increased oxygen flow), so be sure to stand up slowly following your practice. This breathing technique should not be practiced right before eating, and it is advised to wait 1-2 hours after a meal to practice.

The Power of Gratitude

"If the only prayer you said in your whole life was 'thank you,' that would suffice." -Meister Eckhart

One of the most powerful emotional states that can be experienced is that of gratitude. A strong feeling of gratitude is the same vibration as love. While gratitude often wells up within us unexpectedly when someone offers a kind gesture, a few loving words, or an act of kindness, gratitude can also be consciously created through practice. The idea of practicing gratitude may seem counter-intuitive to some people on the spiritual path, as though you are forcing yourself to do something that doesn't initially feel natural. The reason for this is that, although unconditional love truly is our natural state, most of us have been conditioned to repress this natural expression of love for so long, to the point where the repression actually feels familiar, and therefore natural. Because the mind can grow accustomed to many unnatural things, which over time begin to feel "natural," it often actually requires practice to return to this more authentic way of being.

Although being effusive with your love through a gratitude practice may initially feel awkward, over time, you will begin to remember this innately loving part of yourself more fully. The more you practice being grateful for everything in your life (the "good," the "bad," and everything in between) the easier it becomes to view yourself and others with compassion and love. A little gratitude goes a long way, inviting abundance into your life in numerous forms. I like to practice gratitude for about ten minutes at a time, either after my morning meditation, or in the evening before bed.

An Exercise in Gratitude

Begin by closing your eyes and relaxing your body as you take deep slow breaths. Feel the air moving in and out of your lungs, letting go of any tension or stress that you may be holding. Now focus on a person in your life whom you are grateful for. See this person in your mind's eye. See them smiling, being happy, and begin feeling your natural appreciation them for who they are and what they mean to you. Let these positive feelings grow simply by staying present with them. Focus on this feeling of gratitude for as long as feels natural. As the image of this person fades, then, focus your mind on something or someone else that you are grateful for. It can be anything —a person, place, animal, the natural world, or an experience. In your mind's eye see yourself truly appreciating the thing that you are grateful for from you heart. If it is a place, such as a special location on the earth, see yourself being in this location, feeling so joyful and grateful to be there. If it is a person or pet, see their happy smiling face, imagining yourself giving them a hug. See the textures, feel the energy, and let yourself deeply experience what you are grateful for.

The idea is to really allow yourself to generate the positive feelings of love and appreciation through visualization while doing this practice. See how much positive feeling you can generate through focusing your attention on each thing in your life that you are grateful for. This is a powerful practice that can bring you into a very joyful and loving state in a matter of minutes. You may be brought to tears of joy, in which case, let the tears and emotion flow. It may also help to bring one hand to your heart, bowing your head to your heart during the practice.

I also really enjoy singing my gratitude, as it is a fun and effortless way to reinforce these positive emotions throughout the day. Singing (or saying) the words "thank you" out loud, while holding the image of the people, places, and things that you are grateful for, generates powerfully positive and loving feelings. When I do my practice I see myself saying thank you to everything that I am grateful for, deeply feeling the energy of appreciation as I do so. Then as I go about my day I sing the Thank You song as a reminder of these positive feelings. It takes practice to really stay focused on thoughts of gratitude, so keep at it.

It is really amazing to use a gratitude practice to increase your feelings of well-being and positivity, noticing how it can shift your perceptions of the world for the better. Try it for yourself to see how powerful it can be. What you may also notice is that the practice builds momentum over time. You may not see any big shift right away, but over time you will be amazed at how this simple practice can open your heart to the abundance of love and light all around you.

Uncovering Your Soul's Purpose

True religion is real living; living with all one's soul, with all one's goodness and righteousness." -Albert Einstein.

157

Though our primary purpose is to awaken, to dissolve the ego, and to free ourselves from mind-made suffering and limitation, there are also specific experiences that each Soul desires to have in a given lifetime. This could be thought of as your Soul's purpose; particular themes you have come here to explore for the purpose of love, growth, and expansion. This Soul "blueprint" was created by you before you came into this lifetime, and is designed to align you with certain people, situations, and life experiences that allow you the opportunity to grow and bring more love and light into this world. The more you align yourself with your Soul's purpose, the more you feel truly alive, connected, and deeply in the creative flow of life.

Uncovering your Soul's purpose is not found through thinking about it, however, but rather through the intuition flowing from your heart in each moment. You can practice receiving this information directly, simply by holding your attention on the center of your heart for periods of time throughout your day. As you do, you will more clearly receive intuition about what is right for you, and develop a stronger connection with your feelings. Your feelings then become like a divine compass, pointing you in the direction of your Soul's purpose, based on what feels inspiring and right in your heart. An indication of your Soul's purpose can also be detected by noticing all of the experiences in life that you are excited by, inspired by, and feel drawn towards. When we take the time to really feel what is in the heart, and honor what we feel, we are aligning ourselves with our Soul's path for this lifetime.

The first process to uncovering your Soul's purpose, however, is to begin dissolving the ego, which allows for a clearing away of the old patterns of fear, limitation, and imbalance. This creates space for more of your essential self to emerge. As a person moves through this clearing away process, learning to feel more of their true nature, they enter into the next phase of learning; how to consciously create one's life from love and the desires within the heart. And as you move into a more deeply satisfying and authentic way of living, more love and creative energy naturally flows into your life. It is a wonderful upward flowing spiral that becomes more and more rewarding as one progresses along their journey.

How does this look? It takes the form of letting go in many

areas of your life, while also moving in the direction of joy, inspiration, and excitement. Where you used to feel strong attachment to relationships, work or living situations, rigid belief systems, and material possessions as a way of deriving a sense of safety and self-identity, you are now willing to let go of that which no longer serves your growth. You become willing to let go of relationships that are not uplifting, let go of work experiences that no longer inspire you, or lifestyle choices that no longer nourish you, and instead, investigate how your unique Soul's vision can be allowed to unfold in your life.

By clearing away all those elements of your life that don't actually nourish your Soul, you create space for the things that do to enter your life. You begin to live more fluidly, naturally, unafraid of change, and instead, inspired by the myriad of possibility. You may find yourself trying new things, being drawn in new directions, and living life in a new way. As you begin letting go of your old life, however, it may initially seem like not much is happening. Be patient and have faith. It often takes the outer world some time to catch up to the energetic shifts you are making in your inner landscape.

But again, this is not a process that involves thinking about a solution to the question, "how can I manifest my heart's desires?" Thinking cannot connect you with the energy that is in your heart. You must literally feel it. In order to do this you must learn to quiet your mind through meditation, and then actually take your attention to your heart center. While you may need to use your mind to research and learn about different ways of living, different ways to spend your time, new career opportunities, or different ways to nourish your body, these discoveries happen in the right time as you follow your intuition and feelings about what is right for you in each and every moment. It is through developing a stronger connection with the heart that we have access to our intuition, and the higher guidance from within.

As I went through my awakening process I spent hours meditating on my heart, sincerely asking for guidance. Over time I began to receive very clear intuition about the direction to move in. I began investigating different ways to live my life outside the cultural norms, ways that felt more heart-centered. For me this has meant living in nature, traveling for extended periods of time, letting go of many of my possessions, and living simply. My passion in life has become about helping others remember the truth of who they are, bringing more beauty into this world through art and music, and living in love. While this way of living had always been available to me, I had been shut down to it, not aware that I could actually live so simply, and with so much freedom.

While practicing this technique of paying attention to your heart, give yourself permission to shake things up in your life. Do not fret or worry about letting other people down, changing your direction or goals in life, or that you won't find something "better" than your current situation—all common fears that can arise as one begins listening more fully to the inner voice of the heart. If you hold onto the things of your life out of fear, you will likely only continue to experience more of these same limitations in your life.

Take a step into the unknown and see what happens. Find out more about yourself by having new experiences, exploring different ways of living your life, and more expansive ways of perceiving situations and yourself. Is there something that you have always wanted to do but were too afraid to try? Now may be the perfect time. Perhaps you have always wanted to live in an exotic location, travel the world, summit a mountain, work on a farm, build a house, create a business, learn to paint or play a musical instrument. The possibilities are endless.

Even though it may seem frightening, acknowledging your heart's desires is the first step to connecting more fully with your Soul's purpose. There is no need to feel fear about following your heart, it is only the ego that believes that illusion. All you need to do is take that first step of returning your attention to your heart, for all other steps will be made known to you in the right time. If, at any point you feel anxiety or fear during this process, then return to stillness and presence.

You are the creator of your life, and you truly hold the power to mold and change your life in any way that you please. There are over seven billion ways to live on this planet, with so many wonderful experiences to have, places to explore, and gifts to share. The more that you tune into the beautiful song within your heart, the more you will actualize the unique vision that only you can manifest into reality.

Meditation on the Spiritual Heart

To begin tuning into your Soul's unique vision, you can practice the spiritual heart meditation right now in this moment. Sit with your spine straight in a comfortable position, allowing your breath to become relaxed and peaceful. As you breathe allow any tension in your body to be released. Just focus on being present and relaxed, feeling the flow of breath in and out of your lungs....when you feel ready, bring your attention to your spiritual heart, which is located slightly to the right of your physical heart, in the center of your energy field. The spiritual heart is literally the center of you. Take your attention to your center and just notice how it feels. You may find yourself distracted at first, so continue bringing your attention back to your heart center whenever a thought arises.

As you keep your attention in the center of your chest, notice any feelings of vibration, tingling, or energy in this part of your body. You may notice this energy pulsating, gently spiraling, or just vibrating. You also may feel a heaviness, tightness, or the feeling of stuck energy around your heart. No matter what you feel, continue to keep your attention in your center. It is all perfect just as it is. You can practice this meditation as you go about your daily activities, when interacting with others, while working, and while playing. Whatever you are doing, see if you can keep some portion of your attention on your spiritual heart.

The challenge that many people experience initially, is that it is either difficult to actually keep one's attention on the heart, or by doing so it may bring up pain or sadness that feels overwhelming. It is necessary to first feel what you have been holding onto if you want to let it go, and it can actually take quite a bit of practice to keep your attention on your heart center in order to release these repressed emotions. The ego can sometimes be quite sneaky in diverting your attention away from having to feel any potential pain (which the ego views as a threat to your survival), and you may have to bring your attention back to your heart thousands of times throughout your day.

If there is energetic heaviness or pain around your heart, what you may notice as you keep your attention there is that you begin to cry, tremble, shake, or express some other outpouring of emotional energy (which may even take the form of laughter). This is absolutely healthy, and is to be allowed to the best of your ability. Let the emotion flow without getting distracted from the actual feeling around your heart. This is important because many people, as they begin to feel sadness or pain, get distracted by thoughts about what is occurring, or stories about why they are feeling this way. Perpetuating old stories and replaying emotional wounding is not helpful in releasing and healing emotional wounds.

If you find that you cannot stay connected to the direct sensations within your body as you release this emotion, and that you begin having compulsive negative thoughts (either about yourself, other people, or life itself), then stop the practice. Calm yourself down, return to your breath, and find the peace within. Once you have reconnected to the feeling of peace, then start again, bringing your attention back to your heart, feeling for the energy within. Over time this heaviness and pain will lighten and dissolve. Once residual emotional pain has been released from around your heart, you will then be able to experience deeper states of love and connectivity through this practice.

This is a simple technique, and yet it is one of the most direct methods for uncovering the truth of who you are beyond the ego. You may notice that the way you move your body begins to change, the way you speak, express yourself, and behave, all begins to feel more natural, more effortless, and more like You! Do not be surprised to find dramatic shifts occurring in many areas of your life as well, including how you spend your time, and your overall motivation for living.

The Path of Service

"The meaning of life is to find your gift. The purpose is to give it away." -Pablo Picasso

What occurs for many people as they go through the

awakening process is a profound shift in motivation. The shift occurs as a person begins to feel drawn towards being of service for the highest good of all, rather than mainly for the individual self. This occurs most notably in the kind of work that one aspires to do in the world. Instead of being motivated from the desires of the ego to get more material possessions, or achieve more success for oneself, a deep desire to be of service to others begins to blossom within. It feels to me that this is ultimately the will of the Higher Intelligence— to create life in the most beautiful, loving, and uplifting way possible. The more we dissolve the ego, the more we naturally align ourselves with the will of the Universe, and get to participate in the healing of the planet through contributing our own unique gifts.

It may also be that as a person goes through the awakening process, the activities and goals that used to feel satisfying no longer do, and so it takes some investigation to allow oneself to begin living life in a new way. This is not something that you need to think about or plan for, but simply to keep in your awareness. As you go through the awakening process it is quite natural to lose interest in many of the things that you used to enjoy. On the surface this may feel confusing or unsettling, but in time, and through investigation, you will likely begin to open to a much more meaningful way of life, one where your energy is primarily being spent consciously from a place of peace and joy.

The meditation on the spiritual heart as described in the previous chapter is a wonderful practice to help you tune into the unique gifts and skills that are yours to offer this world. The more you follow your unique calling, offering your energy for the upliftment of all, the more meaning you will feel in your life. In order to live authentically and with inspiration, it may mean that you need to change your profession, or it may simply mean that you change how you are doing the work that you do. Just being fully present in each moment of work, play, and while interacting with others, allows the light of consciousness to shine more brightly into everything that you do.

If you are not directly involved in helping people through the work that you do, aspire to incorporate selfless service into your life when you are not working. There are numerous organizations that you can volunteer with to help feed the homeless, work with children or the elderly, participate in ecological restoration projects, or help build low-income housing. Offering your energy in this way can be a tremendously heart opening experience. A few hours a week can make a significant difference in the lives of others, and in the quality of your own life.

To be of service you don't necessarily need to volunteer your time, or become a humanitarian. Simply holding the intention as you go about your day to be in service for the highest good of all life will begin to reorient your motivations towards healing and unity consciousness. Whenever interacting with others, hold the question in your mind, "how can I be of service for the highest good in this moment?" Wait until you receive inspiration from your Higher Self before speaking or taking action. You may be surprised to find how your behavior changes. You may find yourself offering kind and uplifting words in moments where you used to feel hesitation to do so, or perhaps you find yourself remaining silent in times when you used to feel the compulsion to say or do something.

But remember, your state of being is what matters above all. If you take on the task of being of service to others because you feel a sense of obligation or guilt, then it is not the right time for you to engage in these activities. Instead, focus on getting right in your inner state until you firmly establish a foundation of peace and well-being. As the awakening experience becomes more integrated into your day-to-day life, you will naturally feel a strong desire welling up within you to take action for the highest good. It is from this place of love and peace that selfless service is best performed. And what a joy it is to help others. It is a gift of love to give to another, and it fills your own heart with so much love that you just want to keep sharing it with all the world around you.

The Power of Intention

Our intentions are powerful, and create amazing changes in

our inner experience, and in the world around us. Even if your life is not a reflection of your highest expression now, by simply holding the intention to expand into more of your authentic self, the Universe will begin arranging itself to support this goal. While the power of intention is well known among many spiritualists, this phenomenon has begun to garner the attention of some well-known scientific institutions.

For the last three decades Princeton University has been conducting ongoing research through a program known as the Princeton Engineering Anomalies Research project (PEAR). This research has been focused on testing the impact that human intention has on random events. Hundreds of different automated random event generators were created for the study, with the goal of measuring what effect, if any, human thoughts could have on the outcome of random events. The machines underwent rigorous testing to ensure that they did, in fact, create random outcomes under normal conditions in their environment.

The tests involved participants holding the intention for specific outcomes to occur, while simultaneously observing the random event generators in action. For instance, one experiment involved a random event generator that mimicked the tossing of a coin, generating either heads or tails. Participants were asked to hold the intention for the machine to pick tails more of the time. The machine then generated thousands of trials, with researchers tallying the results. There were hundreds of these types of tests performed using different machines, replicated over the course of a few decades.

What these studies uncovered confounded the researchers involved in the project. Over many decades of testing, the conclusion was reached that there is a significantly high correlation between participant intentions and the outcome of random events. In the example of the coin tossing experiment, the results showed that the machine did, in fact, produce the tails outcome more of the time when the intention was held for that particular outcome. The implications of these findings question the foundation of Newtonian physics, and points to the idea that there are other influences in effect beyond what can be measured with current instrumentation.

Researchers noted, however, that even though the outcome

deviation was significantly consistent, it generally produced a minimal effect. The tails outcome, for instance, would occur 55% of the time, versus the expected 50%. Interestingly enough, the deviation was generally increased when a well-bonded romantic couple simultaneously held the same intention. Groups of socially bonded people, such as families or group of friends also increased the degree of deviation more significantly than individual participants.

Another well-known study involving the power of human intention to create measurable effects in the physical world took place in Washington D.C. in 1993. Researchers were curious to see what effect group meditation might have on the incidence of city wide violent crime. A group of over 4000 practiced transcendental meditators traveled to Washington D.C. to participate in the study, which spanned the course of nearly two months. The study was monitored by an independent review board consisting of a 27-member team of sociologists, criminologists, and representatives from the police department in the District of Columbia. Amazingly, over the course of the two-month study, researchers observed a significant drop in violent crimes in Washington, with the decrease averaging a 23 percent drop in comparison to previous years. Researchers noted that the likelihood of these results reflecting chance variation was roughly 2 in 1 billion. No scientific explanation for this phenomenon was reached.

More compelling evidence regarding the connection between intention and the physical world comes from the research of Dr. Masaru Emoto. Emoto spent much of his professional career studying the effects of human intention on various living and non-living substances, most notably, the effects of certain thoughts on water molecules. Emoto's studies involved freezing water samples that had been subjected to different thoughts, and compared the results.

For one water sample Emoto instructed participants to hold loving thoughts and intentions towards the water for a period of time, while for the second water sample, he had participants hold negative thoughts and intentions. The results showed that a frozen water crystal subjected to loving intentions created a symmetrical design similar to that of a magnified snowflake, while the water subjected to negative thoughts and intentions created an asymmetrical mishmash of jagged lines and shapes. Emoto replicated these studies using a variety of different mediums, and achieved similar results in many cases. In 1999 he published his findings in the book "Messages from Water," where he provides photographs of the different water samples.

One of the most incredible phenomenon involving observer intention is that which has been described as the "double slit" experiment. First observed by the physicist Thomas Young in the early part of the nineteenth century, these experiments demonstrate one of the central quandaries of quantum mechanics—a mystery that continues to baffle scientists and challenge the traditional Newtonian approach to how physical matter behaves. The phenomenon in question is an electron's ability to exist both as a wave and a particle, which appears to be dependent on observer expectation and intention.

In the experiments, scientists blasted streams of electrons through a panel with a number of slits in it, observing the patterns where the electrons made impact on a background wall. Because electrons have traditionally been observed as particles, scientists expected to see the electrons form a single band pattern when passed through the slit. What scientists discovered, however, was that when electrons were passed through the slits they behaved as waves (the way in which light and sound travel), creating a spectrum of points of contact on the background wall. This confused and baffled the researchers. How could a particle demonstrate the qualities of a wave? And this is where things get even more strange.

When scientists set up measuring equipment to see exactly how the electrons passed through the slits, the passing electrons reverted back to behaving as particles, making one band on the background wall. When scientists removed the measuring devices, the electrons once again behaved as waves. The mere act of observing the electrons collapsed their wave function back into a particle. It was as if the electrons were consciously aware that they were being watched, and behaved according to what the observers were expecting to see.

While scientists remain baffled by the mystery behind these phenomenon, and tend to discount them, it appears to me that the scientific community is on the verge of having their own spiritual awakening. There may come a time when scientists discover that what they are studying beneath the lens of a microscope is actually the very same essence in which we are all a part. Consciousness studying consciousness in order to know itself. What an amazing and beautiful dance, and what a wondrous way to wake up from the illusion of separation.

The Intention Exercise

Consciously holding an intention is a wonderful way to exercise greater self mastery over your day-to-day experience. Try writing out your intentions every morning, restating them throughout your day with related mantras and positive affirmations. When creating a daily intention, begin by closing your eyes, taking a few deep breaths, and centering your attention in your heart. Ask yourself what your highest intentions are for your life, or simply just for today, and wait to receive intuition and inspiration.

Allow the intention to arise naturally within you, without over thinking it. When it comes to the actual wording of your intention, it works best to focus on what you want, rather than on what you do not want. Focus on affirmative statements, and leave out any words that reinforce a negative or limiting experience, such as "fear," "anger," or "depression." For example, instead of using a phrase such as, "today I won't get angry," say something like, "today I will remember to relax and remain peaceful."

Once you have decided upon an intention, slowly and clearly speak your intention either out loud or in your mind. You can use the same intention each day, or you can change it up. Some days you may feel like saying a short intention, while other days it can be helpful to create more in-depth ones. Write your intention in a journal for greater impact. Here are a few examples of daily intentions:

"Today I choose peace, relaxation, and love in each moment and interaction of the day."

"I allow myself to let go and trust in the Universe today, receiving the abundance that exists all around me."

"I am the creator of my life, creating my thoughts, my emotions, and my actions in every moment."

"Today I am free to create my reality in alignment with the love within my heart."
"I allow myself to be open, happy, and joyful today, relaxing my body and saying 'yes' to all of life."

"Today I choose to see life through the eyes of my heart, to be playful, to be joyful, to be positive and uplifting with my words, emotions, and actions. I choose to say 'yes' to life, with enthusiasm, with excitement, and intention. I choose to follow my heart and listen to my intuition, knowing that my inner guidance will always lead me in the right direction."

"Today I will remember to breathe deeply, feel the energy in my body, and be present. I will remember to relax, let go, and trust that everything will work out as it always does. Today I will allow my body to heal, feeling light and love filling every cell in my body. Today I will live in peace, joy, and harmony with all of life."

Simple day-to-day intentions cultivate your energy over time, laying a foundation for life changes down the road. As you gain more clarity and focus regarding your intentions, the momentum and energy of your intentions will grow, eventually emerging as a greater vision for your life. So take time throughout your day to really understand the motivations for your intentions. What outside forces may be influencing your intentions and desires? What effect do your friends, family, or other cultural influences have on your intentions and desires? Can you tell the difference between a desire of your heart, and a desire of your ego? It may help to keep a written journal of your process, noting what is motivating your day-to-day intentions, how your intentions may shift throughout your day.

The Process of Visioning

"...ask, and it will be given to you; seek and you will find; knock and it will be opened to you." -Luke 11:9

Visioning combines intention with the process of visualization, and is a powerful way to manifest certain experiences into your life that your heart desires to have. Visioning is an innately human expression, one that has been practiced for thousands of years through the act of prayer, sacred ritual, song, and dance. References to the process of visioning can be found in numerous religious texts, and has more recently been described in many New Age teachings as the "law of attraction," or as the process of "manifestation."

Visioning is most effective when you have sufficiently dissolved the ego, removing feelings of lack from your inner experience. When you want something because you believe it will make you happier (be it a romantic partner, a new car, or a bigger house), then visioning will only increase your sense of lack. You can only manifest what you already have found within. And so the first step in visioning is always to return to a state of peace and deep acceptance for your life now, experiencing the natural abundance existing within you and all around you in the present moment. It is from a state of presence, gratitude, and clarity that visioning will be most effective.

In truth, we are always manifesting experiences into our lives, and so it is not so much a skill to be learned, but rather, a natural intuitive process to be refined. Just being alive in a human body, creating thoughts, feelings, and actions, produces change in your inner experience, as well as in the outer world. Every thought and desire you create sends a ripple of energy out into the Universe, which is received by the Higher Intelligence, and then reflected back to you in some shape or form. By holding a vision, you are channeling and distilling your energy into a specific creation. The more clear and focused your energy, the stronger the signal will be to the Universe. So you want to be very clear about your motivation behind the vision, be discerning between heart desires versus ego desires, and be very

170

conscious and responsible in how you use the visioning process.

The difference between using visioning consciously versus unconsciously can mean the difference between happiness and suffering. The more that your vision has been influenced by your ego, the more resistance you will experience in the process of manifestation. When you empower ego desires, you are not aligning yourself with your highest good, or the highest good of others, and consequently, there will be less Universal energy available to you during the process of creation. Using visioning in this way will likely result in some form of imbalance in your life or the lives of others.

However, if after extensive inner reflection you are still uncertain as to the motivation behind your vision, then begin the visioning process anyway. By doing so you give yourself the chance to understand from where your motivations are truly arising. It is by allowing ourselves to take missteps that we afford ourselves the opportunity to discover the correct path.

I would suggest creating some form of ritual around the visioning experience in a way that feels good for you. You might consider designating a small section of a room that has any of the following elements; a comfortable place to sit for meditation, soft fabrics, pictures of spiritual teachers (or any one else with whom you feel a strong loving connection to), crystals, essential oils, or other elements from nature such as flowers, branches, or stones. You also may consider lighting a candle, dimming the lights, or burning a small amount of dried sage or incense to cleanse the energy of the room before beginning. Here are the steps for the visioning process:

1. Meditation

Quieting the mind is an essential aspect of visioning. The quieter your mind, the more in-tune you will be with your heart, and the more energy will be made available for your visioning process. So the first step in visioning is to cultivate a strong foundation of meditation in your life. Practice daily and consistently. Keeping your attention on your heart center during meditation will be most effective for moving on to the next step of the visioning process. When the time is right to move to the next step, you will know it. There is no rush, and a certain amount of inner silence before moving beyond this step is very helpful.

2. Ask Through Prayer

Once your mind has become quieted, you can then ask for guidance from your heart about what wants to be created through you, or what you are here to experience in this lifetime. Close your eyes and ask to be shown your heart and Soul's vision for your life. Once you have asked, wait to receive intuition and inspiration. You may receive images, feelings, or thoughts related to your heart's desires. This may not occur on the first, second, or even third time that you attempt to pray. Because many people have been ignoring their hearts for far too long, the heart can be a bit shy in revealing itself at first. Be patient, open, and sincere in your seeking, and you will be given greater clarity and inspiration in the right time.

3. Cultivate Your Vision

As you begin to receive inspiration through the prayer process in the form of images, thoughts, and feelings, keep a journal of what is coming to you. Write out notes about what it is that you are receiving. Repeat the prayer process multiple times in order to gain greater clarity about what is being revealed to you from within. Be open to your vision changing and expanding as you receive more information from within. Holding on too tightly to preconceived notions about what your heart desires can restrict new inspiration and intuition from coming to you. So be sure to maintain an attitude of openness, innocence, and curiosity. It can also be helpful to engage in the following processes as a way to bring your emerging vision even more fully into focus:

-Visualization

Using the inspirations you are receiving, create a 15-30 minute guided visualization for yourself that describes your life as though you have fully manifested your vision. This can either be a written visualization or an audio recording. The visualization should walk you through the day-to-day experiences of living your vision. As you create the visualization keep the following questions in mind:

-what is the feeling of the environment you live and work in?
-What does it feel like to be doing the work you are doing?
-What is the energy of the people around you?
-How are you interacting with others (what is your demeanor and body language like)?
-What is the feeling of the activities you are engaged in when not working?
-It can even be helpful to notice the kinds of foods you are eating, your exercise habits, and any forms of creative or artistic expression.
-What are the overall feeling tones associated with your life in this vision?
-How does your body feel? Do you feel healthy, energized, alive, and radiant?

Try not to get hung up on the material possessions that may be part of your vision, or get too caught up in specific details of the external world in the vision, but instead, really focus on what it actually feels like to be living this vision. Hone in on the feeling tones of what your heart is wanting to experience, rather than the specific people, places, or things associated with the vision. The purpose of this exercise is to generate powerful positive emotions within you as a way to gain clarity, without becoming attached to specific images or ideas about how you think you should be living. As you construct your visualization, focus on creating a powerful visceral experience for yourself, describing colors, textures, lighting, and other feeling tones. The more you can generate powerful emotions of joy, excitement, connection, peace, and happiness during your visualization, the more effective it will be. The following is an example of a written guided visualization:

"I see myself starting my day in nature, breathing in the fresh air, seeing the sunlight filter through the emerald green leaves of the trees, feeling alive and full of energy. I feel connected to the earth, the soft grass beneath my feet. There is a sense of freedom in this moment, a sense of deep peace as I breathe in this refreshing morning air. I am practicing yoga, feeling fit, healthy, and so happy to be alive.

...I see myself now working in an environment with abundant natural light, plants and flowers, warm colors, and a soothing energy in the space. I feel confident and relaxed here, like I can really be myself. I am smiling, feeling playful and happy. As I work, I am surrounded by caring people, doing work that I love. I see myself connecting with others in a genuine way, feeling so grateful for this connection.

...I see myself with my partner now, cooking dinner in the kitchen, laughing and being playful. We are singing while we cook, feeling joyful like children. There is a sense of adventure in the air, like every moment is new and exciting. My heart is so happy, bursting with love and gratitude in this moment, as I look into the loving eyes of my partner.

...I am standing out under the stars now on a warm summer evening, looking back at the warm glow from the home that I live in with my family. I feel so happy to be here, feeling so much joy for this experience. Taking a deep breath I look up into the night sky at all the stars, feeling so alive, so free, and so peaceful."

This is just an abbreviated example of how you might phrase the visualization. You would likely want to elaborate on the subtlety of the experiences you are wanting to capture in the vision. What does it feel like to be with your future partner? How does it feel to hold each other in your arms? What are the subtle nuanced feelings of doing the type of work that fills your heart? Let yourself begin to really feel that which your heart desires, using as many descriptors as possible.

Repeat particular words and phrases that you really resonate

174

with. Don't worry about repeating positive words too much (such as "love," "joy," or "happiness"). What is most important is that you genuinely feel inspired by your visualization, really allowing yourself to generate the emotional energy associated with each experience. So use whatever words and images work best for this purpose.

What is common for many people as they begin engaging in the visioning process, is the arising of intense emotion. Often tears of joy begin flowing, as well as tears of bittersweet sadness. An emotional outpouring is often the result of having suppressed these heart desires for so long, and now to finally acknowledge them can feel intense. It takes courage and faith to embrace your heart's deepest desires, giving voice to your desire for greater love, intimacy, or joy in your life. No matter what emotions arise, sit with them. Allow yourself to cry tears of joy and tears of sadness. This can be an important part of the clearing away process that will ultimately create more emotional space in your life for your new vision to begin manifesting.

The more detailed you can make your vision, the more effective it will be. As you gain greater clarity about your vision, feel free to continually change and update the visualization. This will not mess up the process, but rather fine-tune it, so that you can be more certain about what you are calling into your life. The more you practice your visualization, the more of a reality it will become for you, and the easier it will be for this "new" version of your life to actually materialize.

-Vision Board

Another technique that helps to bring the vision more fully into focus is called a vision board. This is where you clip out images and words that are representative of the inspirations you receive about your vision, and then paste them onto a board. Magazines work great for finding good images, which can then be pasted onto a simple poster board. Instead of looking for specific images, pay attention to how images feel when you look at them, and if the colors, shapes, and textures seem to match with the overall feeling of your vision. You can create different sections of the vision board for different areas of your life; career, family, personal development, hobbies, etc. When you are finished, hang the vision board somewhere in your house where you will see it often. The more vivid and inspiring you can make your vision board, the more positive feelings it will invoke within you every time that you look at it.

4. Match Your Vision

Once you have fine-tuned your vision, it is time to begin embodying this reality more fully in your life now. Really study yourself in the visualization that you created for yourself, observing exactly how you are living your heart's desires. Then begin to emulate the "you" from your vision with the thoughts that you think, the feelings that you express, and the actions that you take. Essentially, you practice being the "you" from your vision in every way. This may feel strange at first, as though you are trying to be someone else. What you are actually doing through this process, however, is letting go of all those behaviors that previously prevented you from truly being yourself.

Though it may feel strange initially, over time you will begin to see the wisdom in the process, letting go of resistance to making the appropriate changes in your life. When you catch yourself thinking, feeling, or acting in a way that is not in alignment with the "you" from your vision, then change your expression. Interrupt whatever it was you were doing, come back to your breath, feel your inner body, and ask yourself, "How would the 'me' from my heart's vision respond in this situation?"

In addition to changing your day-to-day thoughts, feelings, and actions, it may be necessary to make big changes in your life. If you are working at a job that is not contributing in some way to your vision, then it may be time to let it go. If you are not in a relationship that is nurturing your growth and development, then it may be time to let it go. If you are not eating the kind of diet that is supporting your vision self, then it is time to make some dietary and lifestyle changes. If you are living in an environment that is not supporting your well-being and happiness, then it is time to move to an environment that is more conducive to your vision. Let yourself be bold in the changes that you make in your life. By matching your vision you are showing yourself, and the Universe, that you are truly ready to begin living in this new, more expansive reality.

5. *Let It Go*

The final step to visioning is the act of letting go. This is perhaps the most important step in the manifestation process, and is crucial that it really be practiced. Once you have completed the previous steps, it is time to let go of attachment to your vision even manifesting at all. This may sound like a paradox, but it is not. The idea is that the "goal" of achieving your vision is not as important as the quality of your experience here and now. The emotional experiences associated with your vision are truly what your heart desires (not the outcome), and you can begin allowing yourself to have those experience now. As you practice the last step of embodying your vision, you are allowing yourself to start having these emotional experiences now.

By becoming the "you" from your vision, you are beginning to shift the signal you are sending out to the Universe, tuning into the vibration that is most representative of your natural self. This is the law of attraction in action, in that as you begin vibrating at the frequency of your vision, you are synchronizing yourself with the vibration of all the people, places, and circumstances that match your new reality.

Initially it may seem as though not much has changed. In reality, however, there has been a significant internal shift, and it is only a matter of time before the external circumstances of your life begin to match up to that of your vision. And by the time your outer world catches up with your inner world, it will likely seem more or less inconsequential if you achieve the goals from your vision because you will have enjoyed the journey so thoroughly along the way.

Letting go of desire is crucial in this process, because as long

177

as you are in a state of want, then you are holding onto the belief that there is something lacking in your life that you need to obtain in order to be happy. When you focus on desires that are not yet met, you are sending out the vibration of lack, and the Universe can never fully provide you with what you want, because at a fundamental level you don't truly believe that it can be a reality. So begin acting as though you have already manifested your vision. Embody it fully, and let go of needing to see verification in the outer world. It has been said that you can truly only manifest what you already have, not what you want.

If you find that you doubt your ability to manifest the experiences from your vision, or you believe that you are not worthy of your vision for whatever reason, then continue the process of unraveling the ego and limiting core beliefs as described in the "Awakening" section. Often times as we begin moving more fully into our highest expression of love and joy, we are repeatedly faced with deeper layers of resistance and subconscious beliefs that previously had been preventing us from embodying our dreams fully. This is not a failure, but rather a success, in that it highlights the work that needs to be done, and the healing that needs to take place. Honor your process. Let yourself have the space and time to clear away old ego patterns and limiting beliefs, without attempting to cover over these wounds through the visioning process.

Once you are clear in your vision, and believe in it, be very disciplined with your thoughts and feelings regarding your vision. When you are not engaged in the actual visioning process, do not spend idle time thinking about your vision, or trying to work out how its all going to unfold. The "how" is not so important—let the Universe take care of that. All you have to do is stay alert and present, and take the opportunities that will undoubtedly begin to arise in your life as you practice staying focused, patient, and in a state of acceptance.

When you match your outward expression of energy to that of your vision, you have set the wheels in motion, and it is now time to enjoy the ride. This does not mean that you stop working towards your goals in a structured and organized fashion, but it does mean that you continually let go of attachment to the outcome of life

178

circumstances.

The reason that we let go of our attachment to outcome is because the Universal Intelligence is wise, and surprises us time and time again with twists and turns along our journey—unexpected events that are exactly what we need to experience in that moment for our growth. When we go with the universal flow, we allow ourselves to change, expand, and to grow in a way that is in alignment with our Soul's path. The mind does not have access to this greater wisdom. The mind would rather map out exactly how you are going to get where you want to go, and then fight tooth and nail to get there. The heart, on the other hand, knows that the Universe has a bigger plan, and that everything is happening in perfect divine timing.

Letting go means having deep acceptance for whatever is happening around you, continuing to let go of the ego, letting go of the need to control life, and instead, remaining in a state of non-reaction and non-judgment. When one door appears to close, you continually practice having faith that the right door will open in the right time. You let go of trying to make things go a certain way, of hoping things work out in your favor, or of trying to use any force whatsoever to get what you want. If you find that you are feelings stressed, anxious, or exerting force, then let go, return to your breath, and relax. The path of manifesting from the heart is one of allowance, grace, and deep acceptance.

This does not mean that there will no longer be challenges in your life, however. There will likely be many challenges and obstacles that arise as you begin to follow your heart. But now these challenges are experienced from a higher perspective, and you can see that they are there for a reason—to serve your awakening process, helping you to bring more awareness to those parts of yourself that remain unconscious. When a challenge arises, observe how you respond to it. Does it bother you, does it upset you, does it cause you to get anxious? Why would that be, when every challenge is an opportunity to learn and grow? Life would be very boring if there were no challenges and everything went exactly the way that you wanted it to go.

Law of Attraction in Action

The following story is an account of a client's experience using the visioning process to manifest greater happiness and abundance into her life. Ruth had contacted me because she felt depressed, anxious, and as though she was living a meaningless life. She was 45, had health problems, worked at a job she couldn't stand, and lived in a city that she didn't like. Ruth had been living this way for ten years and was beginning to panic that her life would never change. Over the course of our sessions we worked towards first dissolving the ego, clearing away emotional energy from the past, and then focusing on how she wanted to consciously create her life from her emerging sense of empowerment.

Initially it was a challenging road for Ruth, as she held many deeply entrenched beliefs that were limiting her life experiences. But over time, and with focused spiritual practice, her perspective began to shift. She began daily practices that included meditation, a conscious dietary plan, relaxation techniques, and positive affirmations. During one of our sessions Ruth shared with me that she had long held this vision of living in a small town in Mexico, a place that she had previously visited while on vacation. It was so wonderful to hear her speak about a bright future for herself, and she was excited (yet wary) about the possibility of it becoming a reality.

We took this opportunity to use the visioning process to help Ruth tune more fully into this reality that she wanted to experience. We spent one session fleshing out the details of what her vision entailed; the sights, smells, textures, and feelings of what it would be like to live this vision. She saw herself living in this quaint Mexican town, going to work everyday feeling happy and inspired. One of the main elements from her vision was the image of a beautiful courtyard filled with plants, flowers, palm trees, and cats roaming through the environment freely. It was significant to Ruth to be working in a environment where animals were allowed to co-mingle with humans, which signified to her an air of relaxation and casual living.

We recorded a 20 minute visualization that guided her through the process of seeing, feeling, and experiencing all the elements from her vision, allowing her the opportunity to begin experiencing it in her life now. She listened to the visualization dutifully over the course of a few months, and began making changes in her life to match this new version of herself that had emerged in her vision. Over the course of four months she had cultivated the courage to leave her job, and was able to save up enough money to make the move down to Mexico. Yes there were challenges along the way, inner obstacles she had to face, and many opportunities for her to practice holding a more positive view of life, but she did it. Through the visioning process she had cultivated her inner strength, began believing more fully in herself, and had begun shifting the vibration she was sending out by changing her thoughts, feelings, and reactions towards life.

I received an email from Ruth a few months after she moved to Mexico with two photographs attached. One was of her doing a cartwheel on the beach in Mexico, and the other was a beautiful courtyard filled with plants, flowers, and two cats lounging in the sun. Ruth was elated in her email, retelling a story of incredible synchronicity that involved finding a place to live, a job working at a yoga studio, and many wonderful connections with helpful people. And amazingly, the photograph of the courtyard appeared to match the description from her vision almost perfectly. In her email Ruth no longer sounded like the anxious and depressed person that she was when I first spoke with her. Ruth has begun her journey of awakening, and it has brought her new experiences, challenges, joys, and rewards.

Ruth's story is not a unique one. The process of visioning is systematic and can be practiced by anyone. I have witnessed incredible transformations in myself and others through this process. When you begin expressing the energetic vibration of the reality that you prefer (through your thoughts and emotions), the Universe has no choice but to reflect back to you that which you are sending out. From the viewpoint of the mind, visioning seems superstitious and highly improbable—"how could your imagination effect the physical world, or change the course of random events?" The heart, however, knows that your imagination is a powerful tool, and is actually a part of what creates and shapes reality.

Reconnecting With nature

"One touch of nature makes the whole world kin."
-William Shakespeare

What commonly occurs for many people going through the awakening experience is a deepening desire to return to a more natural way of life. To be with nature is to remember that we are not separate, but a part of everything. We are the same consciousness that is being expressed through the animals, the plants, and the earth itself. We are a part of it all, no more and no less important than any other expression of life. Repairing your relationship with nature, then, can also serve to support the awakening process.

The heart rejoices in the process of reconnecting with nature and awakening to the unity among all of life. The ego, on the other hand, cannot tolerate the seeming uncertainty and chaos that exists in nature, and humanity has gone to great lengths to exert domination and control over nature and the earth. Most westernized cultures have become more and more disconnected from the natural world, creating both psychic and physical boundaries around nature in order to separate and contain it. This is reflected in the commonly held perspective of nature as a place to recreate or visit from time to time, rather than the foundation of our existence on the planet. This subtle erosion of our connection to the natural world, however, has had a profound effect on our collective state of consciousness.

Because we have mostly been living in a mind-dominated culture (a sign of excessive yang, or masculine, energy), we have lost touch with the divine feminine aspect of creation—that of the natural world. Logic, reason, and thought driven processes characterize the "modern" way of living, and do not make much space for the intuitive, feeling based aspect of the human experience. This "left brain" approach to living has collectively shut us off from feeling our shared connection with other forms of life and the earth itself. Mother nature is an aspect of the divine feminine energy of creation, and when we try to control and dominate nature, we are ultimately repressing the feminine aspect of ourselves, causing immense pain

182

and suffering for all life on the planet.

To reconnect with nature is to begin integrating more fully the masculine and feminine aspects of the self. While the masculine energy has sought to rise above and remove oneself from nature, the feminine energy is deeply connected to the natural world. Begin noticing in yourself the masculine and feminine energies, feeling for the balance point. See where your mind might be shutting you off from your shared connection with other forms of life, and even from feeling the earth as a sentient being.

Notice areas of your life where you have sought to insulate yourself from the natural world. Yes, some creature comforts are nice, and can make living more convenient. But perhaps you may also notice how the compulsive need for greater comfort or "padding" around yourself (in the form of material possessions and comforts beyond what are really necessary for your health and happiness), can also perpetuate a sense of separation from the natural world. When you have identified excesses in your levels of comfort, be willing to let them go, and see if your life is really any less enjoyable.

Cycles and Balance

Nature expresses itself through cycles, and the more time you spend in nature, the more you will be reminded of these natural cycles within yourself. All of the problems that we believe are so important do not exist in the natural world. In nature there are no problems, only cycles of birth and death, growth and decay. Even if the human race were to drive itself to extinction, decimating much of the natural world along the way, in time, the earth would regenerate and go on. One cycle would end, and another would begin. Though this may sound extreme, holding this expansive perspective can help dissolve much of the fear or guilt that many people may feel in relation to the natural world.

In addition to the natural rhythms of the day, our bodies are synched up with the cycles of the moon and the seasons of the year. If you are alert and paying attention, these cycles can show you much about how to structure your daily routines in order to live in harmony with the earth, and all of life around you. The more attuned you become to the natural world, the more you may notice how good it feels to align with these natural cycles. You may notice how much better your body feels when you rise with the sun and go to bed soon after it gets dark, or how good your body feels when you eat foods that are fresh and in season. Have you ever noticed how your energy seems to withdrawal in the winter months, while you often experience an influx of creativity and inspiration in the spring? There are many people who try to fight these natural cycles, believing that they should be able to maintain a non-stop productive lifestyle, always being outgoing and full of energy. But this is generally not sustainable, nor a very natural way to exist.

Our bodies are meant to express the inward movement and the outward movement in balance, and nature shows us how to do this. You may notice the qualitative difference, for instance, when you create space for inward activities (such as writing, meditation, or listening to calming music) in the evening hours of the day, rather than in the middle of the day. You may notice that on a full moon you have an abundance of energy, while during the new moon you may feel more inward. Of course there are many variables to why we feel the way that we do, and everyone's constitution is different. But the more that you take your cues from the natural world, in terms of how you structure your life and spend your time and energy, the more of a harmonious experience you can achieve.

Elemental Energy

Each of the elements; water, earth, fire and air, are also within each one of us, connecting us to all of life throughout the history of the earth. The same air, water, and matter that constitutes your physical body, was also present on the earth four billion years ago. These elements have been recycled and re-birthed into new forms of life for billions of years. Elemental energy exists in the cells of the body, the food and water we consume, the air that we breathe, as well as the physical processes involved in birth, growth, and decay. Learning the properties of the four elements and how they relate to the mind, emotions, and body can be helpful in awakening this memory within you. You can use the following information in this way—as a reminder of what you have always intuitively known, yet may have forgotten.

The **air element** is the lightest of the elements, and is associated most strongly with communication. Air is associated with the heart chakra, the breath, and with the formless dimensions of creation. Qualities of air are fluidity, openness, clarity, sociability, and the intellect. Air can spread out quickly, and there is a great sense of freedom associated with this energy. A person embodying strong air element might be able to communicate clearly and succinctly, spreading ideas and information easily among groups. However, when air energy is not balanced with other elemental energy, it can create a feeling of being ungrounded or disconnected from the earthly plane, and a person might feel spacey, confused, or unfocused.

The **water element** is that of fluidity, motion and renewal. Water is associated with the second chakra, and creative energy. Water signifies the ability to flow from one emotional state to another. Just as emotions exist in a wide array of expressions, water also exists in different forms. Water is flexible and transmutable, and moves with the changing tide (literally and figuratively). A person with a strong water element may have an easy time going with the flow, being open to suggestion, and overall, be very accommodating. When the water element is out of balance, however, a person may exhibit indecisiveness, confusion, or apathy.

The **fire element** is that of heat, and is associated with spiritual transformation, as well as the biological processes of transformation—such as digestion, growth, and decay. Fire is associated with the third chakra, and fiery emotions such as anger, excitement and ecstasy. Fire gives fuel to the processes of life, energizing the ever-changing flow of life experiences. A person who is fiery might exhibit strong leadership and vision, feeling an excitement for life. When the fire element becomes imbalanced, however, it expresses as anger, resentment, or jealousy, and can become a destructive force.

The **earth element** is that of physical substance, and is associated with security, connection, growth, and feeling rooted. Earth element is the energy of physical matter—the rocks, minerals, dirt and plants—and is related to calmness, patience, and focus. The earth element is connected to the root chakra, which creates a strong foundation for the human experience. A person with strong earth energy is likely able to create many things in the physical world, moving with focus, commitment, confidence, and determination. Earth energy also exhibits as a strong desire for family and nurturing relationships. When out of balance, the earth element exhibits as stubbornness, stagnation, and steeliness.

Making Space For Your Inner Nature

Simply holding an awareness and appreciation of the elemental energies throughout your day, will begin the process of repairing this fundamental relationship with the natural world. You can also create space and time to focus on each element, deepening your firsthand experience of each elemental energy. When was the last time that you thought about your relationship with fire? Try meditating with your eyes open, while looking at a fire or the flame from a candle. Let your mind fall silent while you merge with the flickering flame. This simple exercise will awaken in you more strongly the fire element—that of transformation.

You can meditate on each of the elements to see how the experience reflects back to you deeper aspects of yourself. What is it like to meditate on the sound of the river, or the sound of the wind? How does it feel to meditate on the earth, sitting directly on the ground, feeling the energy of the earth itself? Create some structure around your relationship with the natural world. Give yourself time each day to simply observe the natural beauty and grace of nature. You can do this by sitting with a tree, taking a walk through nature, or simply by pausing to look at the sky when going about your day. The more you are able to get out into nature, the more clarity and perspective you will gain on the human experience.

If you are unable to spend much time outdoors, you may find it helpful to bring nature into your space by having plants in your home or office. Think of the plants around you as friendly beings. And in fact, compelling research from the last few decades has shown plants to actually have feelings, and to be responsive to emotional energy in a similar way as humans or animals. Think of how many times you have felt lonely or sad and were surrounded by plants. Had you been aware and present, you might have felt their healing energy, you might have felt their deeply peaceful company. Stand next to a redwood tree and you will notice a very still and peaceful energy emanating from the tree. This is not your imagination, but rather the subtler spiritual energies being transmitted from one being to another.

Earthing

In addition to the balancing effects that the subtle spiritual energy of nature has on the mind and emotions, there is plenty of research that validates the positive physical benefits of simply being in nature. "Earthing" is a technique (if you want to call it that—in the not too distant past it would have just been called "walking") where a person walks barefoot on the earth, allowing the energy of the earth to harmonize the systems of the body. The incredible effects of earthing have been well documented in dozens of studies ranging from heart disease to Alzheimer's disease. This healing effect is due to the continual flow of electrons moving up through the earth's surface, which flow into the body most readily through direct skin contact with the ground.

What makes electrons so healing is their negative electrical charge, whereas most free radicals have a positive electrical charge (protons). An inflow of electrons into the body, then, has a similar affect as antioxidants, neutralizing the negative impact of protons, effectively protecting the body from harm caused by free radicals. Because most people spend the majority of their time either indoors, walking with rubber soled shoes, or in their car (which is insulated from the earth by rubber tires) the benefits of this natural phenomenon are not being experienced.

A 2013 study on earthing, published in the Journal of Alternative and Complementary Medicine, showed that the simple technique of earthing effectively reduced blood viscosity, a major factor in heart disease. The study examined 10 adults after engaging in earthing for two hours a day. Blood samples revealed that earthing increased the electrical surface charge of red blood cells, thereby reducing viscosity in the blood. There is an abundance of research which demonstrates that earthing reduces inflammation in the body, enhances immune system functioning, improves sleep, and helps regulate the nervous system.

In fact, just having contact with soil may contribute to increased immune system functioning and increased serotonin production in the brain. Researchers from Bristol University, and the University College of London, looked at the effects that common bacteria found in soil had on neural activity. The study, published in 2007 in the "Journal of Neuroscience," showed that a common strain of soil bacteria, Mycobacterium vaccae, increased the production of serotonin in the brains of mice. Simply by having skin contact with soil, the bacteria was absorbed into the blood stream of the mice, increasing the production of the neurotransmitter in the brain. Byproducts of increased serotonin production include elevated mood, as well as increased immune system functioning. Moreover, because serotonin can be found in the gut, brain, blood, and nerves, increased production of the neurotransmitter can help regulate digestion, sleep patterns, and nervous system functioning.

In addition to the benefits of earthing, the hormones released into the air from plants have also been shown to have a similar positive effect on mental, emotional, and physical health. A popular practice in Japan known simply as "forest bathing," involves going into the forest to absorb the beneficial chemicals released into the air from the trees. Researchers attribute the healing benefits of forest bathing to essential oils specific to trees, such as a-pinene and limonene, both of which have antimicrobial and antibacterial properties. Studies on forest bathing show that just being around trees for a few hours can boost the immune system, improve mood, lower blood pressure, and improve nervous system functioning.

The healing effects of nature may sound too good to be true, until you remember that the human body evolved over millions of years in relationship to the natural world, and so of course our health and well-being would be deeply connected to the earth, plants, animals, and trees. It is only in the last few hundred years that we have begun insulating ourselves so thoroughly from nature. So take time each day to connect with nature in some way, and see how it changes your mental, emotional, and physical state for the better.

Conscious Nourishment

The way that we conceptualize the act of nourishment profoundly affects our mental, emotional, and physical health. Many people think of nourishment in terms of the foods they consume, and perhaps the water they drink. In reality, we are constantly receiving our nourishment from a variety of different sources. In addition to food and water, we also receive energy from the sun, the earth, the air, interactions with other forms of life, and from the Higher Source of energy flowing within. Our overall health and well-being is directly related to our relationship with each source of energy in our day-to-day lives.

The reason why it is helpful to cultivate conscious nourishment is because suffering often arises when a person feels depleted of energy. When you feel tired or drained, you often do not feel very loving or have much energy to share, and are more likely to engage in codependent behaviors. This can take the form of turning to comfort foods, entertainment, or other people to "pick you up," when you are feeling low. When you have an abundance of physical energy, on the other hand, you have more loving energy to share with the world. You can empower yourself, then, by cultivating a stronger relationship with the many sources of nourishment that surround you. By doing so, you are learning how to tend to your own inner vibration and state of being in a healthy way.

Energy From Food

The quality and quantity of the Life Energy obtained from the food you eat can have a significant affect on your ability to maintain a clear mind, stable emotions, and vibrant physical health. There are a few different factors of nutrition to be aware of when understanding how best to nourish yourself; the amount of life energy present in any given food, the elemental energy of the food, and the preparation and processing of food.

-Living Foods

Every type of food has a certain amount of Life Energy. Raw vegetables and fruits, for instance, contain the highest amount of Life Energy, whereas foods that have been dried, cooked, or processed contain far less. Fresh and raw foods also contain an abundance of digestive enzymes, which aid in the digestive process. When a person's diet consists largely of foods that are not "alive," the body has to work much harder to digest these foods, while the pay off is far less. It takes more work to digest these foods, and less energy is obtained through the process. Cooked foods, baked goods, grains, and meat all require significantly more energy to digest than fresh, raw vegetables and fruits. Over time this digestive stress can deplete the body of its energy reserves, causing internal stagnation and disease.

The mind and emotions also often become imbalanced when the body is chronically depleted of Life Energy. The more depleted a person is, the less control they will have over their thoughts, emotional reactions, and subsequent actions. A lack of self-control makes negative mental and emotional states much more likely, often leading to suffering. When the body is receiving plenty of vital energy from living plant sources, however, the mind is sharp, the emotional energy is often positive and balanced, and a person generally feels light and full of energy.

-Elemental Energy

Each type of food contains energy from each of the four elements; earth, water, air, and fire. The body is constantly seeking a balance of its elemental energy, and you may notice how the foods that you are drawn to change over time, depending on the seasons of the year, the people with whom you spend a lot of time with, and your emotional experiences. This is not something you need to necessarily monitor or think about, however. Simply being aware of elemental energy in the food you consume will allow you to notice more closely the relationship between what you eat, and your state of being. As you become more sensitive towards the energy of food, you will naturally gravitate towards the healthiest foods for your constitution, in the proper quantity, and in the right moments that your body requires them.

In general, foods that grow close to the ground or beneath the ground, such as carrots, potatoes, beets, and squash, will have greater earth element. Fats and oils also contain abundant earth energy. Foods that contain higher amounts of water, such as fruits, or the stalks of green vegetables, will contain more water element. Foods that grow higher into the air, such as fruit, leafy green vegetables, or stalk vegetables, will posses greater air element, while the fire element is most readily found in food sources coming from animals, such as meat, eggs, or dairy, as well as spicy foods such as garlic, ginger, or cayenne pepper. Of course, all foods contain some of each element, but can typically be classified by the elemental energy that is most dominant within it.

Your body is wise and knows what it needs. The body holds much more wisdom than the mind when it comes to nutrition, and needs to be trusted. When you actually let go of constantly trying to eat the healthiest foods, or trying to stick to a specific diet (such as vegetarianism, veganism, paleo, or raw), and instead, listen to the ever changing and evolving needs of your own body, you can more easily stay in balance without all of the effort and headache of micromanaging your diet.

Just as foods have dominant elemental energies, so too do people. You may have noticed how some people generally feel more grounded and rooted, some people more fiery and emotional, while other people more fluid and light. Everyone's constitution is different, and each person's Soul has chosen to be born into a body with a particular energetic and physical constitution based on what the Soul desires to experience in a given lifetime. Finding the right diet for you, then, entails understanding the needs of your body, honoring your unique constitution, and eating accordingly.

It is good to be aware that the physical body and emotional body are constantly absorbing elemental energy from many different sources, food being only one source. When you spend time with a person with strong earth energy, for instance, you will begin absorbing the earth element through the emotional energy exchanged during social interactions with this person. You may notice that after spending a lot of time with a person exhibiting strong earth energy, you also begin feeling the earth energy more fully within you. Your body, then, may gravitate towards foods with greater water, air, or fire energy in order to balance out the earth energy for the needs of your personal constitution.

But again, this is not something you need to monitor or think about, but rather, just something to be aware of. The wisdom of the body naturally guides you towards the foods that will keep you in balance. This is why it is extremely helpful to let go of the idea of having a certain type of diet. As soon as you commit to eating only vegetarian, only vegan, only raw, or any other preset dietary practice, you limit the wisdom of your body to gravitate towards the foods that you actually need. There is no formula for the perfect diet, but rather a process of fine-tuning your intuition, whereas you begin to feel the energy of your food, and feel what your body needs at any given time.

A great way to tune into the needs of your body is to open your refrigerator or pantry and just gaze upon the food available to you. As you do, notice which foods your body naturally feels drawn towards. You can do the same process when shopping in the grocery store. Be very honest with yourself while you do this, for there is a significant difference between the foods that your body is actually drawn to, versus the psychological and emotional cravings that would have you eating sweet and fattening foods at every meal.

If you are not sure what foods your body truly needs, consider doing a muscle test on the food. One of my favorite ways to do this is to simply hold a piece of food in front of my heart, and then ask my body, "does this food serve my health at this time?" If I feel an energetic pull towards the food, then it is an indication that the food is what my body needs. If I feel energetically repelled away from the food, then at that moment, that food is not what my body wants. Feeling nothing at all is an indication that, either way, that particular food is neutral, and won't be detrimental to my health at that time. The success of this technique comes down to intention and practice. Repeat the process many times until you get a clear answer.

What you may notice when you look at the culture at large, is that most people are not really listening to their own body's needs, but rather eating the kinds of foods that are being consumed by the people around them, or consuming the diets espoused by health gurus, spiritual teachers, or friends and family. But how could anyone else know what your body needs better than you? You are as unique as each one of the stars above, and only you can know what is best for you.

And so it may be necessary to unravel and dissolve much of the conditioned familial and cultural habits you may be holding regarding your diet, before you reach the point where your body speaks clearly about what it really needs. You may also need to expose yourself to new foods, such as sprouted foods, fermented foods, and different types of fruits and vegetables than what you are currently accustomed to, in order to get more familiarity with what your body actually needs.

And because many people have an adversarial love-hate relationship with their body (we appreciate the body when its healthy and has energy, yet become frustrated with it when it gets sick, tired, or puts on weight), it may be necessary to tend to any unresolved emotional baggage that you may have towards your body. Consider making amends with your body by using positive affirmations daily, such as, "I love my body for all the wonderful experiences it has provided me," or "I love every cell in my body for giving me this gift of life."

-Consciously Preparing Food

The energy that goes into creating, preparing, or processing food also gets transferred to your body when you consume it, and so it is wise to be discerning from where you buy your food. Ideally, we would all be growing the majority of the food we put into our bodies. In the event that you cannot have a garden, research responsible and humane farms in your area, striving to buy local and organic. If possible, develop a relationship with local farmers so that you can get a sense of the energy that is going into the food that you will be eating.

If you are eating meat, be particularly aware of the energy of the farm in which the animal was raised. When animals are mistreated or neglected, that negative energy can easily be passed on to you when you consume the meat of the animal. And of course, you certainly don't want to be supporting a company that increases suffering to any living creature, which is why organic, grass-fed, and free-range production are all essential. Organic and grass fed are good labels, but I have found that these labels have become less reliable over the last decade. Its best to do your own research, and in the case of meat, ideal to visit the farm and see for yourself the conditions in which the animals are living.

Your energy and intentions, as well, have a profound effect on how your body absorbs and assimilates the Life Energy from your food. Be conscious to remain in a peaceful or positive state while preparing and consuming your food. Avoid cooking for yourself or others when you feel agitated, anxious, or any other negative state. Be mindful of how you handle and treat your food. Is it a means to an end, or can you feel the divine and sacred energy of the food as you prepare and consume it? Before eating, consider spending a moment being present with the food, either saying a blessing, or just acknowledging that you are grateful for the nourishment the food is providing. When you bless your food, it blesses you back with the gift of increased vitality and health.

When a person becomes accustomed to an energetically and nutritionally deficient diet, the body can become overloaded with toxic residue. Chronic toxicity in the body makes the mind sluggish, contributes to negative emotional states, drains physical energy, and can eventually cause disease. Fortunately, the process of cleansing the body through detoxification and diet can reverse much of the damage caused by chronic toxicity. Healing the intestinal lining, detoxifying the body from chemicals and heavy metals, and integrating a healing diet into your life can mean the difference between a calm and happy disposition, versus chronic pain, negativity, and suffering.

The last section of this book entitled, "The Holistic Healing Process," contains all of the information, practices, and techniques required for healing the mind, emotions, and body. Although, it is good to remember that no matter what your physical condition, you always have the option and the ability to transmute suffering by coming back to the present moment and bringing acceptance to what is. Maintaining a healthy diet and lifestyle make it easier to do this, however, and by doing so, you are also honoring the sacred vessel that is your body.

Energy From the Water

Water is alive and conscious, and the quality of water that you regularly consume can have a significant affect on your state of mind. There is a big difference between water coming out of the earth, versus water coming from the tap (even if it is purified water, such as water from reverse osmosis or distillation processes). When water flows through the earth it becomes energized by the magnetic field of the earth, and also collects minerals as it travels through the ground and over the rocks. Earth energy is profoundly important for human health, and creates the feeling of being grounded that each one of us needs in order to feel anchored in our bodies and in the physical world. Considering that the human body is over 60% water, imagine how the quality (or consciousness) of the water in your body would affect your mental, emotional, and physical experience.

In addition to the water you drink, bathing in fluoridated water that has long been removed from the underground aquifers of the earth, does not have the same electrical charge, nor does it bring your body the same vitality and sense of aliveness that living water does. If at all possible, find a local river or lake in your area where you can periodically "recharge" through soaking or swimming. Large bodies of water contain an abundance of negatively charged ions, which your body will happily absorb. To search for a local spring in your area where you can obtain fresh spring water, reference the website, www.findaspring.com. Collect water in glass jars for drinking (rather than plastic), being sure to sanitize them on a regular basis with natural products. The energy of the water you drink and bathe in becomes your energy, and when it comes from the earth it provides pure, alive, and radiant energy to you.

Energy From the Earth

Earth energy anchors us in this physical world, providing stability, increased intuition, and support. Anytime we feel lost or confused, we can always turn to the earth for divine guidance, and a reminder of our true nature. In addition, the earth literally energizes the human body through direct skin to earth contact. You can nurture your relationship with the earth by spending more time in nature. Connect with the energy of the earth simply by closing your eyes and holding the intention to feel the earth's presence. Standing barefoot on the ground, or sitting on the ground can help foster this connection

Remembering your relationship with nature can energize and support the process of awakening, igniting the memory of our ancient roots on this planet. There have been times throughout the history of humanity when cultures have maintained a strong connection with the divine aspects of nature, and humans walked on the earth lightly, joyfully, and in harmony with all of life. We are collectively in the process of returning to that way of living now, but this time with more wisdom, and with greater love than ever before. Our relationship with the earth and sun are our primordial relationships, and by nurturing them, we can dissolve much of the feelings of separateness that perpetuate suffering.

While most people experience relationship challenges with

their human parents, the divine father and mother (the sun and earth) are always here for us, and by creating a relationship with them, you can learn to feel at home in this physical experience no matter what your circumstances, or the environment that you find yourself. The sun is always sharing it's light with us, while the mother earth provides energy for all forms of life on the planet. These two beings work in loving synergy together to continue the cycles of life on the planet.

By keeping the earth and the sun in your awareness throughout your day, you offer your gratitude to these divine beings for sustaining life, which also maintains your psychic and emotional connection with them. Being out in the sun, and acknowledging the sun as a healing energy source creates a very loving energy in your mind and body. It may seem insignificant, but your intention to stay connected to the celestial mother and father of the human experience can actually make a profound difference in your life.

Energy From the Sun

Many people take the sun for granted, not fully realizing how much life energy it provides for all living beings on the planet. In addition to supplying all of the plants on the planet with fuel, the sun also directly energizes the human body. The body utilizes the energy from the sun by absorbing it directly through the skin, using this energy to create essential vitamins and nutrients that cannot be obtained very easily from other sources.

While spending time out in the sun is generally a very healthful practice, most people in the U.S. have been conditioned to believe that even moderate sun exposure is dangerous. Surprisingly, much of the fear around excessive sun exposure directly causing cancer is unfounded. While there has yet to be a single study that definitively connects excessive sun exposure to increased risks of skin cancer, there are, ironically, studies connecting excessive sunscreen usage with various types of cancer.

Though sunscreen may not be very healthy for you, you also

don't want to overdo your time in the sun either, and so a good rule of thumb is to gradually increase your time in the sun in order to allow your body to adjust. Start with 20 minutes a day, spending more time in the sun as your intuition guides you to do so. However, try to avoid sunbathing when the sun is high in the sky, but rather, in the morning or late afternoon. As you soak up the healing rays of the sun, feel gratitude for the energy and presence of this powerful being of light.

Energy From the Air

The air is filled with Life Energy, which is measured in the physical world as negatively charged ions. You can access this energy to balance and heal your body through conscious breathing. Indian yogis and Chinese Taoist masters understood the power of the breath to cultivate greater health and well-being, and there are plenty of resources on different breathing techniques available (beyond what I cover in this book) that may be helpful for you. My experience, however, has shown me that simply being aware of the breath, and implementing a few basic breathing patterns throughout your day, can make all the difference in your mental, emotional, and physical health.

The potency of Life Energy in the air (also known as prana, or chi) depends on the quality of air in your environment. Environments where there is an abundance of plant life and large bodies of water tend to contain the highest concentration of negatively charged ions. The areas surrounding rivers, lakes, and oceans, for instance, will contain a higher concentration of negatively charged ions, as compared to regions with less water. In addition, the short wave electromagnetic radiation from the sun creates negatively ionized particles in the air, particularly around large bodies of water.

Conversely, environments devoid of plant life will contain far less negatively charged ions (such as in big cities or deserts), which is one reason why you may feel more drained after spending extended periods of time in urban environments. Air pollutants such as exhaust, smoke, or dust, all take the form of large polymolecular ions, and generally carry a positive charge, thereby negating the healthful effects of the negative ions in the air.

Other factors that compromise air quality are closed spaces where air-flow is restricted, and environments with recycled air (such as planes or automobiles). Metal also tends to strip air molecules of their negative charge, which is why it is common to experience fatigue during or after driving or flying.

According to Chinese Taoist theory, the underlying principle that governs how much Life Energy is available in any given location is related to the relationship between yin and yang energy. It is well established that an electrical field exists between the earth and the atmosphere. This field consists of a positively charged atmosphere (yang) and the negatively charged earth (yin). In western science, the difference in polarity is termed the "potential gradient," which refers to the difference in voltage between the two energy fields. The greater the difference in the potential gradient, the more chi exists in that area.

For instance, the more plant life, water, and open space that exists in an area, the more negatively charged the air close to the surface of the earth becomes. This higher concentration of negative ions allows for a greater charge to build between earth energy and atmospheric energy, increasing the potential gradient. This causes chi to flow more strongly, increasing the availability of Life Energy to all forms of life in that particular area.

If you cannot get out into nature for exercise and deep breathing each day, consider investing in a commercial negative ion generator for your home or office, which will increase the quality of air that you breathe on a daily basis. Oxygen is life, and effects our state of being in a profound way. Breathing good quality air can increase energy, improve concentration, alertness, stamina, and mood.

But remember, just as important as the quality of air you breathe, is your conscious awareness of your breathing process. When you pay attention to the prana in the air as it flows into your body, you feel more alive, vibrant, and connected to life around you. The air that you breathe is the same air coming from the forest, the earth, the ocean, the animals, and the atmosphere. In a certain sense, all of life is sharing the same breath.

Emotional Energy

An often over-looked form of nourishment is the inflow of energy that occurs through the exchange of emotional energy between people. Every time that you interact with another person, you are giving and receiving your life energy with that person. When a person is unconscious of this process it often leads to feeling drained or overextended during social interactions. However, social interaction, when engaged in consciously, can nourish all involved, and is an essential form of energy for each human being.

To engage in social interactions consciously, simply notice your own energetic state, and make your priority that of taking care of yourself first, before extending yourself to another. By honoring your inner energetic state you can remain in balance, allowing yourself to give and receive emotional energy with others effortlessly. Be aware of how much time you are spending with others, and pay attention to when it becomes too much. Conversely, notice times when you have been alone for extended periods, and how that makes you feel. Notice the subtle balance in your life between healthy time alone and healthy social interaction.

There is nothing you need to do in terms of nourishing yourself with emotional energy, except to be aware of this natural phenomenon occurring as you socialize. Just notice how good it feels to exchange emotional energy with others during conversation and social interactions. If you notice yourself becoming drained, return to taking care of yourself in whatever way you may need to, feeling your breath and inner energy field.

Positive emotional energy naturally flows when both people are relaxed and open. As you share your energy with others, also stay alert to moments when it no longer feels productive or uplifting to do so. There is no need to get over enmeshed in another person's experience once the emotional energy exchange doesn't feel positive or productive. This doesn't mean that you stop being there for friends and family when they are in need of support, but rather, make it your priority to tend to your own emotional health and well-being before tending to the well-being of someone else.

Universal Energy

Each one of us also receives our energy from the Universe in the form of loving energy flowing from within the heart chakra. This energy increasingly flows through us the more we dissolve the ego and commit to being a vessel for loving energy. We do this by making the commitment to use our mind, emotions, and body for positivity and love. When we do, we will find that we have access to a never-ending reservoir of energy. It is quite profound to notice how draining it feels when working towards the selfish desires of the ego, and conversely, how energizing it feels when giving your time and energy for the upliftment of others.

There are some days where I have spent the whole day working, engaging in positive and uplifting activities, and find that by the end of the day I feel so happy, and am buzzing with energy. It takes time and practice to integrate this way of being into your life, but by holding the intention to live this way, it will begin to create a container in your life to experience a deeper connection to the Universal Energy.

If you find that you feel drained throughout your day, pay attention to the moments preceding feeling drained. What were your thoughts and desires? What were you feeling? How were you perceiving life in that moment? And then investigate how you could shift your thoughts, feelings, and perceptions of the situation to be more loving, more compassionate, and more accepting. The paradox is that tuning into the Universal energy often requires learning how to tend to your personal needs first. By truly loving and honoring yourself, you are honoring God, which creates more room in your life to become a healing force in the world.

It is through acceptance, forgiveness and love that we dissolve selfish desires, and connect to the Higher Energy. Offer gratitude to all life experiences, and all that you are given in each moment. Know that your Soul is on a journey that is being held by the loving energy of the Universe, and the more that you relax and accept every situation, the quicker you can work through past karma, becoming a divine channel for loving energy.

Conscious Fasting

Fasting, when performed with loving intention, can be a powerful vehicle for increasing self-awareness, dissolving the ego, and purifying the body. The process of fasting, however, is a much deeper practice than simply refraining from eating food. You can use the process of fasting from many different stimuli (such as sex, social interactions, or technology, for instance) as a way to gain a deeper understanding of your relationship with the material world in your everyday experience. By removing specific stimulus from your life for a period of time, you allow yourself the opportunity to see more clearly the mechanisms of the ego, and how the mind works.

One of the foundational aspects of the ego is addiction itself, and by fasting, we can observe the subtle attachment and fear that exists within our minds in relation to the physical world. Many people use the physical world (food, sex, money, and material possessions) to appease and comfort the psychological and emotional anxiety of separation from the Universal connection. Using the physical world in this way actually prevents a person from connecting more fully with the energy of the Universe. The more attachment we have to the experiences of the physical world, the less open we are to receive the abundance of loving energy that exists beyond the world of form.

Ultimately, as a person becomes more awakened, the world of physical forms can be enjoyed in all its facets with little to no attachment. But until a person untangles themselves from attachment to the world of form, the physical world will always be a source of fear. The reason for this is that when a person uses experiences or physical forms to comfort oneself, there exists an awareness that at some point that "thing," whatever it may be, will ultimately leave their life, jeopardizing their sense of safety, identity, and happiness. As you face this fear head-on during the practice of fasting, you will gain greater inner strength, confidence, and connection to a Higher Source of energy. By letting go of attachment to the forms in your life, redirecting your attention to the energy field within, you experience yourself beyond the world of form, as the energy of consciousness itself.

I would suggest brief periods of time fasting in the following areas; food, sex, social interaction, as well as entertainment and technology. Do so, however, only if you genuinely feel curious or inspired by the idea of fasting. The specifics of how to fast from various stimuli will be different for everyone, and are best left to your intuition. However, fasting from food (water fasting) is the one area where specific guidance and support may be needed so that you do not cause yourself harm.

For a water fast be sure to start off slowly, with a half-day fast one week, followed by a full day of fasting the following week. You can work your way up to 2 or 3 days of water fasting, depending on your health and personal constitution. Go slowly, being sure to drink plenty of purified water, giving yourself adequate time and space to be in a relaxed environment where you can be introspective and reflective. The final section of this book, "The Holistic Healing Process," contains detailed instructions for the process of water fasting, and can be referenced before attempting to fast from food.

For the process of fasting from any element of your life, the same general guidelines can be applied. Any time you have a thought or compulsion related to that which you are fasting from, simply bring your attention back to your breath, relax your body, and feel the energy within your body and your heart. By redirecting your attention to your inner energy field, you are retraining your mind to receive energy from the Source within first, rather than from the outside world.

You may experience strong compulsions to engage in other stimulus as a means of distraction, and so you can practice redirecting your attention inward in these situations too. For instance, when fasting from sex (celibacy) you may notice a strong compulsion to eat comfort foods such as sweet, salty, or fattening foods. In these moments, simply pause, bring your attention back to your breath and body, and feel the energy within.

You can also engage in a more proactive form of purification by using a simple energy healing technique. When a compulsion arises take your attention to your breath. As you inhale feel the healing energy of the earth rising up through your feet and root chakra, reaching your heart chakra at the peak of your inhalation. As you exhale, feel your heart purifying this energy, allowing the energy to descend back down through your body and down into the earth. Imagine this energy being received by the earth to be recycled and reused for the highest good of all. Breathe gently and softly, without exerting very much control over the flow of breath. Allow it to move naturally and fluidly on its own.

You may find yourself intuitively beginning a fast without much planning, or it may feel better to engage in some kind of preparation. Honor whatever process supports you best. When planning for a fast, be sure to communicate with the people in your life, letting them know what you are doing and why you are doing it. Setting an intention before a fast, and periodically repeating your intention (in the form of a mantra, or through writing), can be extremely helpful in keeping you focused on your objective.

Try Using an intention such as, "I allow the love of the Universe to flow into every cell of my body," or, "I am purifying my mind, emotions, and body with every breath." You may find that it is helpful to create structure around your fasting experience, deciding on a specific duration of time and specific parameters for your fast. Keep a journal of your experience, keeping in mind that there is no goal to attain, but rather it is the learning that takes place through the process that is the focus.

Fasting, however, is best performed when a person is intuitively guided to do so, rather from the belief that you should fast in order to be more spiritual. If you feel inspired, excited, or curious about the idea of fasting, then it is a good indication that it will be helpful along your spiritual journey. If, however, you feel overwhelmed, frightened, or anxious about the idea, it might not be time for you to attempt a fast. Or, you might feel a combination of both excitement and fear, which may indicate that starting off gradually will best support your process. In either case, do not let the feeling of "should" creep into your decision making process. There is no one path towards awakening, and what works for one person may not be what your Soul needs in this moment for your growth. Always trust your intuition, and always listen to your heart above all else.

Balancing Yin and Yang Energy

The following are generalized examples of both balanced and imbalanced yin and yang expressions. It is important to remember that everyone contains both masculine and feminine energies within, which are constantly seeking to exist in harmony and balance with one another. Apply the following information to your own life in order to see where you may be out of balance in regards to either your feminine or masculine energy.

A balanced masculine expression may best be represented by the father archetype. This is the father figure who is loving, focused, disciplined, and values logic and reason in his decision making processes. This masculine expression allows for action to be taken in the world with confidence, clarity, and determination. The masculine moves methodically, with patience, and an even tone. He uses rational thought processes, creates structured routines, and is unwavering in his commitment and ambition to manifest his goals. The masculine embodies healthy control, the needs of the individual, healthy boundaries, and is able to co-create with others for the highest good of all. In the family constellation, the masculine creates the container for the family to grow, providing the many physical requirements needed for survival.

When masculine energy is expressed in excess, however, it becomes a destructive force. Too much yang energy results in becoming disconnected from one's emotions and feelings, preventing one from feeling their connection to life around. This results in a steeliness of thought and action, insensitivity, and a coldness towards others. The capacities of logic and reason become excessive, causing one to lose touch with the bigger picture, and one's part in the web of life. Imbalanced masculine energy leads to an overactive mind, over analyzing, and judging life circumstances. An emphasis is placed on quantity over quality, on creating for the sake of creating, rather than as a means of improving the quality of life.

Anger, frustration, agitation, aggressiveness, and being overly controlling are all earmarks of excessive yang energy. When the masculine is imbalanced, one seeks to control other forms of life, obsessing over the details of life. From this place of imbalance it is common for fear and resistance to surface towards the seemingly chaotic and unpredictable creative energy of the feminine. What the masculine is truly seeking, however, is to return to balance with the intuitive and feeling capacities of the feminine.

Balanced Feminine expression may best be represented by the archetype of the mother. This is the nurturing mother who is compassionate, loving, kind, and understanding. The feminine values emotions and feelings in her decision making process. Intuition is the guiding force for the feminine, who deeply feels her connection within the web of life. The feminine is flexible, fluid, and able to move with the ever changing currents of life. Feminine energy is focused inward, and has access to the creative energy from the Universe, providing inspiration for the masculine act of creation. The feminine is the bridge between the spiritual realm and the manifest world of form. This is reflected in the act of childbearing (literally bringing spirit into form), as well as being a bridge between family and community members, bringing people together for the purpose of sharing, growing, and greater connectivity.

An excess of feminine energy, however, can lead to becoming over emotional, often resulting in drama and irrational behavior. Logic and reason become trumped by feelings, which can lead to superstitious thought processes, doubt, worry, and anxiety. Imbalanced feminine energy results in a loss of healthy boundaries between oneself and another. Excessive inward reflection often leads to stagnation, feeling lost, hopeless, overly sensitive and powerless. From this sense of powerlessness, it is common for jealousy, anger, possessiveness and depression to arise, as well as the tendency to give one's power away to others.

Becoming manipulative, overly calculating, and deceptive are also common earmarks of excessive feminine energy. From this place of imbalance, fear and resistance often arises towards the seemingly restrictive and controlling energy of the masculine. What the feminine is truly seeking, however, is the structure, order, and rational approach of the masculine.

An indication that you are losing balance between your yin and yang energy is the moment of any arising negativity within you. This negativity can take the form of stress, anxiety, depression, anger, frustration, or boredom. As soon as you feel any negativity in your experience, it is a wonderful opportunity to notice what thoughts or beliefs you are holding which may be repressing either your masculine or feminine energy. There is no need to analyze or monitor how much yin or yang energy is being expressed through you, but rather, it is an opportunity to feel into each moment, holding the intention to find balance between these two aspects of the Self. There is an art to finding balance, which can allow you to return to a state of wholeness and unity consciousness.

Finding Balance with the Breath

One of the most effective ways to begin rebalancing your energy is through the breath. Whenever you find imbalance arising in the form of negativity, return your attention to your breath and inner energy field. Begin by identifying if you are experiencing either excess yin or yang energy, and how the imbalance is affecting your mind, emotions, and body. Pay particular attention to how you are breathing, and the subtle feelings in your body.

When experiencing excessive masculine energy, you will likely find your breathing has become heavy or strained, and you may feel tension or agitation in your body and energy field. If this is the case, then consciously begin taking deep, slow, and relaxed breaths. Relax your body, allowing yourself to become fluid and soft. It may help to shake various parts of your body in order to release any excess tension. Take this moment to truly let go, to surrender your desires in the moment, and your need to control the circumstances of life around you. Feel the peace and calm that arises within you as you do this process. Nothing is more important than returning to peace.

Often times this will be sufficient to integrate more feminine energy into your experience. However, sometimes you may need to shift your focus to other activities that will allow you to continue relaxing and letting go. Meditation, walking, creative projects, journaling, listening to music, or just sitting in peace and observing the natural world around you, are all effective ways to tune into your feminine side. But more important than any particular activity, is your intention to connect to your feminine energy. Give yourself permission to feel the softer, gentler, and more intuitive side of yourself. Slow yourself down and just be for a few minutes. Let your intuition guide you, releasing attachment to your agenda for the time being.

In moments when your feminine energy has become dominant, notice how you are breathing, and the energy in your body. You may notice your breathing has become shallow, and you feel drained or depleted of energy. In these moments take the opportunity to either stand up or sit up tall, bring your chest up, and drop your shoulders back. Then begin taking deep full breaths. If you are standing, it can help to start moving your body. If you need to remain sitting for whatever reason, simply contract and release the various muscles in your body in order to get the blood flowing.

Continue taking deep, activating breaths. Smile, look around, and get engaged in life around you. Ask yourself how you can focus your attention in a productive way that will be nourishing for you and others. Get active, organized, and focused. Bring some structure into your experience by focusing on a goal and then working towards completing it. Physical exercise, a work project, socializing, or cleaning are all great ways to integrate more masculine energy into your experience. But again, the activity is not as important as your intention. So really focus on feeling that empowered, confident and assertive part of yourself, and then don't hesitate to take action.

The Art of Play

While the adult mind is an expression of the masculine, yang energy, the childlike innocence is an expression of the feminine, yin energy. A powerful way to invite the divine feminine more fully into your life, then, is by connecting with your inner child through play. Play transforms the serious adult word into a fun adventure, and opens the door for magic to unfold in your life. While the adult mind can get bogged down with the minutia and details of life, to the child every moment is new and exciting, an opportunity to explore and have fun. The child is open, innocent, loving, ever present, creative, playful, and is an essential aspect of the Self. Do you remember the last time you built a fort or played make-believe? When was the last time you rolled around in the grass, or got really silly and laughed hysterically for no reason at all?

Create some time in your day to engage your creative childlike nature by being silly, illogical, impractical, and totally childish. Allow your heart to truly guide you into this playful realm of magic. If you have access to children of friends or family members, consider setting up a play-date with them. This may seem counter-intuitive or pointless to the spiritual seeker, but it is actually a very powerful way to transform your life and connect with your heart. Look at how serious a person can get about spiritual growth and the idea of "enlightenment," losing touch with the whole purpose of spiritual growth, which ultimately is to be happier, more joyful, and have more fun in life.

Notice how much unadulterated fun children have when they are playing and engaged in fantasy. Children are alive, happy, and exuberant when they are living in a world of their own creation; using their imagination to fight dragons, explore uncharted lands, and create magic. It has been said that "when you play, reality turns to clay," and your construct of reality becomes more malleable, adjustable, and open for discussion. Imagination and play are a form of alchemy, shifting your perceptions of life so that everything becomes lighter, more fun, and much more exciting.

You can either be silly and play by yourself, or find a play partner. Reaching out to a friend with the intention of being playful is a wonderful way to deepen and enrich your connection. The idea is to get out of your head, and enter into the more fluid space of creativity and spontaneity, which you may recall from that faraway magical realm called "childhood." Time slows down in that realm, there's no agenda, no planned activities, just people hanging out, talking about the clouds, watching the ants crawl around in the grass, or making silly sounds. When you decide to let loose and play, anything can be fun.

Try playing "make-believe," where you become different characters for a while. Put on a costume. Walk around on all fours. Howl like a dog for a bit and see how that feels. Roll around on the ground and stretch like a cat, that should be pretty fun. Jump over things, spin around in circles, skip. Skip rocks. Rock, paper, scissors. Cartwheels are great. Somersaults are also fun. Rope swings for sure. Remember running through the sprinklers? How about a slip 'n slide? One word: playdough. Two words: thumb war. Three words: hide and seek. Freeze tag works in a pinch too. Don't forget about building a fort with pillows and blankets, that is absolutely essential. If this all sounds incredibly ridiculous to you, then you should probably stop reading right now and go watch a Disney movie. I would suggest "The Little Mermaid," "Aladdin," "Beauty and the Beast," or one of my favorites, "Tangled."

Other creative expressions such as painting, poetry, dancing, creative writing, acting, singing, and making music are also wonderful ways to tap into the power of your imagination and play. Any activity that gets your creative juices flowing will ultimately be beneficial along your spiritual journey because it allows you to embody more of your true nature, as a creative being. Whether you're playing like a child, or creating some form of art, what is most important is to put down your analytical mind during the process. If a thought arises such as "this is silly," follow it up with the thought, "yeah this is silly, and its great!" and continue on. Yes, it may feel awkward at first to try and play after such a dry spell. You may feel self conscious or uncomfortable trying to be playful, and so you'll have to get past all that. Keep at it, and you will get over the hump. Be okay with other people thinking you look ridiculous, are wasting your time, or are being foolish.

If others are judging you for being playful, it is likely they have yet to uncover the powerful alchemy of play in their own lives. Even if on the surface others react to you as if you're crazy, the act of you being silly and playful might just awaken within them the memory of their own inner child. It may be that a light dusting of your fairy magic is all that is needed to stir the embers of creativity and play within the heart of another. And what gift could be more invaluable to another than the divine reflection of their own childlike innocence.

As you practice play throughout your day you may notice it spreading to other areas of your life. You may find yourself singing while at work, being friendlier with strangers, laughing more with your partner or friends, and just being more playful in general. Remember, wherever you focus your attention (in this case, play) it will energize that experience more fully in your life. So when you focus on being playful, you will find that your life becomes filled with playful moments. And what you may also find is that being playful is actually a very responsible, mature, and logical way to be. The reason is that because the more playful you become, the happier you feel. And the happier you feel, the more productive you become, and consequently, the more empowered you feel. Yay for play!

The Art of Structure

Having adequate and appropriate structure in your life balances out the feminine energy of play with masculine, yang energy. Structure creates a container to allow your life to be filled with the magic, creativity, and love of the feminine principle. Without structure there is nothing to contain the creative energy that you are cultivating and calling into your life. If your heart is the doorway to being more playful, your mind, then, is the tool for implementing structure into your life. Discipline, commitment, focus, and linear and logical thought processes all go hand in hand with living in a structured and organized way, balancing out the childlike energy in your life.

Take the time to understand what kinds of experiences you actually need in order to feel balanced and happy, and then provide a structured routine to give yourself these daily, weekly, and monthly experiences. Having a daily routine of spiritual practices such as meditation, yoga, and deep breathing exercises, as well as an ongoing self care routine that includes conscious exercise, conscious nutrition, and areas of self development, will all enrich your life tremendously.

In addition to personal and spiritual growth, having career

goals and/or creative projects that you are working towards will help keep you grounded in the physical world, keep your mind focused, and help expand your consciousness by giving yourself new experiences. Learning new skills and absorbing new knowledge can empower you along your spiritual path. Without an ordered and organized life there is no place for expansive spiritual experiences to occur. After all, we are here to bring the light of consciousness more fully into the earthly realm, not to lose ourselves in the cosmic spiritual ether.

In my life this has meant creating daily schedules for myself, allotting a certain amount of time for each task, setting timers to keep myself on track, and making organized lists of what needs doing and when to do it. This may sound counter-intuitive to the idea of being present and in the flow. But actually the two align perfectly. Exerting control over oneself through conscious structure is absolutely healthy when it is supporting your growth, expansion, and well-being. Structure actually allows you to sink more deeply into the present moment. When you know there is a container for the experience, you can more fully let go into it, being fully present, rather than becoming preoccupied with other things. Often when we don't have enough structure in our experience it creates anxiety and fear about the future.

Living a structured organized life also just feels really good, and so the "payoff" is in the experience itself, not in trying to get to somewhere in the future that is more satisfying than the present moment. If you find that you are becoming stressed, overly controlling, or anxious on account of too much structure, it is a sign that the ego has returned. If this occurs, simply drop whatever you are doing and rest in the present moment. It's only when we get stuck in our head, trying to exert unnatural control and structure over ourselves, that we begin to suffer as a result of repressing some part of the Self.

Before you create loving structure in your life, however, it is important to first dissolve the ego, which will allow you to begin tuning into the greater themes of your Soul's purpose. If you are not clear about what your Soul's desires are for your lifetime, then return to meditation, mindful-awareness practices, and the visioning process. Working to dissolve the ego first is essential in understanding how to apply structure into your life in a healthy way. Otherwise, you will end up repressing and controlling yourself from a place of anxiety and fear, rather than empowering yourself from a place of love. And as soon as the structure in your life starts to feel restrictive rather than expansive, it is time to be flexible with the structure, using your intuition to restructure your schedule and routine for a more balanced experience.

The awareness of one's yin and yang energy is a lifelong investigation, becoming more subtle and nuanced as one progresses on their journey. There is no goal to attain through this practice, other than greater peace and empowerment in each moment. Your willingness to stretch yourself by engaging in new thoughts, feelings, and behaviors will bring about the quickest transformation. Often times when engaging in new behaviors it can feel unnatural. And though integrating these two aspects of yourself may feel unnatural at first, over time, you will come to see that living in balance between your masculine and feminine energy is truly the most natural way to live.

Neural Reprogramming

One common stumbling block on the path to awakening is the experience of mental and emotional patterns that seem almost carved in stone. While the effects of ingrained habits in the mind can sometimes seem insurmountable, they are not. When you are focused on becoming the conscious creator of your life, you absolutely have the power to rewire your neural processes. The neural pathways that are responsible for what we experience as habits have been learned, and with some effort and practice, can be unlearned as well. By changing how you use your mind, as well as employing some simple techniques for rewiring the brain, you can begin effectively dissolving old patterns that cause suffering, and replace them with positive and uplifting thoughts, emotions and behaviors.

In addition to the biological and chemical aspects of

neurological processing, exist the underlying changes in one's energetic field. One theory regarding this is that the right hemisphere of the brain is connected to the yin (feminine) aspects of our energetic expression, while the left hemisphere is connected to the yang (masculine) expression. Along this vein, many spiritual traditions place an emphasis on creating balance between the two hemispheres of the brain as a way to regain wholeness and energetic homeostasis between the masculine and feminine energies within.

When a person is either described as "left brained" or "right brained," it is in reference to the hemisphere of the brain that is most active within a person's day-to-day life. The left hemisphere is where the logical, practical, and linear processes occur, while the right hemisphere is where the creative, non-linear, intuitive, and spacial processes occur. It is believed that by increasing the communication between the two hemispheres, a person can achieve a greater sense of balance and wholeness within. There are a few powerful techniques for balancing the two hemispheres of the brain.

Pranayama is one such technique, discovered by yogis thousands of years ago. Without the aid of science, these ancient mystics intuitively knew that the hemispheres of the brain could be trained to stay in balance using certain techniques, the breath being one such tool. The theory of pranayama is that the two hemispheres of the brain mainly communicate via a flat band of neural fibers called the corpus callosum. This band of fibers is responsible for sending information between the two hemispheres of the brain. The corpus callosum also behaves like a muscle, in the sense that it can be strengthened to increase the efficacy in which neural signals pass through.

The process for strengthening the corpus callosum is relatively simple, and is reflected in the practice of Pranayama. Essentially, each hemisphere is responsible for processing information that is received from the opposite side of the body. For instance, sensory input on the left side of the body is processed in the right hemisphere of the brain, and vice-versa (although, research now indicates that both sides of the brain actually become activated during most neural activity, with one side predominately active in any given moment). By alternating sensory input from the left and right side of the body in a systematic way, the corpus callosum receives a work-out, having to handle the increased work load of electrical signals as they pass back and forth between each hemisphere of the brain.

You can appreciate this phenomenon of increasing communication between the hemispheres of the brain if you've ever observed an extremely "right brained person" or "left brained person" in action. Often times the person seems stuck and rigid in their way of life. The stereotypical image of a "left brained person" would be that of the brainiac. He or she may be a master of logic, information, and reason, but has little capacity for empathy, feelings, or creativity. Compare this image to that of the right brained "artistic hippy," who is incredibly creative and intuitive, but cannot stay organized or keep an appointment.

Ideally, we can develop and integrate both the masculine and feminine expressions fully in our lives, being able to use the mind for completing tasks, learning skills, staying organized, while not losing touch with our creative, receptive, and intuitive capacities. Creating greater neural elasticity allows for a balance between the right and left hemispheres of the brain, and aids in the formation of new neural pathways. The following techniques can help you master that balance through increasing your neural activity.

Pranayama

In the pranayama practice (also known as "alternate nostril breathing") a person holds the left nostril closed, while only inhaling through the right nostril. At the peak of the inhalation, the person then covers their right nostril, simultaneously releasing their left nostril, exhaling only through the left nostril. The next inhalation occurs through the left nostril. At the peak of this inhalation, the left nostril is once again covered, while the right nostril is uncovered, allowing the person to exhale through the right nostril. The process is then repeated for 5-10 minutes at a time.

Because the function of breathing in each nostril is connected to the opposite hemisphere of the brain, each hemisphere becomes activated alternatively with each breath, causing the corpus callosum to increase it's capacity and "strength," while it allows for more information to fluidly move between the two sides of the brain. This technique takes practice and time to see the benefits. This is a great breathing practice to integrate into your morning routine, and I suggest trying it for at least a month to see positive results.

Binaural Beats

Another wonderful tool for increasing inter-hemisphere communication in the brain is an auditory technology called binaural beats. This technology was developed in 1839 by Heinrich Wilhelm Dove, and utilizes frequencies of sound to strengthen the corpus callosum in a similar way as pranayama. The audio technology involves playing two tones of sound that have a slightly different frequency into the right and left ear simultaneously.

For example, a tone of 300 hz might be played into the right ear, while a tone of 305 hz would be played into the left ear. Because the frequencies are similar, yet not quite identical, the brain sends the signal to the opposing hemisphere of the brain, attempting to synthesize one auditory experience. But because the frequencies are not the same, the signal gets repeatedly sent across the corpus callosum, resulting in a strengthening of the neural band of fibrous tissues. Information (and energy) is then able to flow more fluidly between the hemispheres of the brain.

In addition, the difference in frequencies used in binaural beats is believed to entrain brainwaves into a meditative state. In the example above, the two frequencies of 300 hz and 305 hz, have a differential frequency of 5 hz, effectively entraining brainwaves to this frequency. It is believed that this can produce meditative and healing effects in the brain and body, depending on the frequency used for brainwave entrainment. There have been numerous studies on the effect, little of which has been validated by the greater scientific community at large. Having consistently listened to various binaural beat audio tracks over the course of many years, I know from personal experience the positive effect this audio technology has had on my cognitive functioning and process of integration.

Binaural beats can be listened to during meditation or before bed for 30-40 minutes at a time. It's important to listen to high quality binaural beats, and I would recommend audio tracks by the company Holosync, or the work of Dr. Jeffrey Thompson. Be sure to listen to these audio tracks on stereo headphones that have both a left and right audio output (otherwise the audio technology will not be effective).

Visualizations For Relaxation

Performing regular visualizations for relaxation is a wonderful way to retrain your mind and nervous system to be in a peaceful state, which lends itself to the process of spiritual growth. Because chronic anxiety and stress have become a social norm, the body and nervous system have learned to adapt to these elevated stress levels, keeping a person habitually tense. When the tissue and muscles of the body are tight and contracted, it restricts the flow of energy in the body and emotional field. The process of awakening is about allowing more subtle spiritual energy to flow through you, and primarily occurs through the process of conscious relaxation. When you let go of ego-based thoughts, what you are really doing is just relaxing.

There is abundant research on the efficacy of visualization, showing that the body cannot fully differentiate between an imagined event and a real one. In the classic study of the effects of visualization on basketball players, three groups of players were observed in order to see the effects that visualization had on their ability to shoot free throws. The first group practiced shooting free throws for 20 minutes a day. The second group only visualized shooting free throws, but were not allowed to actually practice. The third group served as the control group, neither visualizing nor practicing. The results showed that the group that visualized improved nearly as much as the group that actually practiced. This type of study has been replicated numerous times in many different contexts, demonstrating the powerful ability of the mind to create real change in our experience through visualization.

A simple visualization that you can do begins with a few minutes of deep and slow breathing (to get your body into a relaxed state), followed by bringing your attention to your heart. Imagine a healing white light filling your heart with each inhalation. As you continue to feel your heart filling with white light, see the intensity of the light increase with each in-breath, and expand with each out-breath. So as you breathe in, the light gets brighter, and as you breathe out, the light expands to fill more of your body. Relax your body with each breath, taking slow, deep, and even inhalations and exhalations.

Stay in this state, breathing light into every cell of your body for 10-20 minutes. Visualizing this light will create a container for you to begin feeling these subtler healing vibrations more deeply. It's not that you are creating a fantasy of the light within, but rather, you are using your imagination to visualize what truly is there, but cannot yet be perceived very fully. The imagination serves as a doorway, allowing you to begin feeling these subtler energies within.

Another variation on this visualization is to imagine you are standing in a meadow encircled by a grove of your favorite trees. See yourself in the center of this ring of trees. As you stand there, feel the circle filling with a healing white light emanating from the trees and the earth itself. Feel the light become distilled to form an orb around your body. As you breathe, take deep and slow breaths, allowing yourself to relax with each exhalation. Breathe the white light into every cell of your body. As you breathe out, feel your body releasing and letting go of any impurities. Let these impurities flow down your body, down through your feet, and back into the earth. On the inhalation, once again breathe in white light, and on the exhalation, breathe out the impure energy.

Both of these visualizations will help retrain your nervous system to be in a state of relaxation, allowing the light within to flow more easily. Learn to relax by making it a priority in your life. Find a recorded visualization that you can listen to that feels natural, uplifting, and inspiring. Remember, your mind and body cannot tell the difference between an imagined event and a real one. So practice, and practice often. I offer many recorded visualizations on my website, which can be found at holistichealth-counseling.com.

Using Your Non-Dominant Hand

This may seem like a relatively insignificant technique, and yet research shows that people who use their non-dominant hand during day-to-day tasks increase the volume of their corpus callosum, effectively increasing inter-hemisphere communication in the brain. A study examining the brains of musicians showed that musicians who used both hands to play their respective instruments had, on average, a nine percent increase in the size of their corpus callosum, as compared to people who predominately used their dominant hand for tasks. Research shows that using the non-dominant hand increases activity in both hemispheres of the brain simultaneously, whereas dominant hand usage tends to only activate one side of the brain.

In addition to strengthening your corpus collosum, using your non-dominant hand also reinforces mindfulness. When you are continually performing tasks using your non-dominant hand, it is like relearning the task all over again, and a higher degree of awareness and attention is required to perform the task. In this heightened state of awareness, you are much less likely to engage in unconscious behaviors in other areas of your life.

Consider using your non-dominant hand for many of your day-to-day tasks, such as brushing your teeth, using utensils, opening doors, using the mouse of your computer, picking up objects, shaking hands, and even writing. You may find it difficult at first, but over time it will become like second nature. As I began this practice many years ago I noticed some interesting changes. Though the effects were subtle, the overall sensation was that of doors opening in my mind. I had the recurring experience of slight and subtle shifts in how I perceived situations, and a general feeling of expansiveness.

Try Something New

Every time that you have a new and unique experience the brain has to process new information. By consistently giving yourself new experiences, you keep your brain on its toes, growing new neural pathways all the while. A constantly changing and evolving lifestyle will make it much easier to let go of the ingrained patterns and habits that often lull a person into less conscious states. This does not mean that you cannot have rituals or repetition in your life (both of which are important for a sense of grounding and rootedness), but merely that you are open to new experiences and challenges entering your life on a regular basis. Learning a new skill, taking up a new hobby, changing your diet, traveling, or even just taking a new route to work, will all contribute to increasing neural elasticity, aiding in your overall spiritual growth.

You can integrate new experiences into your life in a systematic way by allotting time for yourself each week to try something new. Pick one day of the week to take a dance, yoga, or art class, to go somewhere new, volunteer your time for a good cause, or anything else that feels inspiring and exciting to you. While most people experience some form of trepidation or nervousness about attempting something new, it is this heightened state of awareness that contributes to stretching the brain and expanding your sense of self. By giving yourself a new experience, you not only give your brain a workout, you provide yourself with the opportunity to uncover more facets of your divine nature.

Meditation, Intention, and Positive Thinking

Though I have already written on the importance of these practices in previous sections, it is useful to remember that in addition to increasing your moment-to-moment happiness, these techniques also have a profound effect on the neural activity in your brain. When you choose to have a positive thought you are literally rewiring your brain, making positivity a more likely outcome in the future. Research shows that holding a positive thought for at least 10 seconds initiates the formation of a new neurological pathway in the brain, effectively dissolving old mental and emotional patterns.

Use positive affirmations and intentions to keep your attention focused in a way that feels uplifting and positive to you. Write notes to yourself with uplifting phrases or words and post them around your living or work space. Take a moment before starting your car to repeat a peaceful reminder to yourself such as, "I choose peace and relaxation." Before eating each meal of the day, offer some words of gratitude to your body or food. Before you go to sleep at night, review your day, focusing on all the positive aspects and experiences. When you make your state of being your priority, your brain has no choice but to catch up with you.

Sound Healing and the Chakras

Cymatics is the study of how sound waves affect physical matter. The origins of cymatics can be traced back at least a thousand years to African Shamans, who would commonly sprinkle sand upon vibrating drum heads as a means of divination. Though the roots of cymatics are ancient, this phenomenon was first formally documented in 1680 by the English scientist, Robert Hooke. Hooke observed that when he ran a bow along a glass plate covered with flour, the flour created geometric patterns in response to the vibration. These studies were then expanded upon by other researchers, such as Hans Jenny, who observed that when the sound frequency changed, it brought about a change in the geometric patterns created by the particles on the plate. If you've ever seen videos of cymatic demonstrations, you know how amazing and visually stunning the patterns created by sound can be. It's incredible to watch as a metal plate of dancing particles organizes itself into increasingly complex geometric patterns as the frequency of sound changes from one tone to another.

The theory behind cymatics is that frequencies of sound act as an organizing principle of physical matter, including the cells and tissues of the human body. Research conducted at Oxford University in 1972, by the biophysicist Dr. Colin McClare, showed that frequencies of vibrating energy were roughly one hundred times more efficient in creating physiological changes in a biological system, as compared to chemical signals such as neurotransmitters or hormones.

The implications of these findings in the world of metaphysics and alternative healing have led to the creation of sound therapy and color therapy, both of which utilize frequencies of sound and light as a means of bringing order to mental and emotional systems of energy. The idea is that every thought and emotion that a person creates exists as a small burst of energy. The human energy field, then, is constantly being affected and changed by a person's habitual mental and emotional reactions. If sounds and colors are cohesive bundles of energy containing the ability to organize matter, or at least influence the vibration of other sources of energy, then they might effectively be used to harmonize the energy systems within a human being.

This theory might best be encapsulated by the idea of resonance, whereas two frequencies of sound are played together with slightly different tones. The phenomenon of resonance causes the weaker tone to become harmonized to the stronger tone. When a tuning fork with a pitch perfect C is played alongside an out of tune piano, the slightly off C note of the piano will begin to vibrate along with the tuning fork at a perfect C note.

The principles of sound and light healing utilize the phenomenon of resonance to "tune-up" a person's mental, emotional, and even physical energy systems. But you don't have to go to a sound healer to reap the benefits from this natural and simple occurrence. You can explore sound healing for yourself. Try striking tuning forks with specific notes, holding them close to certain parts of your body in order to see what effect it has on your mental and emotional state. Singing bowls and crystal bowls are also wonderful tools for exploring the world of healing vibrations.

Your own voice may be the most powerful way to balance your energy system. Have you ever noticed how singing to yourself often feels soothing? Every time you open up your voice and sing, you are expressing the unique vibration of your Soul, a sound unlike any other in the Universe. And it is my belief that the cells within our body respond most powerfully to our own voice, given that every part within shares the same Soul signature sound. So explore singing and chanting different tones in order to shift the energy within your body and emotional field. With any sound healing technique, keep your attention on the vibration that you feel in your body, take deep and slow breaths, and continue the process for at least 20-30 minutes, providing yourself adequate time to feel the effects.

Balancing Chakras Using Sound

Sound healing is often used in conjunction with a particular intention focused on dissolving energetic blockages in the body. Before imbalance manifests as physical disease in the body, it first occurs as an energetic blockage, often experienced as mental or emotional turmoil. When energy becomes blocked, it prevents the whole system from working in harmony, and can eventually lead to physical illness. By "tuning" up the energy centers of the body through sound and intention, you can keep your body healthy and vibrant.

The chakra model is a system for working with the various energetic centers of the body, and is an aspect of Ayurveda—the holistic medical system developed in India over the course of thousands of years. According to Ayurveda, there are seven main chakra points in the body, each associated with different emotional energies and systems of the body. The chakras are where the subtler spiritual energy from the Universe flows into the human energy system, fueling the emotions and physical body. Chakras are commonly described as spinning wheels or vortices of energy.

In addition to the seven main chakras, there are hundreds of secondary chakras within and around the body as well. Below is an overview of the main chakras, including the commonly associated emotions, colors, and sounds for each chakra. This information is meant to spark a memory within you of what you may always have been aware of. But don't let these descriptions of the energetic centers limit your experience of them. Practice taking your attention to the various chakras to see how they feel first-hand.

First Chakra: The first chakra can be felt at the base of the spine, and is known as the root chakra. This energy center is what grounds you to the earth, and is where your most basal instinctual emotions can be felt, such as those relating to survival. Qualities relating to the first chakra are vitality, connection, courage, and confidence. The color associated with the first chakra is red, and the tone is LAM.

Second Chakra: The second chakra is roughly located in the pelvic area below the bellybutton. This energy center is related to creativity and sexual energy. The energy in this chakra governs how your creative energy flows into your life and the world around you. Qualities relating to the second chakra are joyfulness, creativity, and movement. The color associated with the second chakra is orange, and the tone is VAM.

The Third Chakra: The third Chakra is located in the solar plexus, right below the rib cage, and is related to your personal power. The enegy of the third chakra governs the strength of your will, having clear and healthy boundaries, and your ability to manifest in the physical world. When the energy coming from the third chakra is aligned with their heart and the greater will of the Universe, a soul will feel on their path and have great meaning in their life. Qualities associated with the third chakra are power, assertiveness, courage, and healthy self-esteem. The color associated with the third chakra is yellow, and the sound is RAM.

Fourth Chakra: The fourth energy center is the heart chakra, and is located slightly to the right of your physical heart. The fourth chakra governs your ability to feel your connection to life around you, to feel open, compassionate, and loving for yourself and others. This chakra relates to relationships with others, as well as the divine source of love that is God. Qualities of the fourth chakra are balance, peace, joy, compassion, and unity. The color associated with the fourth chakra is green, and the tone is YUM.

Fifth Chakra: The fifth chakra is located in the throat, and is associated with clear and honest communication. This chakra is where your truth is expressed, where the vision of your heart and Soul is made manifest through sound and the vibration of your voice. Qualities of the fifth chakra are self-expression, communication, clarity, and wisdom. The color associated with the throat chakra is blue, and the tone is HUM.

Sixth Chakra: The sixth chakra is located in your forehead, slightly above and between your eyes. Known as the "third eye," the sixth chakra governs over intuition, knowledge, and insight. The sixth chakra is where you shape your version of reality using your perceptions and mental energy. Some qualities of the sixth chakra are imagination, intuition, integration, wisdom, and clarity. The color of the sixth chakra is purple, and the tone is SHAM.

Seventh Chakra: The seventh chakra is on the very top of your head, and is known as the crown chakra. This is where your personal energy system unites with the divine energy of the Universe. The seventh chakra is associated with spiritual connection, unity, wisdom, integration, and mastery. As a person's awareness expands, so too does their energy field. This spiritual energy fills each chakral center, expanding over time. When the energy system has expanded sufficiently in all other chakras, the energy fully opens the crown chakra, creating a permanent connection to the divine energy of the Universe. The color of the seventh chakra is violet and the tone is OM.

You can use sound to harmonize your energy centers by chanting the tones associated with each chakra: LAM, VAM, RAM, YUM, HUM, SHAM, and OM. Begin by sitting upright, feeling your breath, and sinking into a meditative state. As you relax your body with your eyes closed, bring your attention to each chakra, slowly chanting the sound of each tone. Begin with the first chakra, toning the sound LAM. Feel the vibrations of the tones resonating in each chakra, harmonizing and balancing the energy there.

Continue chanting the tone of each chakra one at a time until you begin to feel a shift, expansion, or opening within the energy center. This may take a few minutes, or it may take longer, depending on how well you are able to keep your attention on each chakra. The more you are able to focus your attention, without becoming distracted by thoughts or outside stimulus, the more effective it will be. This technique will be most effective if you use it on a regular basis.

You can also meditate on the chakras without using sound simply by keeping your attention on each chakra for a period of time. Blockages in certain chakras may be felt as physical discomfort in that part of the body, or you may experience emotions arise, such as sadness, grief, or anger. This is a normal part of balancing the energy in your body, and no matter what arises within your consciousness while meditating, simply allow it to be there. Allow the emotion to subside while returning your focus to the present moment, your breath, and your awareness of the chakra. In this way, you are helping to release and dissolve whatever emotional energy is being held in that chakra and the body. It takes patience to see the shifts in your overall energy system by working with individual chakra points, but is well worth the time and effort.

Heart Centered Communication

There is an art form to communicating from your heart in a way that promotes empathy within yourself and others. This is a simple technique based on a technique created by Marshal Rosenberg in the 1970s called "Non-Violent Communication." Rosenberg worked with prison inmates, observing that almost all conflict arose from miscommunication and misunderstandings between people. By learning to communicate in a clear and straight forward way, it opens up the channels for greater empathy and understanding. In the process outlined below I use the same general format that Rosenberg originally created, but have modified it slightly in order to make it more appropriate for those on the spiritual path.

There are essentially four steps to the process: 1) Observations, 2) Feelings, 3) Needs, and 4) Requests. Whenever any conflict arises between you and another person, you can use this process to resolve the issue in a peaceful way. Before you even begin the process, however, be sure to bring your attention to your heart, relax your body, and feel your breath. Once you have found your center, begin the first step.

1) Observation

The first step is to clearly identify what has just occurred that resulted in conflict or tension between yourself and another, and then express this observation to the other person. When making your observation be sure to stick to the facts, stating exactly what you noticed, rather than making accusations. Be objective and unbiased, as though you were a detective at the scene of a crime, keeping your observations simple and straightforward. One or two sentences will usually be sufficient.

Lets use the example of a romantic relationship where one person felt hurt by the comments of the other person. When stating what you observed, avoid biased interpretation such as, "you were being totally mean to me today like you always do." Instead, say something like, "I noticed that you called me lazy today while we were cleaning the house." Be as specific as possible, using non-dramatic language, and avoid using absolutes such as "always," "never," "completely," or "totally."

Before stating your observation it can be helpful to review the preceding event in your memory to see whether or not you may be holding some bias or emotional charge towards the event. Be honest in your assessment, taking responsibility for where your own ego may be clouding your perceptions of the situation. It helps to speak slowly and deliberately, choosing your words precisely and consciously. Once you have stated your observation, take a moment to breathe, relax, and bring your attention to your heart before moving on to the next step.

2) Feelings

Now is the moment to tune into how you feel. While Rosenberg uses many feeling descriptors, I have found that the negative emotions associated with most conflict can be distilled down to essentially five feelings; either sad, afraid, hurt, confused, or uncomfortable. These feelings are easily identifiable for most people, with the exception of the last descriptor, which has a bit more nuance than the others. The last feeling of "uncomfortable," would be the feeling of when an experience does not resonate with your personal Truth, or does not feel in alignment with what is right for you in that moment. An example might be someone repeatedly hitting on you at a social gathering. At a certain point it may be necessary to tell that person that you feel uncomfortable with their behavior.

Take a moment to notice which of these five feelings you experienced during the conflict, and then use an "I" statement to communicate this to the other person. Perhaps you felt two of the five feelings. Continuing with the previous example, it might sound something like, "I felt hurt and confused when you called me lazy."

Ideally, you will have already connected to your heart, relaxed your body, and dissolved any inner negativity before communicating how you felt, and so you will be speaking peacefully and compassionately. However, we are human, and this is not a perfect process. Work to find your inner peace, but don't discount your need to express yourself or address conflict in situations even when you may still be feeling emotional. If, however, your emotional reaction continues to escalate during the interaction, then it is imperative that you give yourself time to calm down. Focus on your breath, feel your heart, and relax. You may need to remove yourself from the situation in order to calm down. If this is the case, simply explain that you need some personal space, and would prefer to talk about it at a later time.

When speaking your feelings, keep it simple. One or two sentences will usually suffice. Oftentimes, the more succinct and straightforward your statements are regarding how you feel, the more powerful your words will be. Once you have communicated how you feel, return your attention to your breath and your heart, relax your body, and move on to the next step.

3) Needs

Your "needs" are what you require in order to continue relating or working with the other person in a healthy and harmonious way. This is another area in which I depart from Rosenberg's technique. I have found that many of the needs people believe they have are actually artificial needs stemming from the ego. To express an ego need to another person will potentially perpetuate codependency rather than ameliorate it, and so it is wise to be very discerning in how you identify your needs. Honestly ask yourself what you need in a moment of negativity or conflict. Likely you need to feel safe, connected, and ultimately, you need to find your own center, your own source of love within (which cannot be provided to you by anyone else). Many times your need will simply be, "I need to feel safe," or, "I need to feel loved."

Oftentimes it can seem like you need another person to meet your need if you are to feel love within. In the example of being called a name by your partner, you may be tempted to say "I need you to stop calling me names," or, "I need you to respect me." Though these can feel like legitimate needs, they often arise from a place of defensiveness and ego. The more you can keep the focus on your needs, irrespective of the other person's behavior, the more empowering this style of communication will be.

To work towards the goal of self-empowerment, then, ask yourself what it is that you truly need in the moment to continue creating a positive experience for yourself. "I need to know that I am in a respectful relationship," "I need to feel like I can trust the people that I am close with." This is a subtle distinction in wording, and yet profound in how you conceptualize your healing process, as well as your intentions for moving forward in your life as an energetically autonomous person. You are acknowledging what you need for yourself in your life, rather than what you need from another person.

4) Requests

The last step of the process is to make a request. This step is not always necessary, however. In situations of an interpersonal nature, for instance, simply expressing your observation, feeling, and need will be sufficient. Allow the other person to come to their own conclusion about how to move forward, rather than trying to influence them in some way; "will you agree not to call me names anymore?" There is nothing wrong with making this kind of request, and it is absolutely a legitimate approach. However, it can easily lead into codependency when you start making requests that infringe on another person's free will or self expression. Allow another person to make their own decisions about how they treat the people in their life. The purpose of this style of communication is to empower you through identifying and expressing your feelings and needs, rather than as a means for trying to influence or change another person.

In situations of a logistical nature, however, such as how to coordinate the completion of tasks between people, or the specifics of living or working with another person, it can be very helpful to express requests in concrete terms; "will you communicate to me beforehand when you change your plans?" "Can you make sure to always lock the door when you leave the house?" These kinds of requests are practical in nature, let the other person know exactly what you need, and are usually necessary to keep life flowing smoothly for all parties involved.

When expressing your requests to another person, it is important not to expect the other person to actually meet your request in any way. When you expect others to fulfill your needs, it opens the door for codependency, and ultimately, disempowers you from stepping more fully into your own power and truth. If another person happens to help you get what you need, than it is a wonderful blessing, but never something that should be expected from another. Though this may sound contradictory, the idea is that the purpose of expressing your requests is simply to empower yourself (irrespective of whether you actually get your needs met), as a way to help you identify your truth, and then to voice it. Simply by stating your needs and requests, you send a powerful message to the Universe that your needs are important in your life.

Drop expectations of others, and watch as the Universe begins to arrange the circumstances of your life so that you have the opportunity to get your needs met, often in unexpected ways. You must be an active co-creator in this process, however, taking the opportunities when they arise, which may mean letting go of certain relationships or circumstances in your life in which your needs were not previously being met. Every time you identify a need and express it (without trying to hold others accountable for meeting your needs, or having attachment to getting your needs met in specific ways), you are learning to consciously co-create with the greater Universal Intelligence.

So the completed phrase to express from our previous example might be, "I noticed that you called me lazy while we were cleaning the house. I felt hurt and confused when you called me lazy. I need to know that I am in a respectful relationship, and that I can trust those who are close to me." When speaking, take deep slow breaths, feel your heart, and relax. If the other person becomes defensive, or accuses you of being too sensitive, do the process again, "I hear that you think I'm being too sensitive. I feel hurt by this comment. I need to know that my partner honors my feelings." Stick to the process no matter how emotional or upset another person might become.

Empathic Listening

One important aspect of heart centered communication is deeply listening to another person, and then reflecting back to them what you heard them express. Once a person has expressed their feelings or needs to you, take the time to really absorb what it is they were communicating to you. Put yourself in their shoes, and see the situation from their point of view before responding. When you do respond, do so in an unbiased way, reflecting as accurately as possible what you just heard them say. Reflect back with a statement such as, "I hear that you are really upset right now and need your space," or, "I hear that you felt hurt by my behavior and want me to behave differently in the future."

When reflecting back to another person, check in with them to see if you got it right; "It sounds like you felt somewhat disrespected in this situation, is that right?" The idea is to take the time to deeply understand where another person is coming from before attempting to respond. Often times we formulate stories in our mind about how another person must be feeling based on our own interpretations of a situation, without taking the time to look at it from the perspective of the other. By opening yourself up to see multiple angles, you open the door for greater empathy to occur, both in yourself, and others.

It can often take time and patience to implement this new way of communicating. Be easy on yourself, and don't be afraid to make mistakes along the way. It is through our mistakes that we find the right path for ourselves. Hold the intention to use the process with integrity, speaking from your heart, rather than using this technique as a form of manipulation. Communicating honestly from your heart may initially feel very uncomfortable or awkward. But allowing yourself to be vulnerable in this way is one of the most empowering ways to transform your relationships for the better.

Ecstatic Practices

Ecstatic practices have long been used in many cultures around the world as a means of shifting a person's consciousness, and expanding one's awareness to encompass a greater reality. While there is no specific formula for how to enter into an ecstatic state, there are a number of elements that create a suitable environment for letting go and expanding one's consciousness. Ecstatic practices typically involve moving one's attention out of the head and down into the body. The sacred vessel of the body is one way in which these higher states of consciousness can be accessed, usually through some form of repetition. This repetition can occur through making (or simply listening to) repetitive sounds, or engaging in some form of repetitive movement.

A common ecstatic practice in the Sufi tradition, known as Sufi whirling (or Sufi spinning), involves practitioners spinning for hours in worship of the Creator, eventually achieving altered states of consciousness, bliss, and ecstasy through the ritual. The Shakers, a 17th century branch of Protestant Christianity, were known to engage in hours of shaking their bodies as a means of elevating their state of consciousness. Similar practices of shaking exist in tribal societies in Africa, India, and the Middle East. Kirtan (or devotional singing) is another form of ecstatic practice, whereby practitioners repeat various names of God for hours through singing and chanting, which is believed to help dissolve the ego and create an opening for greater divine connectivity.

Laughter yoga is another example of an ecstatic practice that can shift your consciousness relatively quickly. The practice begins by spontaneously laughing. Initially, the laughter is contrived. What occurs over the course of a few minutes, however, is that the fake laughter turns into real laughter, causing a domino effect of positive emotions for all those involved. Research shows that the physiological benefits of fake laughter and real laughter are essentially identical, and that the body cannot differentiate between your intentions when you laugh. Very quickly you can find yourself in a very ecstatic emotional state. The longer you practice, the more energy builds, and the more expansive the experience can become.

In my experience, ecstatic practices can help us tune into the larger reality of Oneness that we are all a part of, and can facilitate the integration of this larger reality into everyday life. By getting out of the head and allowing yourself to let go for a while, the personal self falls away, making space for the Universal Self (or Higher Self) to emerge. Feelings of ecstasy, bliss, and oneness with the Universe are commonly experienced in the ecstatic state, which can last for hours or days, depending on the depth of the experience.

Once you have personally felt the expansiveness that often accompanies an ecstatic state, the everyday reality that most people consider "normal," often no longer seems so real or compelling. To feel this discrepancy can be a bit unsettling at first, but ultimately is a step towards liberation from the limitations of such a narrow version of reality that most people are accustomed to.

In order to tap into the ecstatic state, begin by finding a practice that feels inspiring to you. Whether it is devotional chanting, ecstatic shaking, or something of your own invention, what matters most is that you feel intuitively guided to do it. Once you have decided upon an ecstatic practice that feels good to you, create some space and time in your schedule to give yourself this sacred experience. Wear comfortable clothes, make sure the space is suitable for the activity, and then let yourself go.

The key is to use your breath to keep your attention down in your body. When a thought arises, come back to the breath and relax. It may be helpful to keep your eyes closed, or to deliberately shake parts of your body to keep your attention focused within the body. If you feel self conscious, simply smile and "shake it off." Keep reminding yourself that the altered state accessed through an ecstatic practice is an age-old human expression, one that has only recently been covered over and forgotten in the last few centuries of modern living. You can reclaim this sacred form of expression by being committed to letting go for a time. Stay present with your inner experience, and the feelings and sensations that arise within you as you engage in this repetitive form of devotion.

Release the need to analyze or judge what you are feeling, and instead, let go into the experience, accepting whatever you feel. Stick with the practice, doing it much longer than is "reasonable," or "logical" by your mind's standards (1-2 hours will usually be sufficient to begin shifting your awareness). It is usually when you surrender your need to control your experience that the breakthrough occurs in this practice. Keep your body relaxed, be conscious to take deep, slow breaths, and enjoy yourself. Although unfamiliar to many, ecstatic practices are powerfully transformative, and can expand your experience of yourself and of reality.

Part IV
The Holistic Healing Process

"To keep the body in good health is a duty...otherwise we shall not be able to keep the mind strong and clear." -Gautama Buddha

Overview

The body is a sacred vessel for energy and love to flow through. When the body is healthy, it allows the Universal energy to move through gracefully and easily. A person with a healthy body and energy field will generally have a lightness about them, a sparkle in their eyes, abundant energy, and a calm and alert demeanor. All parts of the system are working in harmony, and so the energy flows without disruption through the entire system. The person is vibrant, clear, focused, happy, and peaceful.

Good health, however, does not begin and end with the physical body. Of profound significance is the mental and emotional energy flowing through a person, which is the real determining factor of a healthy energy system. There are plenty of people who are in very good physical health, and yet their energy is not balanced or peaceful. They are not at ease within themselves, and so their Soul's light does not shine very brightly through their human vessel.

To truly elevate your health is to change the frequency in which the cells of your body vibrate. This happens through changing

235

your thoughts, emotions, as well as purifying the physical body. Each of these processes works hand-in-hand with the other areas. The more you dissolve the ego, for instance, emotional energetic blockages in the body dissolve, allowing the physical body to return to greater homeostasis. Conversely, when you perform specific detox processes, it is quite common to experience emotional releases, or positive shifts in your perceptions and attitudes towards life. The three areas of the human system; mind, body, and emotions, all work synergistically to either allow, or inhibit good health. Working with all three areas holistically, then, creates the most balanced approach to growth and healing.

To begin healing is to begin dissolving the ego. Thoroughly read and reread part II of this book, "The Awakening." As you read this material, really let the information sink in, applying the understanding about the ego to your own experience. Begin to observe your own ego, and all of the ways in which it may be influencing your life. Just bringing awareness to your ego will begin to dissolve its hold over you. This is the first step, which will allow you to begin healing the body from a place of greater love and trust.

Along this path of letting go of the ego, adopting new dietary and lifestyle practices will allow you to integrate into your life a more healthy and natural way of living. Using energy healing practices, as well, will reinforce the awakening and healing occurring within you, bringing you into greater states of health. Your natural state is that of peace, joy, vitality, and well-being. You can absolutely return to this natural state by unraveling the conditioning you have learned throughout your life, and recreate yourself in every moment from a place of conscious awareness.

The information in this chapter is the result of over a decade of research and personal experimentation. This healing protocol is not designed to treat symptoms or specific illnesses, but rather, bring a person's body back into balance. When the mind, emotions, and body are harmonized, vibrant health is the natural result. I have personally undergone every health recommendation I make in this section, often repeating detoxification processes several times (and in some cases, dozens of times), fine-tuning them along the way, in order to ensure the most thorough and comprehensive healing process possible.

If you are uncertain about any of these processes, seek out the guidance of a holistic practitioner to guide you through the journey. What will be more helpful than any third party support, however, is learning to tune into your own intuition with greater confidence and focus. Your body is wise and knows what it needs in order to return to a state of perfect health. Meditate, clear away the ego, learn to feel what your body truly needs in order to be healthy. Don't be afraid to move beyond the traditional model of health care. Much of the health care system in the U.S. has been created from a place of ignorance as to the greater energetic connection existing within all of life. Our bodies are incredibly regenerative, true miracles of creation, and can heal from most any disease. Your thoughts are powerful, as is your intention to heal. Listen to your heart, and always follow your intuition above all else.

The following is an overview of the Holistic Healing Process:

1. **Nutrition and Detoxification**—Increase your physical health by adopting the diet in this section, healing leaky gut, and systematically detoxifying the various organs of the body. Though it may not always be comfortable, adhering to this protocol can dramatically change your life for the better.

2. **Energetic Practices**—The benefits of energetic practices are numerous, including greater mental focus and clarity, increased emotional stability, and increased physical health. There are countless people who have healed themselves from all types of health conditions simply by using energy healing practices.

3. **Mental and Emotional Inventories**—Unravel the myth of your life by deconstructing the mental and emotional conditioning that you received from your family and the culture at large. Healing occurs when we let go of old beliefs and emotional patterns, allowing for new energy to flow into our lives.

Disclaimer: Though the processes described in this section are quite detailed and specific, they are meant to be general guidelines for how to heal using diet and nutrition. Everyone is at a different level of health, and will have different needs in each area of nutrition and detoxification. Because of this, I suggest finding an experienced holistic health practitioner to help guide you through these processes, particularly if you have any doubts or concerns about your current state of health.

The information provided in this section is purely educational, and is not intended as medical advice, or for the treatment of any disease. Please consult with a trained healthcare provider before making any healthcare decisions, or for guidance on healing specific health issues. Recommendations for specific supplement brands can be found on my website, holistichealth-counseling.com.

Healing Leaky Gut

According to Chinese medicine, almost all disease begins through the degradation of the digestive tract. This ancient knowledge has been verified by many well-known researchers and alternative medical practitioners since the early 1900s. This theory is now becoming more widely accepted in western medicine, although there is still much resistance despite the growing body of evidence.

When the intestinal lining becomes compromised due to inflammation, it creates small gaps in the mucosal lining. This allows non-digested food particles and toxins to enter the blood stream. This often triggers the immune system to fight off these foreign invaders, causing increased inflammation throughout other parts of the body. An overtaxed and stressed immune system can begin mistaking bodily tissue for undigested proteins in the blood, leading to chronic autoimmune conditions such as arthritis, ulcerative colitis, Crohn's disease, chronic fatigue syndrome, and lupus.

Over time, other systems within the body can begin to break down on account of systemic inflammation, creating a cycle of inflammation and toxicity. It becomes a perpetual downward spiral.

This is the root cause of most disease from a purely physiological perspective; inflammation and toxicity beginning in the intestinal tract, which spreads slowly to other parts of the body. In order to heal, it is necessary to first heal the intestinal lining. The degradation of the intestinal lining occurs over time as a result of a few different factors:

1) Gluten, Sugar and Dairy

Gluten, sugar and dairy are generally either difficult for many people to digest, or are directly responsible for causing inflammation in the body. These foods affect everyone differently, and may not increase inflammation to the same degree, depending on a person's constitution and overall health. In order to get a baseline understanding of the health of your body, however, it is necessary to cut out all foods that are potentially contributing to inflammation. There is ample research verifying the negative effects of each of these substances, showing a link between these foods and inflammation, as well as many diseases that often arise in the body on account of consuming excess quantities of these foods. In addition, Candida and other parasites tend to feed on sugar, simple carbohydrates, and dairy sugars. The proliferation of parasites in the intestines can perpetuate intestinal inflammation, cause nutritional deficiencies, and increase systemic inflammation, which is another reason why cutting these foods from your diet is so important.

2) Nutrient Poor Diets

The average American diet is extremely out of balance, lacking alive, fresh, and nutrient rich foods. A lack of vitamins and minerals prevent the systems of the body from functioning properly. Even for those with a largely plant based diet, malnutrition can be quite common. Industrial farming has depleted soil quality, effectively reducing the nutritional value of most fruits and vegetables. This is largely due to a century of non-biodynamic farming practices—which often includes many organic farms. In addition, the synthetic vitamin supplements that many people take have been shown to have a very poor absorption rate in the body. Reintroducing a nutrient rich diet, as well as certain "living" supplements can deeply nourish the body on a cellular level, and aid in the process of detoxification.

3) The Accumulation of Toxins and Parasites.

Toxins from the environment, food, air, water, as well as prescription medication (particularly the excessive use of antibiotics) can degrade the intestinal lining, and contribute to creating inflammation in the body. Large amounts of toxins accumulate over the course of a person's lifetime, reducing vitality and health, and setting the stage for disease. Parasites and Candida thrive in a toxic environment, often feeding on the acidity created within the body when toxins are present. Candida and intestinal parasites have been linked to numerous diseases, and can cause long-term health complications if left untreated.

There are countless examples of people who have suffered from cancer, diabetes, heart disease, high blood pressure, and many other conditions, who have regained full health after healing leaky gut and detoxifying from chemicals in the body. I am one of them! Again, this is not new information. This diet and healing protocol are merely a culmination of what has been known for over 100 years in the alternative healing community.

Additionally, when the body is in a state of poor health and toxicity, it can adversely affect a person's mood, causing depression, anxiety, fatigue, and irritability. It should be noted that approximately 80% of the body's total serotonin production actually occurs in the cells of the intestines. Serotonin is a neurotransmitter responsible for mood regulation, nervous system functioning, and proper digestion, which means that when the digestive tract is unhealthy it can directly affect the chemistry within the brain, as well as other important functions of the body. It is easy to see, then, how a downward spiral begins when the digestive tract is unhealthy.

Steps For Healing Leaky Gut:

1. Begin the Holistic Healing Diet as outlined in the next section

2. Begin taking the following supplements and herbs daily (according to the directions on the bottles):

- Slippery Elm Bark (to be taken at least 1 hour before food)
-Marshmallow Root (to be taken at least 1 hour before food)
-Deglycyrrhized Licorice
-L-Glutamine
½ – 1 serving of an organic, raw, green powder

-Ginger and Garlic. Both ginger and garlic are extremely healing. I suggest chewing on a nub of ginger in the morning before breakfast, and consuming either a half or whole clove of garlic (finely chopped) swallowed with a small amount of water, either with your dinner or before bed. Consume ginger and garlic 4-5 days a week, giving yourself a few days off each week so as not to develop an intolerance to them. You can skip this if you include both of these in your daily juice recipe (to be covered in the "Juice Fasting" chapter).

-Probiotics. Fermented foods such as sauerkraut, kombucha, kefir, and kim chee are preferable, however, probiotic supplements can also be taken. Find a probiotic supplement that requires refrigeration, and has at least 50 billion organisms per capsule. Take up to 100 billion organisms per day, depending on your body's tolerance.

-Cayenne Pepper Drink. Combine the following ingredients to make a healing digestive elixir:
    -1/4 teaspoon cayenne pepper
    -1/2 tablespoon apple cider vinegar
    -1 to 2 cups water
    -Drink at least once a day, 20-30 minutes before lunch or dinner. *Though it may seem counterintuitive, cayenne pepper is one of the best remedies for healing leaky gut. While it might be assumed*

that cayenne is an irritant, it is not. The pepper is actually a stimulant, meaning that it does not harm tissue in any way, but rather stimulates blood vessels within the tissue. The active compound in cayenne, capsaicin, tricks the body into believing it has a wound. While no damage is actually being done to the tissue, the body responds as if there were, increasing blood flow and initiating the healing response.

-Turmeric Ginger and Cinnamon Tea—combine turmeric, ginger, and cinnamon into a cup of warm water and sip. Add a pinch of black pepper (which significantly increases the healing effects of the active compound in turmeric, curcumin). Drink this tea in the morning or before going to bed, stirring occasionally, as cinnamon has a tendency to coagulate. Each of these ingredients contains powerful healing properties that will help to reduce inflammation, repair damaged tissue, and cleanse the blood.

3. Begin a Liquid Diet

Put 60-70% of your meals through the blender with just enough liquid to blend it up (with a majority of your food being blended raw vegetables). You can also make blended soups out of cooked vegetables (remember, just enough liquid to blend it up). Experiment with the liquid diet by doing either a full day of liquid diet for 2 or more days at a time, followed by 1 or 2 days of eating solid foods in between. You can also do a liquid diet for the first half of each day, and then have a dinner of solid foods. You may feel so good on a liquid diet, that you want to continue for weeks at a time. However, you also may experience a healing reaction as your body adjusts to the increase in enzymes present in raw foods. Listen to your body, move at a comfortable pace, and go for it!

4. Less Food, More Chewing

Try to reduce the size of your meals between 10-20%. Most people, in general, overeat at each meal. If you know you overeat, you may need to reduce your food intake more than 20%. When eating, chew your food slowly and thoroughly. As soon as you begin to feel slightly full, stop eating. The body may be telling you to eat more, but this is usually due to psychological or emotional factors, more so than based on true physical need. After a few weeks of slightly reducing your food intake, your body will begin to adjust, and you will require less food in order to feel full. Research shows that slight caloric restriction is the healthiest way to live, decreasing the likelihood of disease, and prolonging life.

When eating meals, eat in a relaxing environment without too much distraction or stimulus. Eating slower and chewing more thoroughly will also allow your body to feel full, making it easier not to overeat. When you prepare meals, practice proper food combining, which most notably includes eating fruit separately from all other types of foods, not combining protein with starches, and limiting liquid intake during meals. There are numerous online resources for the specifics regarding food combining.

5. Intermittent Juice or Water Fasting

Fasting can be one of the most powerful ways to let the intestinal lining heal, as well as to begin detoxifying the body of accumulated toxins. Fasting gives the body a chance to repair itself, and rest from the processes of digestion. For the process of juice fasting, drink 1-3 glasses of vegetable juice a day, limiting the amount of sweet vegetables that you use (such as carrots or beets) to a minimum. Be sure to drink plenty of water throughout the day, relaxing and taking it easy. Although juice fasting allows the intestines time to heal, this type of fast will not detoxify the body to the same degree as a water fast.

The Holistic Healing Diet

The following diet eliminates all foods that potentially cause inflammation in the intestines which may be contributing to leaky gut.

243

Healing leaky gut is essential for further detoxification and healing processes. By strictly following this diet for at least 30 days, you allow your body to begin repairing your intestinal lining. Though these guidelines are meant to be followed rather strictly, as time goes on, do not be afraid to modify them based on what your intuition may be telling you. And remember, this diet is not permanent. Once leaky gut has been healed, you can enjoy some inflammation causing foods in moderation. Try to buy organic, GMO free, and locally grown whenever possible.

Foods To Consume:

-Raw and cooked vegetables (except for corn, tomatoes, potatoes, or eggplant). Raw and cooked veggies should consist of roughly 60-80% of your diet.
-Organic chicken, turkey, eggs (in moderation, 1-2 times a week) beef, or lamb. No fish, due to high levels of heavy metals.

-Moderate amounts of grains and legumes such as rice, quinoa, buckwheat, beans and lentils.

-Fermented foods and drinks, such as sauerkraut, kimchee, kefir, kombucha and miso, all of which are amazingly beneficial for the intestines and body.

-Tempeh. If possible, find a brand that does not contain sweeteners or other additives. Do not consume tofu or other soy products.

-Fresh veggie juice. 1-2 glasses to be consumed every day, or every other day. Listen to your intuition, taking breaks when your body is telling you to.

-Nuts, seeds, and nut butters (in moderation). Rinse and soak nuts for a few hours before ingesting (this helps make them more digestible). Avoid peanuts and peanut butter, due to the high mold content of most store bought peanuts. Be sure to use only fresh nuts, as nuts will go rancid if they are stored for longer than a few weeks.

-Hemp protein powder, rice protein powder, or pea protein powder. These are all a good source of easily digestible protein, which can be mixed with water, or added to smoothies or cooked dishes for an extra protein boost.

-Coconut oil, olive oil, flax seed oil, or sunflower oil. Coconut oil is the only oil to be used for cooking, and one of the best oils for reducing inflammation and reducing intestinal fungus and parasites. The oils listed here are healthy and part of reducing inflammation in the body.

-Unsweetened almond milk, unsweetened hemp milk, and unsweetened coconut milk. Use these in place of cow's milk (avoid soy milk).

-Beneficial spices: garlic, tumeric, ginger, cardamom, cinnamon, cayenne, coriander, nutmeg, basil, rosemary, and fennel seed. Use pink Himalayan salt, or grey sea salt, rather than table salt. Limit salt intake to 1-2 teaspoons a day. Absolutely no sugar or sweeteners of any kind. For a sweetener substitute use Stevia in moderation.

Grains and Legumes

There is some research showing that all grains and legumes (including non-glutenous grains such as rice and quinoa) cause low levels of inflammation in some people. For this reason, all grains may need to be avoided completely by some individuals. For those who feel they tolerate grains and beans, be sure to sprout them first (this releases the phytic acid and lectins, which are linked to increasing inflammation in the body). Sprouting makes nutrients from the grains and beans more bio-available and easily digestible.

Salt Quality and Quantity

One of the most important minerals within the human body is

salt. Salt is essential for countless processes, as well as maintaining energy levels, and good health. Salt has gotten an undeserving bad rap, and was previously believed to be the cause of health problems such as high blood pressure and heart disease. It is now understood that it is not necessarily excessive salt intake that causes inflammation in the body, but rather salt in combination with excess sugar and unhealthy oils which contribute to inflammation.

However, what is of the utmost importance, is to be consuming the right type of salt in the proper quantity. Begin using pink Himalayan salt, or Celtic sea salt that have not been processed, heated, or treated in any way. There are many commercial Sea Salts that have been heated or treated, both which change the molecular structure of the salt crystal, and changes how your body is able to utilize it as well. In general, 1 teaspoon a day of Himalayan or Celtic sea salt will be adequate to provide your body with the proper amount of salt. However, if you are more physically active, sweating a lot, or under increased stress, than you may need between 1-3 teaspoons a day.

Foods and Liquids to Completely Remove From Your Diet:

If you are able to adhere to the diet previously listed, then you are doing fine and can disregard the information below. The following is a list of foods that should NOT be consumed (in case there is any question or doubt).

-Remove all dairy, gluten, wheat, bread, pasta, tofu (or other soy products aside from tempeh), sugar, honey, agave, maple syrup (or any other sweetener besides stevia) alcohol, caffeine, nicotine, tap water, non-organic food products, and all GMO's.

-Remove all types of fats and oils, except for sunflower oil, olive oil, flax seed oil (not to be heated), and coconut oil (used for cooking).

-Really cold or really hot beverages, as both can aggravate digestion.

Particularly avoid liquids with meals, as this will compromise your digestive juices, making it more difficult for your body to digest food properly. Wait 30 minutes after drinking anything before eating food, or 1-2 hours after eating food to drink liquid. When drinking tea, cool it down with a bit of cold water first.

-Be sure to read labels on processed foods to check for gluten, sugar, chemicals, and hydrogenated fats, as these are all common ingredients in tomato sauces, soups, almond and soy milk, and many other processed products.

-It is very important that all of these foods listed above be completely removed from the diet. Many of these substances wreak havoc on intestinal tracts and digestion. Some of these foods can be moderately re-introduced into one's diet only after intestinal healing has occurred, but during the time of healing they must be strictly avoided.

Supplementation

Because most people are deficient in vitamins and minerals, it can be helpful to nourish the body with adequate levels of both. Even if you are taking a vitamin or mineral supplement in pill form, there is a good chance that you are still deficient. This is because most vitamin and mineral supplements are not sourced from living foods, nor do they exist in a form that is bio-available to the body. Research on the efficacy of most forms of highly processed supplements show that they actually have very little impact on health, which is why it is so important to take the proper kinds of supplements; those derived from living, raw, organic sources, which have not been heated, and have only been minimally processed. This ensures that the nutrients are alive and can be easily assimilated by the body.

The best way to get living vitamins into your system is through juicing and smoothies. In addition, begin integrating the following supplements into your daily regimen. If you have been suffering from serious digestive illness, such as crohn's disease or ulcerative colitis, you will want to make sure that you are on the mend first (through the previous steps outlined) before introducing any supplements. The supplements listed below will strengthen the intestines once they are on the mend, but can irritate them if there is still too much inflammation present. For anyone healing from a digestive disease, I would suggest doing the previous practices for a few months before moving on. It is essential to let the intestines heal before attempting to introduce any substance which may cause irritation or inflammation. This often times takes between a few months, and up to a year in some cases.

Supplements To Begin Taking:

-Vitamin C— between 500 and 1000 milligrams daily.
-MSM capsules—between 1000-3000 milligrams daily with food.
-Liquid Mineral Drops—Follow the recommended dosage on the bottle.
-Krill Oil—follow the recommended dosage on the bottle.
-Adaptogenic herbs, such as mushroom extracts, ashwaganda, schizandra, or ginseng. Follow the recommended dosage on the bottle.

Supplement Details

Vitamin C- Vitamin C helps to heal the intestinal lining (when taken in moderation) and boost the immune system, promoting regular immune functioning, and overall good health. Vitamin C in conjunction with MSM will begin detoxifying the body in a gentle way. It's best to find a natural and bioavailable source of vitamin C.

MSM- Methylsulfonylmethane is a naturally occurring sulfur based compound, which helps relieve inflammation, improve joint flexibility, reduce stiffness, improve circulation, and reduce pain and swelling. The supplement is also believed to aid the body in detoxification. MSM is thought to increase cell permeability, allowing

248

cells greater respiration, which is essential during periods of detoxification.

Liquid Minerals- Minerals are essential for thousands of processes in the body. Due to nutritional deficiency, industrial agriculture, and environmental toxins, most people are deficient in minerals. In order for your body to adequately absorb minerals, they must be in the proper form (ionic). In recent years new technology has been able to reduce the size of particles in mineral solutions, allowing the body to more readily absorb them.

Krill Oil- Krill are small crustaceans found in the world's oceans, and one of the largest biomass on the planet. Krill oil is one of the best sources of EPA and DHA, also known as Omega 3 fatty acids. Omega 3's are hugely important for so many functions of the body, and is also a compound that the body is not able to produce on its own. Krill oil helps reduce inflammation, increase cellular respiration, and allows cells to maintain a greater electrical charge. Omega 3's improve memory, circulation, concentration, increase mood, and help the body detoxify. Krill oil is superior to fish oil because it contains a potent antioxidant called astaxanthin, which prevents the oil from becoming rancid (a common problem with most fish oils).

Adaptogenic Herbs- The term "adaptogenic" refers to a compound's ability to modulate and balance the immune response, nervous system, and to increase the body's ability to handle stress. Adaptogenic herbs have numerous health benefits, which include lowering cortisol levels, reducing blood pressure, and increasing mood. Ginseng, Ashwaganda, and Schizandra are just a few examples. Do your own research and experimentation to find the adaptogenic herb that suites your body best.

Juice Fasting

Juicing is one of the best ways to provide the body with

essential vitamins, minerals and enzymes required for healing. It is also one of the gentlest ways to begin detoxifying the body. What makes juicing so effective is that juice is readily absorbed through even the most unhealthy intestinal tracts, and is loaded with a higher concentration of nutrients, vitamins and enzymes than would be possible to eat in solid form. Juicing also gives the intestines a break from digesting solid food, allowing them time to begin healing. You can either juice fast for 24 hours once or twice a week, or start your day with fresh pressed vegetable juice, while continuing to eat three meals a day. While juice fasting be sure to drink plenty of water, in addition to vegetable juice consumed throughout the day.

For optimal results juicing should be done almost everyday, or every other day, for at least a two-month period. Juicing vegetables low in sugar is ideal, such as leafy greens, cucumbers, and celery. If you cannot go without sweet veggies, such as carrots or beets, I would suggest consuming a serving of protein powder with the juice, in order to help maintain balanced blood sugar levels. Although, for anyone suffering from candida, a juice blend with the least amount of sugar is ideal.

To begin juicing it is important to have the right type of juicer. There are two kinds: a centrifugal style juicer, and the masticating juicer. A masticating juicer is preferable to the centrifugal juicer (no heat or friction is created during the juicing process when using a masticating juicer, which allows for the enzymes and phyto-nutrients to remain intact and un-oxidized). I've used both types of juicers and can actually taste the difference in flavor and potency. A centrifugal juicer will work if that is the only option. However, I highly recommend investing in a masticating juicer if possible.

Vegetable Juice Recipe

Begin with one full glass of juice a day—more if you feel inclined, but at least one glass a day. Dilute juice with a small amount of water if you find that it is too strong to drink on its own. It's best to juice fresh each morning (rather than juicing a two or three day supply at a time). Try to include each of the ingredients listed below with every juicing, as they all serve an important function due to their specific nutritional and healing qualities. Always use fresh veggies and try to buy organic whenever possible. Amounts based on enough ingredients for 1-2 glasses of juice:

-Cucumber (1/2-1)
-Celery (2-3 stalks)
-Kale (1/3 of a bunch)
-Parsley (1/3 of a bunch)
-Red cabbage (1 cup chopped)
-Spinach (1 handful)
-Lemon (1/2)—Cut into wedges (do not peel) and put through the juicer.
-1 or 2 carrots for sweetness
-Ginger, turmeric, and garlic—*a little goes along way–with the exception of turmeric, you can juice about a 2-inch stub of turmeric without it changing the flavor too much. Experiment to find out how much garlic and ginger you can tolerate without making it too strong to drink. If you are worried about garlic breath, then don't juice garlic, but rather consume one medium sized clove of garlic, 1-2 hours after dinner, finely chopped, with a small amount of water.*

Optional additions:
-wheat grass, barley grass, chard, broccoli, or any other non-root veggies that appeal to you. Avoid juicing fruit or drinking fruit juice due to high levels of sugar.

Green Smoothie Recipe

Another alternative to juicing that also lightens the strain on digestion are smoothies. With any smoothie recipe, you want to be sure to limit your sugar intake, and try to include as much nutritionally dense food as possible. The following recipe is a delicious and hearty breakfast smoothie that works well during the liquid diet. I like to juice in the morning and have a smoothie for lunch. I find that when I do a liquid diet for the first part of the day I have tons of energy and feel really good throughout the day. Put the following ingredients into a blender and puree until smooth and creamy.

-1-2 cups filtered or spring water
-1/4 avocado
2-3 handfuls of a combination of spinach, kale, chard, or salad greens. *Use whatever greens you have available, being sure to mix it up so as to receive a good variety of nutrients. Avoid kale if you suffer from any thyroid issues, as kale can disrupt thyroid function when consumed in excess.*
-1 serving of green powder (chlorella, spirulina, or a blend of the two)
-1 to 2 servings of rice, hemp, or pea protein powder
-dash of himalayan pink salt
-dash of olive oil
-a few nubs of ginger

-Optional additions: Stevia, coconut milk, maca, chia seeds, cucumber, or any other vegetables that appeals to you. *You can also substitute blueberries for some vegetables, in order to add a little sweetness. Blueberries are one of the few fruits that can be consumed due to their high quantity of fiber, which slows down digestion, allowing your body to absorb the fruit sugars before the Candida does.*

Therapeutic Water Fasting

Water fasting has been practiced by many cultures around the world for thousands of years, including Egyptian, Indian, Greek, Chinese, and Russian cultures. Fasting for spiritual purposes has been documented in numerous religious and spiritual texts. Historical figures such as Hippocrates, Socrates, Plato, Confucius, Gandhi, and even Benjamin Franklin were all advocates of water fasting for

252

spiritual and physical health. It has only been in the last century that this technique has begun to receive the attention from western medicine.

Though there has yet to be any concrete scientific data showing exactly how or why water fasting is effective, there are a few viable theories. One theory is that fasting is actually the body's natural healing mechanism. Though it may seem counter-intuitive, fasting has been shown to increase immune system functioning, reduce inflammation, and initiate a healing response in the body. The idea is that digestion requires a fair amount of energy, energy that could otherwise go towards healing. When food is removed from your system, then the body has more vital energy to heal.

Another theory is that fasting is a biological adaption for survival, allowing the body to rid itself of all extraneous tissues, cells, bacteria, or viruses that would otherwise impede survival during times of food scarcity. This would have allowed early humans to have survived periods of famine without losing vital muscle mass or tissue related to organ functioning. If there is a diseased part of the body, for instance, the cells and tissues of this part of the body would be the first to go during a fast, allowing the body to remain in optimal health in order to ensure survival.

A 2002 review of studies on fasting published in the health journal, "Alternative Therapies," showed positive results from this technique. Researchers examined the effects of water fasting on patients with auto-immune conditions, with results showing a significant decrease in inflammation, pain, and swelling associated with each condition. There are numerous healing centers around the world that utilize water fasting for the treatment of various health conditions.

If you are wondering why you have not heard about the powerful benefits of water fasting before, think about the significance of this healing modality on the mainstream medical model. Because fasting is a free and simple process that anyone can undergo to significantly increase their health, no one stands to make any money in the process. It would be understandable, then, that there might be a lack of interest by the mainstream health industry, if not an overt resistance to the practice.

However, therapeutic water fasting is not for everyone. The information in this section is for educational purposes only, and is by no means medical advice. Water fasting may pose potential health risks for diabetics, people who are hypoglycemic, pregnant, or suffering from conditions related to cortisol dysregulation. Speak with your health care provider before attempting a fast if you have any concerns about the practice.

The Process For Water Fasting

If you have never water fasted before, begin with a half day fast in order to see how your body responds. Drink plenty of purified water or spring water throughout the day, being sure not to overextend yourself during your first fast. Break the fast in the late afternoon or early evening with a light dinner. Completing a half day fast will help prepare your body for the full day fast, without triggering any of the detoxification symptoms that commonly occur during a full day fast.

For the full day water fast drink only purified or spring water throughout the day. Pick a day where you are able to remain meditative and relaxed, focusing on being calm and peaceful. Drink water whenever you feel thirsty, and a little extra for good measure. Some people choose to drink tea or put lemon in their water. I believe that a water fast will be most successful when you simply stick to pure water. Throughout the day be sure to focus on your breath, relaxing your body, and staying present. Take deep, full, natural breaths, allowing yourself to be calm and peaceful. If you feel light headed or dizzy, find a place to sit and breathe peacefully until it passes.

It is common to experience a healing reaction that may include any of the following symptoms: headache, weakness, fatigue, racing heart, cold sweats, chills, nausea, diarrhea, abdominal cramping, rash, and irritability. A slight fever can also accompany a healing reaction. However, if any of these symptoms are severe, or persist longer than a few days, seek the support of a trained medical professional. Be sure to drink plenty of water during your fast, and keep water by your bedside for moments when you awake feeling thirsty. Drinking water can often alleviate the symptoms associated with the healing reaction.

The following morning be sure to drink at least a full glass of water, if not more, and then wait 30 minutes before breaking your fast. To break your fast begin by consuming either vegetable juice or a light salad. Fermented foods are good to consume accompanying your first meal as well. This will help to repopulate your intestines with beneficial bacteria. The day following a fast eat lightly and simply—raw or cooked vegetables accompanied by rice and a protein source. Though it may be tempting to indulge, avoid eating excess fat, salt, or sweet food, being sure to eat slowly and consciously.

Therapeutic water fasting can be used for intense periods of detoxification, as well as for regular maintenance. I generally fast one day a week, or one day every other week, just to keep my system feeling light and healthy. Listen to your intuition regarding how long to fast for. I would recommend not fasting for longer than 1-2 days at a time unless strongly guided by your intuition to do so. For those with serious medical conditions, consult a trained health care provider before attempting a fast of any duration.

The Importance of Probiotics

Though it's hard to fathom, the bacteria that comprise your body's microflora actually outnumber the cells in your body by 10 to 1. Having adequate beneficial bacteria in the body are crucial for healing leaky gut and fortifying your intestinal lining. The beneficial bacteria in your body are so important, in fact, that researchers now believe that microflora significantly effects brain functioning, mood, and stress levels.

A study from the University of California, Los Angeles, observed the effects of probiotics on 36 women. Researchers discovered that the women who regularly consumed probiotics experienced a decrease in activity in two regions of the brain responsible for processing emotion and sensation; the insular cortex, and the somatosensory cortex. A decrease in these two parts of the brain resulted in a reduction of stress, and greater regulation of the nervous system. In addition, it was noted that the test participants showed an increase in activity in an area of the prefrontal cortex associated with sensory processing. This could have important implications for the treatment of conditions such as obsessive compulsive disorder, anxiety disorder, and depression.

It is also estimated that roughly 80% of the body's total serotonin production actually occurs in the gut, so when intestinal flora is not in balance, it can cause mood swings, irritability, depression, anxiety, and fatigue. In addition, roughly 60-70% of your immune system cells exist in your gut. This takes the form of a vast network of lymph tissue known as GALT (gut associated lymph tissue). So when gut flora is imbalanced, it can be detrimental to the health and functioning of the immune system, effecting mood, sleep, and other aspects of physical health. When researchers examined the various diets of different cultures around the world, with the aim of finding the healthiest diet, they found that those who ate fermented foods on a regular basis ranked as some of the healthiest and longest living folks on the planet!

Fermented Foods and Probiotics

I highly recommend making your own fermented foods, rather than spending a lot of money on store bought probiotic supplements. The main reason is that fermented foods are a superior source of beneficial bacteria, as compared to probiotic supplements. One serving of sauerkraut, for instance, has upwards of 1 trillion healthy organisms, while most probiotic supplements have an organism count in the billions. Ideally, it would be best to take supplements in addition to fermented foods, in order to get a full spectrum of probiotics.

In Addition, you can make fermented foods for much less money than store bought probiotics, and when you do so, you can ensure the quality, as well as ensure that the healthy bacteria are living and thriving (versus supplemented probiotics, which you can never be sure as to the quality of cultures in the product). My basic approach is to trust mother nature whenever possible, and go with the most natural route available. People have been consuming fermented foods for ages, and the incredible health benefits are well documented. There are a few things to consider when making your own fermented foods:

-The first thing you want to be sure of is that all of your equipment is properly sterilized with boiling water, to ensure no unhealthy bacteria contaminate your fermentation process.

-Avoid using metal containers or spoons, as metal inhibits the fermentation process.

-Be sure to keep fermented foods in the proper temperature range during the fermentation, as well as properly covered (allowing for some air flow, which helps release gasses during the ferment).

-Be sure to adequately ferment your product in order to reduce the sugar content as much as possible. Beneficial bacteria consume sugars, and so the longer you ferment, the more good bacteria are produced. In general, the more sour or vinegary the taste is, the more beneficial bacteria it contains. If the product still tastes sweet, it needs to ferment longer.

-Variety is key. Ideally, you want to get the greatest spectrum of beneficial bacteria into your diet through a variety of different fermented foods. There are hundreds of strains of healthy flora, and the more variety you consume, the heartier your health will be.

My favorite types of fermented foods are homemade sauerkraut, kombucha, and water kefir. It's best to avoid dairy kefir, on account of most people's inability to properly digest dairy sugars. You don't need a starter for sauerkraut, while for kombucha and water kefir you will need to start with a colony of bacteria. Starters for kombucha and water kefir can be bought online for relatively inexpensive. If fermenting seems intimidating, there are numerous resources online which can walk you through the process step-by-step. If there is only one change you make in your life for better health, make it learning to ferment your own foods and liquids. There is a small learning curve with the process, however, and it did take me a few tries to get a final product that was uncontaminated and palatable.

If you choose to buy fermented foods, be sure that the product actually says "raw" on the label. If it does not, it means there is a good chance the product has been pasteurized, which will have partially or completely destroyed the beneficial bacteria in the product. I recommend consuming 1-2 cups of solid cultured foods, or one 8-ounce glass of liquid cultured drinks each day. Although, the more the better, and it is best to listen to the needs of your body. Research indicates that it is best to take probiotics at the same time as consuming food or liquid with some quantity of healthy fats. This helps to ensure the survival of the probiotics as they travel to your intestines.

Although I strongly recommend fermented foods over supplements, in some cases store bought probiotic supplements are more tolerable for some people. When buying probiotics, try out a variety of brands to see which ones your body reacts better to. Opt for a refrigerated variety of probiotics when possible, with an organism count between 50 and 100 billion. I suggest taking up to 100 billion organisms a day, divided into two servings.

The Importance of Oxygen

Getting adequate oxygen into your body is one of the most essential elements for healing. Increased oxygen speeds up the healing process, improves cardiovascular health, improves neurological functioning, reduces inflammation, regulates hormone production, increases energy levels, improves sleep quality, and aids in the elimination of toxins from the body. There is ample research highlighting just how important oxygen is in the process of healing. While you can pay to receive oxygen therapy, there are two free ways to increase the oxygen in your body that are readily available to everyone; belly breathing and exercise.

Belly Breathing

Many people have developed patterns of shallow breathing from the chest, which restricts oxygen absorption in the lungs. Deep belly breathing, on the other hand, allows a greater inflow of oxygen into the body, activates the parasympathetic nervous system, releases endorphins in the brain, and calms an overactive mind. Take the time to master belly breathing by following the steps below.

1. Place your hand on your belly, sit up straight, and take a slow, deep, natural breath, allowing your belly to expand outward with each breath.

2. As you exhale, allow all of the oxygen to be released from your lungs, contracting your belly back towards your core. The breath should be relaxed, natural, and slow. Consciously slow down your breathing, taking deeper breaths than what you may be accustomed to. This doesn't need to be forced in any way, but rather, a gentle and conscious allowance to take deeper breaths.

3. Practice makes perfect! This may seem simple, but really pay attention to how you are breathing throughout your day, and continually bring your attention back to the flow of breath in your body, being sure to breathe from your belly. As you go about your day notice your breath, and any time you find yourself feeling anxious, or notice that you are breathing from your chest, take the time to straighten your spine and take a deep and relaxed belly breath.

Aerobic Exercise

Aerobic exercise is another way to effectively increase the oxygen in your body. You have probably heard the benefits of exercise extolled a thousand times, and yet most people still do not get enough daily exercise. Try to get at least 30 minutes to an hour of exercise each day. The quality of exercise you perform is equally as important as duration. When exercising, be sure to stick mostly to aerobic exercise. What this term means is that you are taking in enough oxygen in every moment to supply your body with adequate oxygen for all the functions of the body.

The key to making sure that you are doing aerobic exercise (versus anaerobic exercise) is belly breathing. Try to maintain belly breathing throughout the duration of your workout. As soon as your breathing primarily moves up into the chest (in the form of gasping or panting for air), your body begins using oxygen faster than you can inhale, depleting your energy reserves. This puts stress on the body, releases cortisol, and can contribute to burnout, rather than a build-up of your energy reserves.

This technique of maintaining belly breathing (even during strenuous activity) is commonly used among marathon runners (including the well known marathon runner, Stu Middleman), who reported having an abundance of energy even after running a 100 mile race. In order to work up to a 100 miles, however, you need to increase your exercise level gradually, never pushing yourself beyond what is comfortable to breathe from your belly.

Detoxification Overview

In many cases, simply adhering to the previous health recommendations will be sufficient to heal many health conditions. If, however, you have not seen any positive shifts in your health after two months, continue with the following detoxification processes. In order for the body to regain homeostasis, good health, and the ability to properly absorb nutrients, it is often necessary to do regular and thorough detoxification processes throughout the year.

Depending on your environment, lifestyle, and history, the depth to which you will need to detoxify will vary. It is safe to say that, in general, most people have an excess of toxins in the body, and could greatly benefit from the detoxification processes in this section. Below is an outline of what will be accomplished in this step of the healing journey. Each of these items will be covered more thoroughly in the following chapters, and detailed instructions provided for the correct order of operations.

It is essential to detoxify in the proper order. This is a very commonly overlooked factor that can mean the difference between a successful detox, versus further auto-intoxication (the process that occurs when the body reabsorbs toxins expelled through an improperly performed detox). The processes for detoxification are as follows: 1) Environmental detoxification, 2) Skin and Intestinal cleanse, 3) Liver Flush, 4) Deep Tissue Cleanse, and finally, 5) Parasite Cleanse.

Environmental Detoxification

You can spend much time, energy, and money trying to heal, but if your environment is what is contributing to poor health, then it will be nearly impossible to regain optimal health. There are numerous ways in which environmental toxins interfere with good health, including putting additional strain on the liver, interfering with the elimination of waste material from cells, interfering with hormone production and distribution, compromising the immune system, and interfering with neurological processes. This inventory serves as a guideline for detoxifying your environment from potential health hazards.

Skin and Intestinal Cleanse

Once leaky gut is on the mend, it is time to clear the intestines for further detoxification. The skin and intestines are complementary organs, in that they each serve as the barrier between the outside world and your inner world. By cleansing and strengthening this barrier, it helps to prevent further toxicity from occurring down the road. It is important to clear the intestines before doing any deeper levels of detox, for the reason that if the gut is compacted with mucoidal plaque, there is less peristalsis (the rhythmic contraction of muscles surrounding the intestinal lining, which helps transport waste out of the body), and the body is more likely to reabsorb toxins as they pass through the intestines. The intestinal cleanse consists of specific herbs, clays, and juice fasting to clear the intestines of built-up debris.

Liver Flush

The liver is one of the most important organs in the body, as it is responsible for filtering and purifying the blood. In order to help the body eliminate toxins, the liver and gallbladder must be cleansed periodically to reduce built-up bile. Again, this step should only be done after healing leaky gut, and the intestinal cleanse, so that toxins expelled from the liver do not get reabsorbed by the intestines.

The liver flush consists of a day of juice fasting, and a liver cleansing preparation in order to eliminate gallstones. You will need two full days for this process. Depending on the toxicity of your liver and how many gallstones are expelled, you may need to repeat the liver flush two to three times over the course of a few months, in order to fully evacuate toxins from the liver.

Deep Tissue Cleanse

Once the liver has been flushed, it is safe to begin evacuating toxins at a deeper level. Often times heavy metals, pesticide residue, and other toxins can accumulate in the body faster than the body can naturally evacuate them, and so it can be necessary to perform a deep tissue cleanse periodically. In addition, the body has an ingenious mechanism for storing certain toxins in a way that minimizes the harm they cause. The body hides toxins away mainly in the fatty tissue, bones, and organs of the body, preventing these substances from circulating through the bloodstream, causing additional harm. Though they are stored in the body's fat reserves for safe keeping, they still continue to do some damage in the form of disrupting hormonal production and distribution, interfering with nervous system functioning, causing inflammation, and feeding candida and parasites. The deep tissue cleanse can take anywhere from one month to a year, and involves specific herbs and supplements to chelate these toxins from the body.

Parasite Cleanse

This is the most intense cleanse of the detox processes outlined in this book, and should only be performed once every other aspect of the detox has been completed. The reason is that parasites do not like to give up their home so easily, and if you try to cleanse too early (when the body is still relatively toxic and acidic) they can put up quite a fight, or come back with a vengeance if not fully eradicated the first time. The previous detox and cleansing steps will have weakened the parasite's defenses, as well as improved the overall health of your body, allowing you to get rid of them much more easily. This process takes about one month and can be repeated many times throughout the year.

Environmental Detoxification

An often overlooked form of detoxification is the removal of toxic elements from your home and work environment. If complete elimination is not possible, it is best to to take steps to limit and mitigate the harmful effects of toxic exposure. The process for removing toxicity can be tedious, time consuming, and labor intensive. However, the payoff may very well be a significant improvement in your health, and so it is usually well worth the time and effort.

While some environmental toxins are not harmful enough to do damage on their own, there is an accumulative effect that occurs over time, which can disrupt the systems of the body in significant ways. Environmental toxins have a negative effect on the nervous system, immune system, hormone production, and on neurological functioning.

The following list highlights areas where environmental toxins may be affecting your health. Each of these factors will likely affect everyone differently, depending on one's constitution and current state of health. Take the time to thoroughly evaluate your home and work space, taking each of these items seriously. Do your own research, and listen to your intuition in order to determine which factors may be effecting your health in a negative way.

-**Non-organic Food.** Pesticides, GMO's, and chemical fertilizers all wreak havoc on the body, and over time can contribute to poor health. Buy organic, non-GMO, and local whenever possible.

-**Tap water.** Most municipal water sources contain numerous chemicals including fluoride, lead, aluminum, arsenic, VOCs, copper, nitrates, pesticides, herbicides, plastics, and pharmaceuticals, to name a few. The counter-top filters do little to filter out the majority of these chemicals. Drink spring water, or reverse osmosis filtered water whenever possible.

-**Mercury dental fillings.** Mercury is incredibly toxic to the body, and can cause many symptoms, which are often mistakenly misdiagnosed. Find a holistic dentist to replace mercury fillings with composite fillings. Follow the procedure with a heavy metal cleanse.

-**Household mold.** Mold often exists behind walls and under carpets, invisible to the naked eye. Mold can have serious adverse health effects, compromising immune system functioning over prolonged periods of time. Hire an expert to evaluate your living situation if you suspect the presence of mold.

-**Cosmetics and personal hygiene products.** Commercial shampoo, toothpaste, lotions, sunscreen, and deodorant commonly contain toxic chemicals that can get absorbed through the skin and mucous membranes. It's best to buy organic and natural products if possible.

-Cookware. Cooking with certain types of metal pots and pans can leech metal into food, disrupting hormone production, and causing neurological damage over time. Eliminate all teflon, aluminum, and copper cookware. Limit use of stainless steel and caste iron. Glass and ceramic cookware are the healthiest.

-Plastic residue. Exposure from water bottles, storing food in tupperware, and food microwaved in plastic can all leech plastic materials into your water and food. Opt for glass food storage whenever possible.

-Wifi signals. Research shows wifi signals can disrupt nervous system functioning and hormone production, particularly in children. Opt for a cable plug-in connection if possible.

-Electromagnetic frequencies (EMFs). have also been shown to disrupt the nervous system and neurological functioning. Utilize "earthing" techniques to mitigate the harmful effects from EMFs.

-New construction "off gassing." Traditional construction uses large amounts of different types of toxic chemicals, which according to research, takes approximately 70 years to properly "off gas." Natural structures such as cob and strawbale do not contain the same level of toxicity as traditional construction.

-Poor air quality. Indoor air pollution is estimated to be one of the greatest sources of harm to the lungs. Some possible culprits are poor ventilation, household chemicals, carbon monoxide, unvented gas heaters, poorly maintained furnaces and stoves, and pressed wood products containing formaldehyde, such as particle board.

-Household cleaning products. Most household cleaners are extremely toxic, particularly to children. Use organic and natural cleaning products whenever possible.

Skin and Intestinal Cleanse

Here are the beginning detoxification practices for the skin and intestines. The colon cleanse formulas are generally only necessary if you suffer from chronic constipation, or have a bowel movement less than two times a day, on average. Integrate the following practices into your daily and weekly schedules. Below the following list is a description for each of these practices and why they are important.

Saunas or epsom salt baths. 3-4 times a week.
Bentonite clay and psyllium husks. 3-4 days at a time, with 3-4 days off during the week.
Skin brushing. This is best to do daily, preferably before a bath or shower.
Colon Cleanse Formula. I recommend Dr. Christopher's Colon Cleanse Formulas. Follow the directions on the bottle (only to be performed if you experience constipation, or have a bowel movement less than two times a day, on average).
Supplements for support. You may find it beneficial to increase your intake of MSM, vitamin C, and adaptogenic herbs for immune system support through the detoxification process.

Saunas and Epsom Salt Baths

Both of these practices have the same goal; to pull toxins from the lymph tissues and subcutaneous layers of fat within your skin. The body stores heavy metals and other toxins mostly in fatty tissue, much of it in the fat beneath the layers of the skin. Heat opens up pores, and sweating expels toxins through the pores of the skin. Infrared saunas are preferable, but if you do not have access to a sauna, then an epsom salt bath will do, and is considered by many to be just as potent a detoxifier as saunas. For regular Sauanas, stay in for 15 minutes at a time, for multiple rounds, 3-4 times a week. Be sure to drink plenty of water, as well as get adequate salt and mineral supplementation following a sauna.

For the Epsom salt bath, put 2 cups of Epsom salt into a hot bath and soak for 15-30 minutes at a time, 3-4 times a week. Be sure to get adequate hydration, as well as proper amounts of salt and mineral supplementation. Epsom salts can be bought in bulk at any drug store. If you are dealing with any topical fungal infections (yeast infection, jock itch, or toe fungus) then try adding a cup of baking soda to the bath as well. You may find that a combination of sauna and epsom salt baths are most effective for drawing toxins out of the body.

Bentonite Clay and Psyllium Husks

One of the most effective ways to begin cleaning the intestinal tract, as well as pull toxins from your body is through the use of bentonite clay. Combined with psyllium husks (which help to loosen mucoid plaque on the intestinal walls, and move it through the intestines), bentonite clay can help remove blocked fecal matter from the gut. Bentonite clay is best taken early in the morning on an empty stomach, accompanied by adequate water. It is best not to eat any food or other supplements for an hour after the clay. Start with 1-2 teaspoons of the clay a day, and then gradually increase over time to 1-2 tablespoons. Take bentonite clay for 3-4 days at a time, with 3-4 days off for no longer than a month at a time. Add 1 tablespoon of psyllium husks to the bentonite clay in a jar with a lid, shaking the mixture vigorously in water to thoroughly dissolve. Be sure there is enough water so that the liquid is quite runny and easy to drink. Follow by drinking another full glass of water.

Skin Brushing

Skin brushing is an ancient practice that has been used in numerous cultures around the world. The technique involves lightly massaging and scrubbing your skin with a skin brush in order to remove dead skin cells and stimulate the lymphatic system. Between 20-30% of toxins are stored in the lymphatic system at any given time, and by lightly brushing the skin, it aids in releasing the toxins from the skin. It is best to skin brush right before a shower, or during a shower. You may experience less irritation by skin brushing dry, versus in the shower. Spend about five minutes a day covering the entirety of your body with the brush.

Colon Cleanse Herbal Formula

For those who experience constipation on a regular basis, it may be necessary to do a 1-2 week colon cleanse. The herbs in the colon cleanse formula will help induce peristalsis, the muscular contractions lining the intestinal wall, which help move waste matter through the gut. Dr Christopher's colon cleanse is one of the better colon cleansing products on the market at an affordable price. This formula contains Aloe, Cascara Sagrada Bark, Garlic Bulb, Senna Leaves, Ginger Root, Barberry Bark and Cayenne (90,000 H.U.) in an all vegetarian Capsule. Follow the instructions as described on the bottle.

The Liver Flush

The purpose of a liver flush is to release gallstones that have accumulated in the liver and gallbladder. A liver flush is recommended 1-3 times a year, depending on your overall health and lifestyle. The following is the protocol for a gentle and effective liver flush. This will require two days to do, and it is advised not to schedule any other activities for the duration of the two days. The liver flush is only to be performed once the skin and intestinal cleanse has been implemented for at least two weeks.

Preparation For Liver Flush:

-Skin and intestinal cleanse.

-A week of eating a low fat diet (only good fats such as coconut, olive, flax, and sunflower oil in moderation) as well as eliminating all sugar, dairy, and gluten.

-A week of taking an herbal formula designed to support liver health and liver detoxification.

-In addition to cleansing the intestines, give yourself at least a week of taking bentonite clay and psyllium husk to clean out the intestines before the liver flush (take the clay 1 week leading up to the flush, giving yourself 48 hours between the last bentonite clay dosage and the first day of the flush).

-Continue taking MSM, vitamin C, and any adaptogenic herbs up until the day before the flush.

What You Will Need For the Liver Flush:

-2 days time (one for the flush, one day to recuperate)

-4-5 organic lemons

-1-2 liters fresh pressed vegetable juice (refer to the "juicing" recipe)

-1 bag of Magnesium Sulfate, or Magnesium Chloride (to be used as a laxative).

-4 ounces of organic olive oil

-Fresh spring water or reverse osmosis water

-Enema kit (optional)

-MSM

-An herbal formula for liver detoxification and regeneration

Day 1 of the Liver Flush

The first day of the flush do not eat any solid food. Only juice and water are to be consumed during the day. Start the day with 1/2 liter of filtered water with 2000 milligrams of MSM. An hour later drink your first glass of vegetable juice (being sure to completely remove any pulp from the juice). Drink the juice no later than 12 noon, then switch over to water for the next two hours. At 2pm have your first serving of the laxative solution (magnesium sulfate or magnesium chloride, as described below).

-Laxative solution—At 2pm dissolve 1 teaspoon of either the magnesium sulfate or magnesium chloride into 1/2 liter of water. Wait 30 minutes and drink another 1/2 liter of water. It's important to drink enough water, in order to flush out the intestines. Repeat this step again at 5pm and 7pm. You may drink herbal teas throughout the day in addition to water, but absolutely no solid food. Within a few hours you should begin having bowel movements, eventually evacuating mostly water.

-By 8 pm have your last liquids for the day.

-Between 9 and 10pm, prepare the olive oil and lemon juice mixture by combining a 1/4 cup of olive oil into a jar with a lid, adding 1/4 cup of freshly squeezed lemon juice to the olive oil. Secure the lid on the jar and shake vigorously to thoroughly combine the olive oil and lemon juice. Drink the mixture right before going to bed, being sure to immediately lie down on your right side directly after drinking the olive oil solution. Continue laying on your right side while drifting off to sleep.

Day 2 of Liver Flush

Upon rising on day two, immediately drink the laxative solution of 1/2 liter of water with 1 teaspoon of magnesium sulfate or magnesium chloride dissolved in water, followed by 1/2 liter water 30 minutes later. Wait one hour and repeat. Flushing out your intestines in the morning with more laxative solution will keep the body from absorbing any of the toxins released from the gallstones.

Continue drinking water periodically until your first bowel movement. If you do not have a bowel movement within three hours of your first laxative solution of the morning, drink another dosage of magnesium sulfate or magnesium chloride. Do not eat any solid food until after you have begun passing the gallstones. Your first or second bowel movement of the day should begin expelling gallstones (which will look like hardened green, gray, and black stones). It is common to release hundreds of stones over the course of a few hours. Some people will continue releasing gallstones in their stool for a day or two following the flush. Relax and take it easy on the second day, being sure not to do any exercise or strenuous activities.

After you have passed a significant amount of gallstones, drink a glass of vegetable juice and wait 2 hours. Have a light dinner of salad, or lightly cooked vegetables with limited quantities of protein or fat. Do not overeat on the second day, as this can put undue strain on your liver after the cleansing process. On day three you can mostly return to your regular diet, with the exception of minimizing your protein and fat intake. For a few days following the liver flush reduce fat intake, and by day five, return to your normal diet.

Deep Tissue Cleanse

Once the intestines and liver have been flushed, your body is now ready to begin detoxifying and eliminating chemicals that have been stored in the cells, tissue, and organs of your body. Heavy metals, pesticide residue, plastics, and other chemicals are the toxins being targeted through this cleanse, and it can take some time to draw all of the toxins from the body. This is an ongoing cleanse that you can perform for months at a time, and requires patience and consistency. Do not try to rush through this, but rather, take a methodical and balanced approach. I would strongly suggest seeking guidance and support from a health professional before attempting a deep tissue cleanse. When performed improperly, this cleanse has the potential to cause some harm to the body, and so it is best to have support for the process from someone who has gone through it themselves.

A common occurrence during this cleanse is what is often referred to as the "healing reaction," whereas your body experiences the negative effects from the chemicals as they are reintroduced back into your blood stream on their way out of your system. This is why having a healthy intestinal tract and liver is crucial–these two organs help extricate chemicals from the body in the most efficient manner. The bentonite clay is one of the most important supplements during this cleanse, as it will absorb toxins as they pass through the intestines, preventing them from being reabsorbed as they pass through the gut. Here are the supplements to begin taking for the deep tissue cleanse. Be sure to drink plenty of water throughout the day and to get adequate rest as your body detoxifies.

Foundational Detoxification Supplements

Vitamin C, MSM, Adaptogenic Herbal Formula—These supplements will support your body in detoxing and healing. For most people, vitamin C and MSM can be increased to daily doses of 4000 mg of each, divided into three dosages throughout the day. Increase slowly over the course of two weeks, cutting back if the healing reaction becomes too intense. Pay attention to how your body feels, reducing the dosage, and taking breaks for days or weeks at a time, depending on how your body is responding to the detox process.

Bentonite Clay and Psyllium Husks—One of the most effective ways to begin cleaning the intestinal tract, as well as pull toxins from your body is through the use of bentonite clay. Combined with psyllium husks (which help to loosen mucoid plaque on the intestinal walls and move it through the intestines), bentonite clay can remove a lot of blocked fecal matter from the gut. Bentonite clay is best taken early in the morning on an empty stomach, accompanied by adequate water. It is best not to eat any food or other supplements for an hour after the clay. Start with 1-2 teaspoons of the clay a day, and then gradually increase over time to 1-2 tablespoons. Take bentonite clay for 3-4 days at a time, with 3-4 days off. Add 1 tablespoon of psyllium husks to the bentonite clay in a jar with a lid, shaking the mixture vigorously in water to thoroughly dissolve. Be sure there is enough water so that the liquid is quite runny and easy to drink. Follow by drinking another full glass of water.

An Organic Green Powder—Green superfood powders contain chlorella, spirulina, and other minerals and nutrients which aid in chelating heavy metals from the body, as well as nourish the body on a deep level. It is best to find a brand that is organic, has not been heated during processing, and contains no fillers or processed sugars. A good green powder will be dark green in color, and have an earthy or grassy flavor (it may not taste great, but it is good for you). In order to avoid developing a potential allergic reaction to any of the components of the green powder, you may consider taking a day or two off from the supplement each week. For a more intense detox regimen, buy pure chlorella or spirulina (powder or capsules), taking the recommended dosage on the bottles.

Nascent Iodine–Iodine is crucial for detoxifying the soft tissue within the thyroid. Most people are deficient in iodine, which can eventually lead to hormonal imbalance and thyroid dysfunction. While thyroid medications are often prescribed for hyperthyroidism and hypothyroidism, it is a deficiency in iodine that is commonly part of the thyroid imbalance. However, because iodine is a very potent substance, it is strongly advised to seek the guidance of a trained professional before making it a part of your supplement regimen.

The Parasite Cleanse

A parasite cleanse can be one of the more intense cleanses, and takes adequate preparation before attempting. The cleanse itself takes roughly 4-6 weeks, and can be performed 1-2 times a year. Before beginning a parasite cleanse, you should have completed all of the other processes, including the healing leaky gut section, and the detox section. Once you have completed all other sections, and are continuing to maintain the inflammation-free diet (as described in the Healing Leaky Gut section), then you are ready to do a parasite cleanse. If you attempt a parasite cleanse before your body is ready, you may do more harm than good. Partially fighting off parasites can make them come back even stronger, and make it more difficult to get rid of them when the time comes.

Parasite Cleanse Herbs and Supplements:

Diatomaceous Earth—Diatomaceous earth is essentially ground up fossilized diatoms (a type of algae). This soft siliceous sedimentary rock, when ground up, creates microscopic particles that have abrasive edges. When the powder comes into contact with candida and other parasites, it effectively shreds their exoskeletons, killing parasites and their eggs. Diatomaceous particles, however, are too small to cause any abrasion to the mucosal lining of the intestinal tract, and is considered a benign and safe substance to consume. Be sure to buy "food grade" diatomaceous earth, and begin by mixing 1/2 tablespoon of Diatomaceous earth with a small glass of water in the morning on an empty stomach. After a few days, up the dosage to 1 tablespoon. After two weeks, up the dose to 2 tablespoons and continue for another 2-3 weeks. Be sure to wait at least 30-40 minutes after drinking the solution before eating any solid food.

Wormood, Black Walnut Hull, and Clove Oil—These three herbs will eradicate most all parasites at different stages of their development (parasite eggs, as well as mature parasites), and can oftentimes be found in a herbal blends specifically targeting parasites. I don't have a recommendation for any specific quantity of these herbs, however. The reason for this is that they are quite strong, and everyone's body will likely react differently to them. Its best to do your own research to find a brand that works for you, and a quantity that works for you as well. Find someone with experience using these herbs to fine-tune the dosage or timing of the herbs.

Immune System Support:

Because eradicating parasites puts extra strain on the body, it is important to do everything that you can to strengthen your immune system during a parasite cleanse. In addition to the supplements I've already listed for immune support (vitamin C, MSM, and adaptogenic herbs), here are two practices to strengthen your immune system during a parasite cleanse.

Baking Soda Soaks/Hydrogen Peroxide bath—You can use both baking soda and hydrogen peroxide simultaneously, or on their own to help facilitate the detox process of candida and parasites. Baking soda is extremely alkaline and will help kill candida on the skin. During a soak, both baking soda and hydrogen peroxide will get absorbed into the skin and help oxygenate and alkanize an overly acidic body. For baking soda, use one 16oz bag per bath. For hydrogen peroxide, use either 1/8 cup 35% hydrogen peroxide, or 1 cup of 3% hydrogen peroxide. Soak in a hot bath for 20-30 minutes, being sure to drink adequate water to stay hydrated. 35% hydrogen peroxide is extremely caustic and can cause serious harm when used undiluted. Take extreme caution when handling 35% hydrogen peroxide, and when bathing be sure not to get any water in your eyes or mouth.

Also limit yourself to no more than 2-3 baths per week, for only a few weeks at time. This should not be an ongoing practice, as both baking soda and hydrogen peroxide will eventually wipe out the microflora on your skin if continued long term. It can be beneficial to apply coconut oil on the skin after a bath, which has anti-fungal properties, and will help to nourish the skin.

Deep Breathing—Parasites cannot survive in an oxygenated environment, which means the more you breathe, the more oxygen gets into your body, and the harder it is for parasites and candida to thrive. Practice the deep belly breathing (as described in previous sections) and use it throughout your day. Whenever you feel tired, anxious, or compulsive cravings for food, turn to your breath to relax and revitalize yourself. Oxygen is one of the most healing "nutrients" that your body needs in order to detoxify and regain homeostasis.

Balancing the Thyroid

A crucial part of the endocrine system, the thyroid gland is responsible for creating and distributing essential hormones related to metabolism, growth cycles, tissue health, reproductive health, mood regulation, and sleep patterns. Two of the most common types of thyroid imbalances, hypothyroidism, and hyperthyroidism, occur when the gland becomes exhausted, leading to a chronically depleted, or over-active thyroid.

There are different approaches to healing the thyroid. While western medicine uses the approach of supplementing the specific hormones that are out of balance, a more holistic approach is to treat the thyroid as part of the entire system, understanding how imbalance occurred in the first place, and then making dietary and lifestyle changes to remedy the imbalance.

One prominent theory regarding the cause of thyroid imbalance relates to intestinal health and liver health. The primary hormones that the thyroid gland produces are triiodothyronine and thyroxine, commonly referred to as T3 and T4. The body however, can only use the hormone in its T3 form, while T4 needs to be converted into T3. So as these two hormones travel through the blood stream, T3 is readily absorbed and utilized by the body, while T4 is sent off to the intestines and liver, where it is then converted into the more usable T3 form.

In order for the intestines to properly convert T4 into T3 a specific enzyme called sulfatase is required, which is produced by bacteria in the gut. When the gut is unhealthy, lacking the proper intestinal flora, T4 is unable to be converted into T3, and instead, remains in the blood stream, inactive. The same process applies for the liver. A generally healthy liver is able to convert T4 to T3, while a toxic and overburdened liver is not so equipped to do so.

With an abundance of unusable T4, and a lack of T3 in the blood stream, the hypothalamus triggers the pituitary gland, sending the signal to the thyroid gland to create more T3 and T4 to make up for the deficit. Over time this increased work load on the thyroid leads to burnout, and the gland loses it's ability to properly modulate hormone production and distribution (leading to hypothyroidism or hyperthyroidism).

So in order to heal the thyroid it is first essential to heal leaky gut by repopulating the intestines with healthy flora. Once the intestines have been fortified, a liver flush will begin to allow T4 to be converted into T3 more readily. By repairing the two areas of the body that convert these essential hormones (the intestines and liver), over time the hormone imbalance will naturally correct itself. Though this process of healing the thyroid by first healing the gut and liver is not a quick fix (and in some instances medication may be necessary to maintain homeostasis in the meantime), overall, this holistic approach will actually heal the thyroid, rather than simply cover up the symptoms of imbalance with medication.

In addition to healing leaky gut and detoxifying the liver, it is essential to reduce stress as much as possible. Be sure not to overextend yourself, or physically push yourself. Gentle and moderate physical exercise will help to keep your body healthy, but should not be overdone. Maintaining balanced blood sugar levels have also shown to aid in the healing of the thyroid. Make sure to balance out carbohydrates with adequate protein intake, reducing or eliminating sugar and sweet foods from your diet. Supplementing with cinnamon, fenugreek, and holy basil can help modulate insulin levels in the blood as well.

Spiritual and Energetic Practices

The role that spiritual and energetic practices take in a person's healing journey will vary depending on the person. Some people may not feel very drawn to work with subtler spiritual energy in this way, while others may experience powerful healings through these techniques. Experiment with each practice in order to see how it can best serve your growth and healing. I would suggest implementing a few practices into your daily schedule at any given time, maintaining them for at least a month's time. Using your intuition, rotate in other practices in order to keep the process interesting and engaging.

Let your intuition guide you on this journey, and feel free to modify or change any practice when you receive an inspiration to do so. More is not necessarily better when it comes to energy practices, and the power of these techniques will be in the quality of presence that you maintain while you do them. By turning your attention inward you cultivate greater inner awareness, as well as greater self-mastery over how you focus your attention. The more you focus on feeling your own inner energy field, the stronger and more vital your energy becomes. The more you learn to be in control of your thoughts, emotions, and actions, the more the body naturally comes into alignment with this empowered and healthy way of being.

I would suggest that you make daily meditation and yoga the foundation of your spiritual practices, in addition to implementing other techniques into your daily routine. If you find that one technique becomes too monotonous, let it go and move on to another. Oscillate between different practices to keep your attention focused on what's important—you. The secret is that the technique is not nearly as important as your intention and commitment to honoring, healing, and loving yourself.

-Meditation and Yoga (Pg. 145-148). Developing inner stillness and greater self-awareness through meditation and yoga will create a powerful foundation for healing in your life. Though it may be challenging to practice both each day, committing yourself to these foundational practices will expedite the healing process tremendously.

-Breathing Techniques (Pg. 152). The breath is the doorway to good health, vitality, inner peace, and happiness. Breath awareness is an ongoing practice that builds momentum over time, incrementally increasing health and vitality. Practice these breathing techniques often throughout your day, and notice the incredible benefits of conscious breathing.

-Power of Gratitude (Pg. 155). Practicing gratitude is similar to meditating on the spiritual heart, in that you are practicing focusing your attention on very high vibrations of loving energy within.

Cultivate a practice of feeling gratitude everyday in your life for your health, your body, your relationships, nature, and all the amazing experiences of being alive.

-Meditation On the Spiritual Heart (Pg. 161). A very powerful meditation practice that will open your heart, and help heal your mind, emotions, and body. Practice this meditation throughout your day and witness an amazing transformation in your life.

-The Intention Exercise (Pg. 168). Focusing on an intention is the first step in consciously changing your life. As you learn to focus your intention and attention on the experiences that you desire, you can manifest anything into your life—including good health, happiness, and inner peace.

-The Process of Visioning (Pg. 170). Visioning is the complete process for manifesting experiences into your life. You can use the visioning process to manifest a life of good health and vitality, as well as for tuning into the experiences that your heart and soul came here to have.

-Conscious Nourishment (Pg. 189). Nourishment goes far beyond the food and liquids that a person consumes. Everything you put into your body potentially affects your health and state of being. Take the time to bring deeper awareness to all the ways in which you can consciously nourish yourself.

-Neural Reprogramming (Pg. 213). Use these simple techniques to rewrite the programming of the mind using loving intention. The mind is like a computer and can be used as a tool when we learn to take back conscious control over our thoughts.

-Sound Healing and the Chakras (Pg. 221). The vibrations of sound can have very positive effects on your mind, emotions, and body, creating healing in your life. You can use sound to balance and harmonize your chakras. Learn to use sound as a transformative tool, practicing these techniques on a regular basis.

-Ecstatic Practices (Pg. 232). Getting out of the head and into the body can be powerful medicine for releasing stored emotional energy. Using age-old ecstatic practices helps you shift your focus, and your experience of reality, waking up your entire energy system. Expand your mind and heart through these techniques, and allow greater vitality to flow through you by creating a stronger connection to the Universal Energy.

Additional Healing Practices

The following practices are each powerful in their own right, and the more you integrate the right practice for you into your life, the more you will see healing results. While these descriptions are brief, this in no way reflects their healing potential. Use your intuition to guide you towards the specific modalities that call to you.

Qi-Gong

Qi-gong is an ancient form of moving meditation used for healing and revitalizing the body. Created over 4000 years ago, the term qi-gong roughly translates as "life energy cultivation." The practice involves slow and methodical movements accompanied by deep and relaxed breathing. There are different branches of qi-gong, which each contain variations in style and emphasis. There are hundreds of studies extolling the benefits of qi-gong for increasing mental, emotional, and physical health. Qi-gong has been shown to reduce inflammation in the body, improve circulation, increase immune system functioning, and increase cognitive functioning.

I have spent time over the years learning some of the different styles of qi-gong, and have come to the conclusion that the healing effects of this practice are largely a result of keeping your attention within your own energy field. By doing so you increase the chi flowing throughout your entire system, balancing mind, emotions, and body. In this sense, the specific technique you employ is not as important as simply learning to focus on your own energy field. Though many qi-gong masters might debate this point, I feel that it can be more powerful, in fact, to develop your own style of qi-gong, rather than trying to adhere too strictly to specific techniques. There are many online tutorials to get you started with the essentials for this practice, which you can then branch off from.

The basic posture of qi-gong is to stand with spine straight, feet shoulder width apart, and a slight bend in your knees and elbows. While keeping all of your joints soft and loose, slowly begin moving your body, being sure to keep your attention on the energy within your body as you do so. Use your hands to gently guide your attention all throughout your body by slowly waving your hands in front of various parts of your body. As you move, allow your body to become fluid, loose, and relaxed. Feel as though your body is the ocean, and each breath is the in and out flow of the tide.

I often combine qi-gong with dancing, allowing myself to freely move while always keeping my attention on the energy within. It may help to keep your eyes closed for this process, allowing you to really concentrate on your own energy within. Find your own flow and go at your own pace. You will achieve the best results by adhering to a regular routine of qi-gong.

Acupuncture and Acupressure

Both acupuncture and acupressure were created by ancient Chinese health practitioners thousands of years ago, and work with the energy channels of the body (known as meridians) to restore health and vitality to the body. The 12 primary meridians are each associated with a particular organ in the body. Acupressure uses gentle pressure applied to different meridian points on the body, while acupuncture uses needles to stimulate these same points.

Although Acupuncture and acupressure are very healing and regenerative, and there are hundreds of studies validating their healing effects, I believe they work best for symptom control, pain relief, and as a complementary form of treatment, rather than as a primary treatment. Also, because regular acupuncturist sessions can become costly, it may be equally effective to learn a few healing acupressure routines that you can apply to yourself. Acupuncture is actually an offshoot of acupressure, which was widely used before the more invasive acupuncture treatments came into existence. Research appropriate meridian points that target the systems and organs of the body associated with your particular health challenges. And again, this form of healing modality will be most effective if used on a regular basis.

Massage

Massage is a wonderful way to get the energy flowing through your body again. Energetic blockages are reflected in the physical body as tight muscles, stiff joints, and sore or tender organs. Going to a massage therapist is a wonderful option to help open up the energetic channels in the body. However, massage therapy can become quite expensive in the long term. Another option is to practice self massage, spending 10-20 minutes a day gently massaging various parts of your body. As you massage, really take the time to tune into your body and offer yourself loving touch. Using your thumbs, knuckles, and the base of your palms, slowly and methodically apply pressure to different parts of your body that need healing attention. It can be helpful to do self massage in conjunction with a morning practice of yoga or qi-gong.

Aroma Therapy

Aroma therapy has been used in numerous cultures around the world for centuries, including the Egyptian, Greek, Indian, and Chinese cultures. Best used as a complementary form of treatment, aroma therapy has been shown to help regulate hormones, relieve tension, relax muscles, reduce inflammation, improve sleep quality, aid in digestion, and improve energy and concentration.

Aroma therapy involves inhaling the aroma of essential oils, but can also include topical application as well. In certain circumstances, applying the extracts to specific parts of the body may have a more significant healing effect. Some common essential oils used for healing include lavender, eucalyptus, tea tree, frankincense, bergamot, cedar, chamomile, rose, rosemary, ylang-ylang, and sage. Be sure not to get essential oils too close to sensitive areas such as the eyes, or directly into open wounds. Although some essential oils can be taken internally, others may have toxic effects, so be sure to consult with a trained aromatherapist before taking essential oils internally.

Mental and Emotional Inventories

These inventories are meant to be practiced on an ongoing basis. Start with one a week, while simultaneously integrating the dietary and energetic practices outlined in the previous sections. Write your responses to each inventory in a healing journal designated for this purpose. As you progress along your healing journey it can be beneficial to revisit certain emotional inventories, in order to uncover deeper layers of conditioning that may be contributing to your illness.

These inventories are meant to be followed up with the guided meditations and visualizations as found on my website, holistichealth-counseling.com. Complete the inventory first, and follow it with the accompanying visualization. Really allow yourself to reflect on the experiences of your life when answering these questions. The deeper your self reflection, the more energy you will free up to allow healing in your mind, emotions, and body. Repeat these inventories as you progress along your journey of healing. Every time that you revisit these questions, it will deepen your self-awareness, allowing you to go deeper.

If at any point you find yourself becoming emotional during this process, allow the emotion to flow. Hold the intention to consciously observe your emotional release, remaining as neutral as possible to whatever is flowing through you. If strong emotions such as anger or fear arise, come back to your breath, relax your body, and take a few deep, slow breaths. The purpose of allowing emotional energy to flow is to consciously release it, rather than to perpetuate the trauma and pain from experiences of the past.

Inventory I: Ego Mechanisms

Take the time to reflect on how the ego may be influencing your life and experience of yourself (as described in the "Ego and the Mind" section). There is no need to feel shame, guilt, or any negative feeling about yourself when you identify the ego operating in you. In fact, if you do, notice how any negative feeling you may have toward the ego is also the ego at work. This is an example of some profound paradoxes that exist as you start becoming more aware of the ego. Remember, the ego is not personal. It exists within each person in varying degrees. It is a part of the field of collective unconsciousness, and is expressed through each one of us at different times.

A good strategy for not getting wrapped up in the drama of the ego is to simply smile and laugh at yourself in the moment you catch the ego in action. Adopting a light-hearted approach helps you see how absurd, and even funny, the antics of the ego can be. It also helps you to create space between who you are as awareness, and the ego thought pattern. The more you can see the ego for what it is, the less control this part of your mind will have over your energy, your health, and your happiness. Answer the following questions in your healing journal.

Q: Can you identify the voice in your mind right now? What is this voice saying to you now? How can this voice be you, if it is speaking to you—which would imply that there are two of you; the one speaking, and the one listening? Can you create space between the voice in your head, and who you are as the field of awareness in which the thought is being experienced? Try it now....

Q: Looking back over your life, can you see how the voice in your mind has influenced your life decisions? How has this voice controlled you, and in what areas of your life does the voice still have control over you?

Q: What kinds of judgments, criticisms, or comparisons do you find yourself making throughout your day? What behaviors in others (or yourself) elicit these negative thoughts?

Q: What situations do you find yourself annoyed, frustrated, angry, or upset over? Write down what kinds of "triggers" cause you to create these negative states within you. How does this negativity make your body feel? Where in your body do you feel this negativity?

Q: What stories do you create in your mind about yourself and other people on a regular basis? Can you be certain that these stories are true without a doubt? Can these stories be proven? If not, are they stories that feel positive, uplifting, and ones that you wish to continue telling yourself?

Q: In what areas of your life do you role-play in order to meet the expectations of your friends, family, coworkers, boss, romantic partner, children, neighbors or community? Make a list of all the various scenarios in your life where you fill different roles.

Q: How does it feel to fill these roles? How do you notice your behavior changing from one role to another? Do you notice tension or anxiety in your body when you feel the need to fill certain roles? Where in the body is this tension felt?

Now, make the commitment to yourself that from this moment forward, whenever you observe the ego within yourself, that you will come back to your breath, and feel the stillness and peace of the present moment. It may help to use the mantra, "I am the creator of my life with every thought, emotion, and action…and I choose love."

-Follow this inventory by listening to the audio Guided Meditation, provided on my website, holistichealth-counseling.com

Inventory II: Family History and Values

Begin by spending some time reflecting on your family history, thinking about the kinds of experiences that your family and ancestors went through. Was survival difficult for them? Were they involved in any wars or traumatic experiences? Was there physical abuse, sexual abuse, or drug or alcohol abuse present? Now think more specifically about your immediate family, and the types of experiences you had growing up. Write your answers to the questions below in your healing journal.

It is important while doing this exercise not to become attached to any stories you have about yourself, or other family members as being victims. Bringing awareness to familial patterns is a technique for freeing yourself from unconsciously acting out the same patterns. When you see from where you have learned these patterns, it can be easier to realize that they are not who you are, and you can more easily let them go.

Q. What types of expectations did your parents have for you and your siblings? What roles did they expect you to fill? Do you remember messages that you needed to be tough, strong, hold back your feelings, or maintain control? Did you receive the message that it wasn't okay to express what you wanted, that you needed to be passive, or be perfect in some way?

Q. What kinds of sayings or attitudes does your family have about life? What core beliefs would you say your family has about what it means to be a good person, to be a successful person, or to be acceptable in the eyes of your family or society? What similarities do you notice in your own beliefs? Do you wish to release these core beliefs?

Q. What sorts of behavior or attitudes are unacceptable to your family? What kinds of expressions or lifestyle choices would make them uncomfortable? Is it okay to cry? Is it okay to get angry? Is it okay to feel sad, joyful, or hurt? Is it okay to sing, dance, laugh and celebrate life? What similarities do you notice in your own attitudes about what are acceptable forms of expression?

Q. How does your family deal with anger? Is anger expressed openly, or is it repressed? Is there a general feeling of guilt or shame about feeling angry? Does anger get expressed in hurtful ways or abusive behaviors? Do you notice any similarities with how you experience anger?

Q. Reflect back on times when you needed love and comfort from your parents but did not receive it. Do you have memories of feeling angry or confused by your parent's actions (or lack of attention) towards you? How did they discipline you? Did you feel loved and cared for even when you were being punished? What types of punishment did you receive?

Q. If you could change one aspect about your childhood, or how your parents treated you, what would it be?

Q. When you think about your family and childhood now, what sensations and thoughts come up for you? What do you feel in your body, and where in your body do you feel it? Are there unresolved emotions within you relating to your family experience?

After reflecting on your family experience take a few moments to sit in silence, feeling your inner energy field, taking deep, slow breaths. As you breathe, make the commitment to yourself that from this moment forward that you will no longer allow the past conditioning or beliefs from your family to unconsciously shape your experience and perceptions of reality. It may help to use the following mantra, "I am recreating myself in every moment, and I choose love, peace, and joy." When you notice yourself acting habitually based on outdated conditioning, come back to your breath, and use this mantra.

-Follow by listening to the audio Healing Light Visualization, as provided on my website, holistichealth-counseling.com.

Inventory III: Physical Healing

This inventory is designed to help you deepen your awareness of your relationship with your body, as well as any health conditions that you may be challenged with. The thoughts and feelings you have about our body and physical health profoundly affects your health. By bringing greater awareness to the negative beliefs you may have about your body, you will begin to dissolve these limiting attitudes and energetic patterns. So take this time to reflect on how you have thought and felt about your own physical state, and answer the following questions in your healing journal:

Q: Are there any parts of your body that you feel judgment towards, or do not accept in some way? Make a list of any parts of your body that you do not feel acceptance for, or have some negative feelings towards.

Q: How long have you held these beliefs, and can you think back to where they originated? Answer this question for each part of your body that you feel critical of, taking the time to trace back in your memory to when each negative belief began.

Q: How have these beliefs about your body been reinforced by your family, your friends, or popular culture?

Q: Can you think back to a time before you held these beliefs about your body? How old were you, and what were the circumstances in your life? Do you remember what changed that caused you to begin feeling negativity towards your body? And why do you imagine this might have occurred?

Q: Now take the time to reflect on the circumstances and time in your life when you first developed your current health condition? Do you remember what was happening in your life prior to developing this health condition?

Q: Continuing to think back on this time, can you see any connection between your beliefs and attitudes, or the circumstances of your life at the time, and the onset of your current health condition?

Q: How do you currently feel about your health condition? Do you have any negative feelings about your physical state? Do you feel that being sick is a sign of weakness, failure, or that you have let yourself down in some way? Do you feel disappointment for being unhealthy?

Q: Honestly reflect on the experience of dealing with your health condition. Is there some part of you that perhaps enjoys (even in a very subtle way) being unwell? Do you feel any sense of satisfaction in feeling like a victim of disease? Do you notice yourself often talking about your illness to others, or enjoying the attention or sympathy from others?

Take a second to connect to your breath, quiet your mind, and be still for a few moments…Now ask yourself from a place of sincerity and openness…"why is this dis-ease or imbalance manifesting in my life, and what can I learn from it?" There will likely be no single answer to this question, but rather an awareness of how the process of going through dis-ease serves to awaken you to more of your authentic self. To genuinely get to this place of understanding may take time, so continue asking in meditation, letting go of any expectations of a particular answer that should come to you.

Now, make the commitment to yourself to love your body unconditionally, no matter what state of health you are in. Any time you notice a negative thought about your body or your health arising, come back to your breath, relax your body, and find the peace and stillness that exists in this moment. If you find it hard to drop negative thoughts about your body or health, use the following mantra, "I love my body unconditionally, and feel deeply grateful for the health and vitality in every cell of my body."

-Follow this exercise by listening to the audio, Healing Light Visualization, provided on my website, holistichealth-counseling.com.

Inventory IV: Healing Emotional Wounds

When most people think of trauma, they think of some type of abuse, a painful accident, or the loss of a loved one. The word "trauma," however, can also refer to those times in your life when you felt helpless, unloved, or alone—particularly in times when you were expecting to feel safe, loved, and supported. As children, most of us experienced moments of not receiving the love and attention that we needed. Just the experience of being a child in an uncertain and unpredictable world can be traumatic. These experiences of trauma, if left unresolved, are often carried over into adulthood. Many adults go about their days feeling this sense of anxiety, uneasiness, and abandonment as the result of unresolved emotional wounds from earlier in their life. These repressed emotions can contributes to a negative energetic charge in the body, and disease.

While many people spend years in therapy rehashing old wounds, they are often still left unresolved. In order to heal the energetic component of trauma, it is necessary to move beyond the mind, and the "story" of trauma. Focusing on the story often only reinforces a sense of helplessness or victim mentality, keeping the trauma active in a person's emotional field. To heal and release the repressed energy of trauma, it is necessary to let go of any stories you may have about the traumatic event, bringing as much acceptance and love for the experience as possible.

This means that you do not need to focus on why the trauma happened, or who was at fault. Instead, the process begins by first allowing yourself to feel the repressed emotion associated with the trauma from a conscious and aware state—meaning that you do not get pulled into emotional reactivity, but instead, stay present with whatever it is you are feeling, without labeling, judging or reacting to what it is you are feeling. As the emotional energy moves through you, you then have the chance to offer yourself love from a higher perspective. This feeling of love will naturally harmonize your energy system.

This process can be done through simple visualizations, which anyone can learn to do. The following exercise will guide you through the process of healing an emotional wound. It may be necessary to repeat these visualizations until resolution is felt at a deep level within you. If you feel emotional during the visualization, allow yourself to release and express it, even if it disrupts the visualization. If you find that the emotional release does not feel cathartic, but rather seems to be perpetuating drama in your mind or emotional field, then relax and come back to your breath. Attempt the visualization again once the emotion has naturally subsided. Continue repeating this visualization until your emotional charge is no longer present. Once an emotional wound is healed within you, you will know it. The memory will become neutral, no longer creating any emotional reaction in you.

Preparing For the Visualization

1. Make a list of the most traumatic events in your life that still feel unresolved. It does not matter how insignificant they may seem. What matters most is how you feel when you think about it. Do you still feel some form of emotional charge when you think about the situation? If the answer is yes, then you can address this event to heal it through this visualization.

2. Once you have a list of traumatic events that you would like to heal, label them in order of significance, assigning the number "1" to the event which feels the most unresolved in your emotional experience, and the number "2" to the second most unresolved event, and so on. Continue rating the events, until each one has been assigned a number.

3. Now decide which event you would like to focus on for this visualization. Some people find it easier to start with less emotionally charged events for their first visualization, and work their way towards the more emotionally charged events. A good indicator of where to start is by following your intuition. By just looking at the list you've created, feel which event would be the best for you to start with. Let go of thoughts such as "I really should heal this trauma

first." Instead, trust your intuition to guide the way.

4. Once you have decided which event you would like to focus on, briefly recall the circumstances, people, and places involved (1-2 minutes only). For each person involved in the experience, reflect on how this person has contributed to your growth through the events that played out. Write your thoughts in your healing journey. This may feel challenging to do, particularly if you experienced a great deal of trauma, but finding this higher perspective is the first step towards forgiveness.

As you bring greater awareness to all the ways in which this event has made you the person you are today, offer your forgiveness to those people involved, one by one. It may help to close your eyes, put your hand to your heart, and say the words, "I forgive you," or "thank you." Let your heart open up to each person again, acknowledging that they have served your growth and evolution. Feel as much gratitude for this person and what you have learned from them as possible. Take your time with this step, truly allowing forgiveness to move through you. If no forgiveness arises, then return to reflecting on how you have grown from this experience until the higher perspective is reached.

Once you have completed this step, you are ready to practice the visualization.

-Follow this exercise by listening to the audio Healing Emotional Wounds, provided on my website, holistichealth-counseling.com.

Inventory V: Healing Codependency

The dynamics of codependency are explained in-depth in previous chapters, which may be helpful to review before beginning this exercise. After reading the chapter on co-dependency, answer the questions about your own relationships in your healing journal, taking a good amount of time to honestly reflect and examine any patterns of codependency. Remember, almost everyone experiences this phenomenon to varying degrees, and these exercises are not meant to cause anxiety or guilt, but rather begin the process of liberating you from unconscious behaviors that may be draining your energy, and potentially contributing to poor health. Write the answers to the following questions in your healing journal:

Q: In what ways are you sacrificing yourself in order to make other people in your life happy; your partner, your family, your friends, your boss or coworkers, for instance?

Q: In what way do you seek validation from outside yourself, or put other people's needs ahead of your own? In what ways do you expect others to take care of you, or compromise their own needs for your well-being.

Q: In what ways do you take care of others with the belief that they should then take care of you?

Q: How does it feel in your body when you feel the pressure to take care of someone else? Is there a specific part of your body where you feel stuck emotion when engaged in codependent behaviors (your stomach, abdomen, throat, shoulders, or head, for instance)?

Q: Do you notice a relationship between co-dependent behavior and your energy levels? How might this be related to your own health conditions?

Q: What dreams and goals have you put aside because you felt you had to take care of others in some way, or meet the expectations of others? Are you holding a belief that by following your dreams, you might jeopardize being loved and accepted by others?

Q: Do you ever feel worried that by being successful (or unsuccessful) with your life goals, that others may not love or accept you anymore? With whom do you notice this pattern in your life?

Q: What types of activities or life goals have you always wanted to focus on, but have pushed aside? Reflect on why have you pushed them aside.

Now that you have identified these patterns, begin to choose more wisely about how you are expressing your energy. When you notice a co-dependent thought, feeling, or behavior arise, take a moment to stop and consciously breathe. In that moment bring your attention to the field of energy within your own body. Feel the subtle vibration of energy in your hands, feet, and the space around your heart. Breathe that energy in more fully, and take a few more breaths before continuing with whatever you were engaged in.

Ending codependent behaviors does not mean, however, that you stop giving your energy for those you care about. Rather, it simply means that you begin rediscovering your own source of energy first before extending your energy to another. As you re-establish this connection within, you will have more loving energy to give to those around you. Over time this will begin to have a positive effect on your relationships, your energy levels, and your health.

In order to prepare for the Healing Relationships visualization, briefly review your life for relationships where you have given your power away to others. Notice the connections you have with people in your life where you have compromised your own needs and have failed to honor yourself in some way. Choose a relationship with one person, in particular, with whom you would like to heal any codependent dynamics. Once you have chosen a person from your life, you are ready to listen to the guided visualization.

-Follow this exercise by listening to the audio, Healing Relationships

Healing and Beyond

More important than following any specific regimen for healing, is to deeply understand that it is the energy in which you live your life that either allows good health, or restricts it. Is your ego running the show, or are you tuned into the voice of your heart? Do you choose love or do you choose fear? When you take action from a place of fear, anxiety, or negativity, health and vitality are restricted. It is the energy of love, allowance, relaxation, and peace that are synonymous with health and healing.

Healing is essentially a process of letting go of fear, limitation, negativity, and restriction, and allowing your natural self to emerge more fully in your life. And by making love a conscious decision, you will see the greatest results in your physical health. It can be extremely helpful to have guidance through the process of healing, and so it may be beneficial to seek out the support of someone who has gone through the process themselves.

Your heart is constantly calling to you through your intuition and feelings, guiding you back to your most essential Self. Follow this call, moving towards what your heart is showing you about how to live your life in harmony and balance. Quiet your mind, simplify your life, and let go of aspects of your life that are not in alignment with who you are. Do not be afraid to make changes in your life, dramatic changes even! There is no need to listen to those who would cast doubt, or who would spread the energy of anxiety and worry.

Love is the animating energy of the Universe, and there is an infinite supply. There is a Higher Intelligence that is lovingly holding all of life, and so have courage and have inner strength to follow your heart. Re-member the deepest parts within yourself that are connected to the the magic, beauty, and love of the Universe, and your part in it. Trust and have faith in what you have always known, but may have buried deep within you; that you are the creator of your life, an aspect of the Divine that flows through all of creation. You can create your life any way that you choose. You are free, you are whole, and you are love! Blessings and peace to each one of us, to all of life, and to the ever unfolding magic and mystery of the Universe.

References

Tolle, Eckhart. *A New Earth: Awakening to Your Life's Purpose*. New York: Plume, 2006. Print.

Gibran, Kahlil. *The Prophet Kahlil Gibran*. New Delhi: Rupa, 1993. Print.

Emmanuel, Pat Rodegast, Judith Stanton, and Shizhen Wang. *Emmanuel's Book II: The Choice for Love*. Taibei Shi: Fang Zhi Chu Ban She, 1995. Print.

Rosenberg, Marshall B. *Nonviolent Communication: A Language of Compassion*. Del Mar, CA: PuddleDancer, 1999. Print.

Johnson, Luke Timothy, and Daniel J. Harrington. *The Gospel of Luke*. Collegeville, MN: Liturgical, 1991. Print.

Hafiz, and Daniel James. Ladinsky. *The Gift: Poems by the Great Sufi Master*. New York: Arkana, 1999. Print.

Shakespear, William, William George Clark, William Aldis Wright, and Israel Gollancz. *Shakespear's Complete Works*. New York: Dumont, n.d. Print.

Rumi, Jalal Al-Din, and Kabir Edmund Helminski. *The Rumi Collection: An Anthology of Translations of Mevlana Jalaluddin Rumi*. Boston: Shambhala, 2005. Print.

Serling, Rod, Beaumon, Charles. The Twilight Zone. *A Nice Place to Visit*. Dir. John Brahm. 15 April. 1960. Television.

Pilgrim, Peace. *Peace Pilgrim: Her Life and Work in Her Own Words*. Santa Fe, NM: Ocean Tree, 1983. Print

About The Author

Mica Akullian is a spiritual and holistic counselor, writer, and artist who spends his time on the West coast of the U.S. He received his master's degree in marriage and family therapy from San Francisco State University in 2008, and has written hundreds of articles on spirituality, health, and healing for a variety of online and print publications. In 2009 Mica experienced a profound spiritual awakening that healed him from a chronic disease. Mica now devotes his time to the awakening and healing of the planet through simple spiritual teachings, energetic practices, and nutritional and lifestyle guidance.

Contact:

holistichealth-counseling.com
holistic.mica@gmail.com